SYNTAX OF
NEW TESTAMENT GREEK

SYNTAX OF
NEW TESTAMENT
GREEK

James A. Brooks
Carlton L. Winbery

Library of Congress Cataloging-in-Publication Data

Brooks, James A.
Syntax of New Testament Greek.

Includes bibliographical references and indexes.
1. Greek language, Biblical—Syntax. I. Winbery,
Carlton L. II. Title.
PA836.B76   1983   487'.4   78–51150
ISBN 0–8191–0473–6 (pbk. : alk. paper)

TABLE OF CONTENTS

Preface   ii

Introduction   1

Part I   The Substantive

Characteristics   1
  Number   1
  Gender   1
  Case   2
    Nominative   3
    Genitive   8
    Ablative   21
    Dative   31
    Locative   37
    Instrumental   42
    Accusative   49
    Vocative   64
  Appendix: Prepositions   65

Kinds   69
  Noun   70
  Adjective   70
  Article   73
  Pronoun   80

Part II   The Verb

Characteristics   82
  Tense   82
    Present   83
    Imperfect   90

Future   95
Aorist   98
Perfect   104
Pluperfect   108
Voice   109
Active   110
Middle   111
Passive   113
Mood   114
Indicative   114
Subjunctive   118
Optative   124
Imperative   127
Person   130
Number   131

Kinds   131
Finite   131
Infinite   132
Infinitive   132
Verbal   133
Substantival   139
Participle   143
Attributive   143
Substantival   144
Predicative   144
Adverbial   145

Part III Aspects of Greek Sentences

Kinds of Sentences   154
Simple Statements   155
Sentences with Connective Verbs   156
Sentences with Objects of the Verb   156
Sentences with Indirect Objects   157
Interrogative Sentences   158
Commands and Requests   159
Sentences with Participles and
Infinitives   160

Complex Sentences   161
Compound Sentences   162

The Expansion of the Subject   163
  By the Use of Adjectives and Adverbs   163
  By the Use of Nouns and Pronouns   164
  By the Use of Phrases   167
  By the Use of Clauses   168
    Relative Clauses   169
    Clauses Introduced by
      Adverbial Particles   170
    Clauses Introduced by
      Subordinating Conjunctions   171

The Expansion of the Predicate   172
  By the Use of Nouns and Pronouns   172
  By the Use of Adjectives and
    Adverbs   174
  By the Use of Phrases   175
  By the Use of Clauses   175
    Relative Clauses   175
    Clauses Introduced by
      Adverbial Particles   177
    Comparative Clauses   178
    Clauses Introduced by
      Subordinating Conjunctions   179
    Conditional Clauses   181
  By the Use of Indirect Discourse   184
    Employing a ὅτι Clause   184
    Employing a ἵνα or ὅπως
      Clause   185
    Employing a Clause Introduced
      by τί   185
    Employing an Infinitive   186
    Employing a Participle   186

Subject Index   188

Scripture Index   190

PREFACE

There are a number of grammars of the Greek New Testament which deal with the subject of syntax. Major works include the following:

F. Blass and A. Debrunner, *Greek Grammar of the New Testament and Other Early Christian Literature,* translated and revised by Robert W. Funk (Chicago: University of Chicago Press, 1961)

James Hope Moulton, *Grammar of the Greek New Testament,* Vol. III, *Syntax,* by Nigel Turner (Edinburgh: T. & T. Clark, 1963)

A.T. Robertson, *Grammar of the Greek New Testament in the Light of Historical Research* (Nashville: Broadman Press, [4]1923)

Smaller, handbook-type editions include:

William Douglas Chamberlain, *Exegetical Grammar of the Greek New Testament* (New York: Macmillan Company, 1941)

Robert W. Funk, *A Beginning-Intermediate Grammar of Hellenistic Greek,* Vol. II, *Syntax* (Missoula, Montana: Society of Biblical Literature, [2]1973)

H.E. Dana and Julius R. Mantey, *Manual Grammar of the Greek New Testament* (New York: Macmillan Company, 1927)

J. Harold Greenlee, *Concise Exegetical Grammar of New Testament Greek* (Grand Rapids: Wm. B. Eerdmans Publishing Company, [3]1963)

William Sanford LaSor, *Handbook of New Testament Greek: An Inductive Approach Based on the Greek Text of Acts,* Vol. II *Grammar* (Grand Rapids: Wm. B. Eerdmans Publishing Company, 1973)

C.F.D. Moule, *Idiom-Book of New Testament Greek* (Cambridge: University Press, [2]1963)

A.T. Robertson and W. Hersey Davis, *New Short Grammar of the Greek Testament* (New York: Harper & Brothers Publishers, [10]1933)

Curtis Vaughan and Virtus E. Gideon, *A Greek Grammar of the New Testament, A Workbook Approach to Intermediate Grammar* (Nashville: Broadman Press, 1979)

Maximillian Zerwick, *Biblical Greek,* translated and adapted by Joseph Smith (Rome: Biblical Institute Press, 1963)

Works on particular subjects include:

Ernest de Witt Burton, *Syntax of the Moods and Tenses in New Testament Greek* (Edinburgh: T. & T. Clark, [3]1898)

In the opinion of the present writers none of the above grammars is altogether satisfactory for the seminary or college student who begins a study of syntax during the first or second year of Greek. The volume by Dana and Mantey is perhaps the best, but it still leaves something to be desired. It is the purpose of this book to introduce the student to Greek syntax with maximum exposure to examples in the New Testament. An attempt has been made to improve upon other grammars by (1) better descriptions of the various syntactical categories and (2) the presentation of more examples of each category of use, printing each example in Greek and English translation, and italicizing the word or words involved. The descriptions of the various categories owe something to all of the grammars mentioned above, and no attempt has been made to document. The examples have been taken from these grammars and from the present writers' own reading of the Greek New Testament. The Greek text is that of The United Bible Societies' *Greek New Testament* ([3]1975).[1] In some instances, however, its punctuation has been altered, and various introductory words such as γάρ and δέ have been omitted, in order to make the examples as brief and clear as possible. The translation has been made for the purpose of illustrating syntactical usage, not to provide the best translation for general use. In most instances

---

[1]Cited with permission of the publishers.

five examples are given of each use. In the case of substantives used with prepositions, only two examples under each preposition have been cited.

The writers desire to express their appreciation to Mrs. Cheryl Walters Rahaim for her invaluable assistance in typing the manuscript. They also express appreciation to Drs. Ray Frank Robbins and J. Hardee Kennedy and the New Orleans Baptist Theological Seminary for providing extra funds for securing typing services and for their encouragement.

INTRODUCTION

Accidence or morphology is that aspect of grammar which deals with word formation. In the case of Greek, accidence involves inflection, which in turn involves declension and conjugation. Syntax is that aspect of grammar which deals with the relationship and use of words and larger elements in a sentence. This book attempts to treat certain aspects of Greek syntax. No attempt is made to be exhaustive. Not treated are the more elementary aspects of syntax, which are best learned in connection with accidence.

It is usually possible to give the accidence of, i.e. to parse, or analyze, or locate, an individual word apart from its use in a sentence. Accidence involves a rather mechanical type of study which yields a high degree of certainty. The syntax of a word, however, is always dependent upon the context in which it is used. Syntax therefore always involves interpretation, and interpretation usually involves a subjective element. In some instances there will be uncertainty or even disagreement. Gramarians do not always agree about the various syntactical categories, and exegetes do not always agree about the syntax of a particular word. Although certainty and agreement are not always possible, an attempt must be made to determine the syntax of key elements in the Greek New Testament. Translation and exegesis often depend upon such determination.

Part I
THE SUBSTANTIVE

A substantive is a noun or any word or group of words which may be used as a noun. The adjective, the article, and the pronoun function as substantives. Certain participles and infinitives also function as substantives. Prepositions as such are not substantives, but they are used with substantives and are usually treated along with them. Phrases and clauses which function as substantives will be treated separately.

CHARACTERISTICS

There are three characteristics or qualities or elements which are inherent in the Greek substantive.

NUMBER

Number is that aspect of a substantive which indicates whether it is singular (one person or one thing) or plural (two or more). During the Classical Period there was a third category, the dual. The dual referred to two persons or things, the plural to three or more. The dual, however, was a luxury the language could not afford, and it died out during the Koine Period. There is no example of it in the New Testament. Number can usually be determined mechanically by observing the form of the word.

GENDER

Gender, in English at least, is that aspect of a substantive which indicates its sex: masculine, feminine, or neuter. The sex

1

of a Greek substantive, however, does not always correspond to that of an English substantive, and in Greek gender is more a matter of grammar than sex. Gender can usually be determined mechanically by consulting a lexicon and/or by observing the form of the word.

CASE

Case is that aspect of a substantive which indicates its grammatical relationship to the verb and/or other elements in the sentence. The Greek substantive appears in four, or in some instances five, case forms which are often referred to as the first, second, third, fourth, and fifth inflected forms. Grammarians are divided as to whether case is determined by form or use. If the former, there are five cases which correspond to the five inflected forms: the nominative, the genitive, the dative, the accusative, and the vocative. If the latter, there are eight cases. The nominative employs the first inflected form; the genitive and ablative the second; the dative, locative, and instrumental the third; the accusative the fourth; and the vocative the fifth. (If there is no fifth inflected form the vocative also employs the first inflected from in both the five- and eight-case systems.) This book will employ the eight-case system but will provide cross references to the five-case system.

Words in the fourth and fifth inflected forms will always be accusative and vocative respectively. In all other instances the case of a substantive must be determined by its use in the sentence. A word in the first inflected form may be nominative or vocative; a word in the second genitive or ablative; and a word in the third dative, locative, or instrumental. Inasmuch as neuter nouns have only three case forms—the first being used for the nominative, accusative, and vocative; the second and third as above—their case must be determined in every instance by use in the sentence. And in every instance the particular syntax of the case of a word must be determined by the way in which it is used.

Prepositions are function words which assist substantives in expressing their case relationship. They help interpret the syntax of case. They help define case usage. Prepositions are also prefixed to verbs to form compound verbs, but such use in composition is not relevant to the present subject. There are also a number of adverbs which are used with substantives in exactly the same way as prepositions. When so used they are sometimes referred to as improper prepositions or adverbial prepositions. Such adverbs differ from true prepositions in that prepositions were originally adverbs and even in the New Testament are occasionally used as adverbs, but in the development of the language they more and more came to be orientated toward substantives rather than verbs. In the following discussion of syntactical categories an indication is made of which prepositions and adverbs, if any, are used with each category. Also, at the conclusion of the treatment of the cases, there is a complete list of both true prepositions and adverbial prepositions together with an indication of the cases with which they are used and of their particular function(s) with each case. Prepositions are used only with the oblique cases, i.e. those other than the nominative and the vocative.

In the following discussion of syntactical categories an attempt is made to give five examples where the substantive is used by itself and two examples where the substantive is used with a preposition. Where an adverb is involved, however, only references are given.

THE NOMINATIVE

The basic idea expressed by the nominative is that of designation, naming, pointing out. It has the following uses.

Subject Nominative

A word in the nominative which functions as the subject of a finite verb indicates who or what produces the action or is involved in the state of being expressed by that verb. Of course the verb ending also indicates a subject, but when the verb is in the third person there is often a need to be more specific, to actually designate or name the subject.

τὸ φῶς ἐν τῇ σκοτίᾳ φαίνει. (John 1:5)
The light shines in the darkness.

οἱ λοιποὶ ἐπωρώθησαν. (Rom. 11:7)
The rest were hardened.

οὗτος ἦν ἐν ἀρχῇ πρὸς τὸν θεόν. (John 1:2)
This man was in the beginning with God.

ὁ ἐναρξάμενος ἐν ὑμῖν ἔργον ἀγαθὸν ἐπιτελέσει ἄχρι ἡμέρας
Χριστοῦ Ἰησοῦ. (Phil. 1:6))
The one who began in you a good work will continue (it) until
the day of Christ Jesus.

τὸ θέλειν παράκειταί μοι. (Rom. 7:18)
To will is present with me.

Predicate Nominative

The object of a copulative or linking verb employs the nominative rather than the accusative case and is called a predicate
nominative. Copulative verbs express a state of being rather
than an action. The most common are εἰμί, γίνομαι, and
ὑπάρχω. These verbs link together a subject and an object which
are in apposition, which are closely related if not identical.
(Some grammarians would also look upon καλέω as a copulative verb, but it is preferable to describe the syntax of its object
as a nominative of appelation. See below.)

αὐτός ἐστιν ἡ εἰρήνη ἡμῶν. (Eph. 2:14)
He himself is our *peace.*

ὁ θεὸς ἀγάπη ἐστίν. (I John 4:8)
God is *love.*

ὁ λόγος σὰρξ ἐγένετο. (John 1:14).
The Word became *flesh.*

γίνεσθε ποιηταὶ λόγου. (James 1:22)
Become *doers* of the word.

οὗτος ἄρχων τῆς συναγωγῆς ὑπῆρχεν. (Luke 8:41)
This man was *a ruler* of the synagogue.

Nominative of Appelation

Ordinarily a proper noun appears in whatever case is required by its use in the sentence. Sometimes, however, a proper noun is given in the nominative case regardless of how it is used. Such usage is called a nominative of appelation. Inasmuch as the nominative is the naming case, this use is quite logical and natural.[1]

ἐκλήθη τὸ ὄνομα αὐτοῦ Ἰησοῦς. (Luke 2:21)
His name was called *Jesus.*

ὄνομα ἔχει Ἀπολλύων. (Rev. 9:11)
He has the name *Apollyon.*

φωνεῖτέ με Ὁ διδάσκαλος καὶ Ὁ κύριος. (John 13:13)
You call me *Teacher* and *Lord.*

Note: *In the preceding examples the nominative* Ἀπολλύων *is in apposition with the accusative* ὄνομα, *and the nominatives* διδάσκαλος *and* κύριος *are in apposition with the accusative* με. *All nominatives of appelation have an appositive quality. Also, the words Jesus, Apollyon, Teacher, and Lord could very well be put in quotation marks in a modern language.*

ἐγένετο ἄνθρωπος ἀπεσταλμένος παρὰ θεοῦ, ὄνομα αὐτῷ Ἰωάννης. (John 1:6)
A man appeared who was sent from God, whose name (was) *John.*

Note: *The syntax of* Ἰωάννης *could also be interpreted as a predicate nominative by understanding the verb* ἦν.

χάρις ὑμῖν καὶ εἰρήνη ἀπὸ ὁ ὢν καὶ ὁ ἦν καὶ ὁ ἐρχόμενος. (Rev. 1:4)
Grace and peace to you from *The One Who Is* and *The One Who Was* and *The One Who Is Coming.*

Independent Nominative

This use is also called nominative absolute or hanging nominative. It has no grammatical relationship to a complete sen-

---

[1] Indeclinable proper nouns should not be treated as nominatives of appelation but should be given whatever case is required by their uses in the sentence.

tence. This kind of nominative appears in at least six types of constructions.

1. *Where a change of construction suddenly takes place.* Some grammarians refer to this use as the nominative of apposition because the word in the nominative is in apposition with a word in another case.

ὁ νικῶν ποιήσω αὐτὸν στῦλον ἐν τῷ ναῷ τοῦ θεοῦ μου . . . καὶ γράψω ἐπ᾽ αὐτὸν τὸ ὄνομα . . . τῆς πόλεως τοῦ θεοῦ μου, τῆς καινῆς Ἰερουσαλήμ, ἡ καταβαίνουσα ἐκ τοῦ οὐρανοῦ. (Rev. 3:12)
The one who conquers I will make him a pillar in the temple of my God, and I will write upon him the name of the city of my God, the new Jerusalem, *which comes down* from heaven.

πᾶν ῥῆμα ἀργὸν ὃ λαλήσουσιν οἱ ἄνθρωποι ἀποδώσουσιν περὶ αὐτοῦ λόγον ἐν ἡμέρᾳ κρίσεως. (Matt. 12:36)
Every idle word which men shall speak, they shall render an account for it on the day of judgment.

Note: *In the above examples observe how the nominative* ὁ νικῶν *is in apposition with the accusative* αὐτόν, *the nominative* ἡ καταβαίνουσα *is in apposition with the genitive* τῆς καινῆς Ἰερουσαλήμ, *and the nominative* πᾶν ῥῆμα ἀργόν *is in apposition with the genitive* αὐτοῦ.

2. *In the salutations of letters.*

Παῦλος δοῦλος Χριστοῦ Ἰησοῦ . . . πᾶσιν τοῖς οὖσιν ἐν Ῥώμῃ . . . . χάρις ὑμῖν καὶ εἰρήνη ἀπὸ θεοῦ . . . . (Rom. 1:1,7)
Paul a servant of Christ Jesus to all who are in Rome. *Grace* to you and *peace* from God.

Note: χάρις *and* εἰρήνη *could possibly be construed as subject nominatives by understanding the verb* ἔστω.

3. *In the titles of books.*

Ἀποκάλυψις Ἰωάννου (the title of Revelation)
The Revelation of John.

4. *In proverbial expressions and quotations.*

κύων ἐπιστρέψας ἐπὶ τὸ ἴδιον ἐξέραμα, καὶ, ὗς λουσαμένη εἰς κυλισμὸν βορβόρου. (II Pet. 2:22)
A *dog* returns to its own vomit, and, a *pig* is "washed" by rolling in the mire.

Note: *Although it is necessary to translate them as such in English,* κύων *and* ὗς *are not subjects of a finite verb.* ἐπιστρέψας *and* λουσαμένη *are participles, not finite verbs as the English translation might lead one to think.*

ὁ δρασσόμενος τοὺς σοφοὺς ἐν τῇ πανουργίᾳ αὐτῶν. (I Cor. 3:19)
Literally: *The one who grasps the wise* in their own craftiness.
Idiomatically: God traps the wise in their own craftiness.

5. *In exclamations.* It is uncertain whether the use of the nominative in exclamations should be treated as a separate category or a subdivision of the independent nominative.

Ἴδε ἡ μήτηρ μου καὶ οἱ ἀδελφοί μου. (Mark 3:34)
Behold my *mother* and my *brothers*!

Ὦ Βάθος πλούτου καὶ σοφίας καὶ γνώσεως θεοῦ. (Rom. 11:33)
O *the depth* of the riches and wisdom and knowledge of God!

6. *In expressions of time where the use of the accusative might be expected.*

σπλαγχνίζομαι ἐπὶ τὸν ὄχλον ὅτι ἤδη ἡμέραι τρεῖς προσμένουσίν μοι. (Mark 8:2)
I have compassion upon the multitude because already they have remained with me *for three days.*

Apposition

A word in any of the cases may stand in apposition with another word in the same case. For example in Rom. 1:1 (above) δοῦλος is in apposition with Παῦλος. It would be correct to call δοῦλος a nominative of apposition, but it is not customary to provide a separate category for words in apposition with another word in the same case. There are special kinds of apposition, however, such as the genitive of apposition (below), which demand a separate category.

THE GENITIVE

The basic function of the genitive is to describe and define. It does so by attributing a quality or relationship to a substantive. It limits the meaning and application of a substantive. It does so by answering the question, What kind? Therefore the genitive functions very much like an adjective. It has the following uses.

Genitive of Description

All genitives are to a greater or lesser degree descriptive. Therefore some grammarians prefer to call this use the genitive of quality or the attributive genitive. Whatever the name, this use of the genitive is the nearest to the basic meaning of the case as described above. This category employs the substantive without a preposition.

τὸ σῶμα τῆς ἁμαρτίας (Rom. 6:6)
the body *of sin*

υἱοὶ φωτός (I Thess. 5:5)
sons *of light*

λόγοις τῆς χάριτος (Luke 4:22)
words *of grace*

καρδία πονηρὰ ἀπιστίας (Heb. 3:12)
an evil heart *of unbelief*

ἡμέρᾳ ὀργῆς (Rom. 2:5)
a day *of wrath*

σκεῦος ἐκλογῆς (Acts 9:15)
a *chosen* vessel

Genitive of Possession

This use of the genitive defines, describes, and limits by denoting ownership. A test for the genitive of possession is whether the expression "belonging to" can be substituted for the preposition "of" with which the genitive is usually translated but which is often ambiguous. This category employs the substantive without a preposition.

ἀπέσπασεν τὴν μάχαιραν αὐτοῦ καὶ πατάξας τὸν δοῦλον τοῦ ἀρχιερέως ἀφεῖλεν αὐτοῦ τὸ ὠτίον, (Matt. 26:51)

He drew out *his* sword and having struck the servant *of the high priest* cut off *his* ear.

Παῦλος ἀπόστολος Χριστοῦ Ἰησοῦ (II Cor. 1:1)

Paul an apostle *of Christ Jesus*

πάντα ὑμῶν ἐστιν. (I Cor. 3:21)

All things are *yours.*

ἐγώ εἰμι ἡ θύρα τῶν προβάτων. (John 10:7)

I am the door *of the sheep.*

ἔδωκεν αὐτοῖς ἐξουσίαν τέκνα θεοῦ γενέσθαι. (John 1:12)

He gave to them power to become children *of God.*

Genitive of Relationship

Despite the fact that most grammarians make a separate category of it, this genitive is really a specialized use of the genitive of possession. It indicates some aspect of marital or genital or even social relationship. The exact relationship (son, daughter, brother, sister, etc.) is not stated but must be determined on the basis of other knowledge. This category employs the substantive without a preposition.

Ἰάκωβον τὸν τοῦ Ζεβεδαίου (Matt. 4:21)

James the (son) *of Zebedee*

τὸν Ἰούδαν Σίμωνος Ἰσκαριώτου (John 6:71)

Judas the (son) *of Simon Iscariot*

Σίμων Ἰωάννου (John 21:15)

Simon (son) *of John*

Μαρία ἡ Ἰακώβου (Luke 24:10)

Mary the (mother) *of James*

οἱ τοῦ Χριστοῦ (Gal. 5:24)

the (followers) *of Christ*

Adverbial Genitive

Sometimes the genitive modifies a verb rather than a substantive. In such case it is an adverbial genitive and functions in
much the same way as does an adverb.

1. *Adverbial Genitive of Time.* A genitive which is used
adverbially to express time usually indicates kind of time,
time within which, or one time as opposed to another time.
Time is also expressed in Greek by the locative, the instrumental, and the accusative (and even the nominative—see page 7).
Theoretically the locative is used to indicate time at which—a
particular point in time, the instrumental to indicate time
within which—two points of time separated by means of a
period of time, and the accusative to indicate time throughout
which—duration or extent of time. During the Koine Period,
however, such distinctions were not always maintained. This
category employs:

(1) The Substantive without a Preposition.

ὁ δὲ θεὸς οὐ μὴ ποιήσῃ τὴν ἐκδίκησιν τῶν ἐκλεκτῶν αὐτοῦ
τῶν βοώντων αὐτῷ ἡμέρας καὶ νυκτός; (Luke 18:7)
And will not God make a vindication of his elect who cry to him
day and *night*?

προσεύχεσθε ἵνα μὴ γένηται ἡ φυγὴ ὑμῶν χειμῶνος. (Matt. 24:20)
Pray that your flight may not be *in winter.*

νηστεύω δὶς τοῦ σαββάτου. (Luke 18:12)
I fast twice *during the week.*

οἱ πυλῶνες αὐτῆς οὐ μὴ κλεισθῶσιν ἡμέρας. (Rev. 21:25)
Its gates shall not be shut *by day.*

Καϊάφας, ἀρχιερεὺς ὢν τοῦ ἐνιαυτοῦ ἐκείνου (John 11:49)
Caiaphas who was high priest *that year*

(2) The Substantive with the Preposition διά.[2]

---

[2]A complete list of prepositions and adverbial prepositions cited in
this section appears on pp. 65-96.

δι' ὅλης νυκτὸς κοπιάσαντες οὐδὲν ἐλάβομεν. (Luke 5:5)
Although we have toiled *throughout the whole night*, we have
caught nothing.

ἔπειτα διὰ δεκατεσσάρων ἐτῶν πάλιν ἀνέβην εἰς Ἱεροσόλυμα.
(Gal. 2:1)
Then *after fourteen years* again I went up to Jerusalem.

(3) The Substantive with the Preposition ἐπί.

ἐπὶ ἀρχιερέως Ἄννα καὶ Καϊάφα, ἐγένετο ῥῆμα θεοῦ ἐπὶ
Ἰωάννην. (Luke 3:2)
During the high priesthood of Annas and Caiaphas the word of
God came to John.

ἐγένετο ἐπὶ Κλαυδίου. (Acts 11:28)
It came to pass *during the (reign) of Claudius.*

(4) The Substantive with Adverbial Prepositions.

ἄχρι (Luke 1:20; 4:13); ἕως (Matt. 27:8, 45); μέχρι(ς) (Matt.
28:15; Acts 10:30); ὀψέ (Matt. 28:1 only—but this use may be
an ablative of separation)

2. *Adverbial Genitive of Measure.* This use of the genitive
indicates how much and how far. It includes what some grammarians call the genitive of price or genitive of value or genitive
of quantity. It also includes what some grammarians call the
genitive of penalty. This category employs:

(1) The Substantive without a Preposition.

οὐχὶ δύο στρουθία ἀσσαρίου πωλεῖται; (Matt. 10:29)
Are not two sparrows sold *for a farthing?*

χοῖνιξ σίτου δηναρίου, καὶ τρεῖς χοίνικες κριθῶν δηναρίου.
(Rev. 6:6)
A measure of wheat *for a denarius* and three measures of barley
for a denarius.

ἠγοράσθητε τιμῆς. (I Cor. 6:20)
You were bought *for a price.*

οὐχὶ δηναρίου συνεφώνησάς μοι; (Matt. 20:13)
Did you not agree with me *for a denarius?*

μισθοῦ ἐξεχύθησαν. (Jude 11)
They abandoned themselves *for financial reward.*

(2) The Substantive with Adverbial Prepositions.

ἄχρι (Acts 22:4, 22); ἕως (Matt. 26:38; Mark 6:23);
μέχρι(ς) (II Tim. 2:9; Heb. 12:4)

3. *Adverbial Genitive of Place.* Place is most often expressed by the locative case. When a genitive is used to denote place the emphasis is usually upon kind of place, one place as opposed to another place, here and not there. The locative simply indicates a particular place, a spot, an area. This category employs:

(1) The Substantive without a Preposition.

ἐκείνης ἤμελλεν διέρχεσθαι. (Luke 19:4)
He was going to pass along *that (way).*

οὐ μόνον Ἐφέσου ἀλλὰ σχεδὸν πάσης τῆς Ἀσίας ὁ Παῦλος οὗτος πείσας μετέστησεν ἱκανὸν ὄχλον. (Acts 19:26)
Not only *in Ephesus* but *in* almost *all of Asia* this man Paul having persuaded (them) has perverted a large multitude.

Note: Ἀσίας *could be interpreted as a partitive ablative (below page 30).*

μετὰ τὴν μετοικεσίαν Βαβυλῶνος (Matt. 1:12)
after the deportation *to Babylon*

μὴ εὑρόντες ποίας εἰσενέγκωσιν αὐτόν (Luke 5:19)
when they did not find *what* (way) they could bring him in

Πέτρος ἀπόστολος Ἰησοῦ Χριστοῦ ἐκλεκτοῖς παρεπιδήμοις διασπορᾶς Πόντου, Γαλατίας, Καππαδοκίας, Ἀσίας, καὶ Βιθυνίας. (I Peter 1:1)
Peter an apostle of Jesus Christ to the elect who sojourn *in the dispersion, in Pontus, in Galatia, in Cappadocia, in Asia,* and *in Bithynia.*

(2) The Substantive with the Preposition διά.

ἔδει αὐτὸν διέρχεσθαι διὰ τῆς Σαμαρείας. (John 4:4)
It was necessary for him to pass *through Samaria.*

παρεπορεύοντο διὰ τῆς Γαλιλαίας. (Mark 9:30)
They went *through Galilee.*

(3) The Substantive with the Preposition ἐπί.

ἐξουσίαν ἔχει ὁ υἱὸς τοῦ ἀνθρώπου ἀφιέναι ἁμαρτίας ἐπὶ τῆς γῆς. (Mark 2:10)
The Son of Man has authority *on earth* to forgive sins.

ἐθεώρουν τὰ σημεῖα ἃ ἐποίει ἐπὶ τῶν ἀσθενούντων. (John 6:2)
They beheld the miracles which he performed *on the sick.*

(4) The Substantive with the Preposition κατά.

φήμη ἐξῆλθεν καθ' ὅλης τῆς περιχώρου περὶ αὐτοῦ. (Luke 4:14)
A report concerning him went *throughout all the surrounding territory.*

ἡ ἐκκλησία καθ' ὅλης τῆς Ἰουδαίας. . . εἶχεν εἰρήνην. (Acts 9:31)
The church *throughout all Judea* had peace.

Note: *This use is found only in Luke-Acts and always in connection with* ὅλος.

(5) The Substantive with Adverbial Prepositions.

ἄντικρυς	(Acts 20:15 only)
ἀντιπέρα	(Luke 8:26 only)
ἄχρι	(Acts 11:5; 13:6)
ἐγγύς	(Luke 19:11; John 11:54)
ἔναντι	(Luke 1:8; Acts 8:21)
ἐναντίον	(Luke 1:6; 20:26)
ἐντός	(Luke 17:21 only)
ἐνώπιον	(Luke 1:15; Rev. 4:10)
ἐπάνω	(Matt. 5:14; Luke 10:19)
ἔσω	(Mark 15:16 only)
ἕως	(Luke 2:15; Acts 11:19)
κατέναντι	(Mark 12:41; 13:3)
κατενώπιον	(Eph. 1:4; Jude 24)
κυκλόθεν	(Rev. 4:3-4)
κύκλῳ	(Rev. 4:6; 5:11)
μέσον	(Phil. 2:15; Matt. 14:24 variant reading)

μέχρι   (Luke 16:16; Rom. 15:19)
πλησίον   (John 4:5 only)

4. *Adverbial Genitive of Reference.* Some grammarians limit this category to those instances where the genitive functions as an adverb which modifies an adjective. There are other instances, however, when the genitive means "with reference to." This category employs:

(1) The Substantive without a Preposition.

πᾶς γὰρ ὁ μετέχων γάλακτος ἄπειρος <u>λόγου</u> δικαιοσύνης. (Heb. 5:13)
For everyone who partakes of milk (is) inexperienced *with reference to the word* of righteousness.

ὁ γὰρ θεὸς ἀπείραστός ἐστιν <u>κακῶν</u>. (James 1:13)
For God is not capable of being tempted *with reference to evil things.*

(ἡ γλῶσσά ἐστι) μεστὴ <u>ἰοῦ θανατηφόρου</u>. (James 3:8)
The tongue is full *of deadly poison.*

ποιήσατε καρπὸν ἄξιον <u>τῆς μετανοίας</u>. (Matt. 3:8)
Produce fruit worthy *of repentance.*

πλήρης <u>χάριτος</u> καὶ <u>ἀληθείας</u>. (John 1:14)
full *of grace* and *truth.*

(2) The Substantive with the Preposition περί.

αὐτὸς ἱλασμός ἐστιν <u>περὶ τῶν ἁμαρτιῶν ἡμῶν</u>, οὐ <u>περὶ τῶν ἡμετέρων</u> δὲ μόνον ἀλλὰ καὶ <u>περὶ ὅλου τοῦ κόσμου</u>. (I Jo. 2:2)
He himself is the expiation *for our sins,* and not *for ours* only but also *for those of the whole world.*

<u>περὶ ὧν</u> ἐγράψατε .... (I Cor. 7:1)
Concerning the things about which you wrote. ...

(3) The Substantive with the Preposition ὑπέρ.

οὗτός ἐστιν <u>ὑπὲρ οὗ</u> ἐγὼ εἶπον. (John 1:30)
This is the one *about whom* I spoke.

εἴτε <u>ὑπὲρ Τίτου</u>, κοινωνὸς ἐμὸς καὶ εἰς ὑμᾶς συνεργός. (II Cor. 8:23)
As for Titus, (he is) my partner and fellow worker for you.

Genitive with Nouns of Action.

A noun of action is a noun the definition of which contains a verbal idea. Often there will be a cognate verb which has the same root. The following are examples of nouns of action: ἀγάπη (cf. ἀγαπάω), ὀργή (cf. ὀργίζω), δέησις (cf. δέομαι). Contrast the following nouns which imply no action: ἄνθρωπος, καρδία, καρπός. Most nouns which end in -σις or -μος are nouns of action, but there are many others which must be recognized by their meaning. This category employs the substantive without a preposition.

1. *Subjective Genitive.* If the word in the genitive produces the action implied by the noun of action, it functions as the "subject" of the verbal idea contained in the noun of action and is therefore a subjective genitive. To put it another way, if the noun of action were replaced by a cognate verb in the active voice, the word in the genitive would be put in the nominative case and would become the subject of the verb.

τίς ἡμᾶς χωρίσει ἀπὸ τῆς ἀγάπης τοῦ Χριστοῦ; (Rom. 8:35)
Who shall separate us from the love *of Christ?*

ἀποκαλύπτεται ὀργὴ θεοῦ. . . (Rom. 1:18)
The wrath *of God* is revealed. . .

ἐν τῇ ὑπομονῇ ὑμῶν. . . (Luke 21:19)
by *your* endurance. . .

ἡ πίστις σου σέσωκέν σε. (Luke 18:42)
Your faith has saved you.

τὴν πάντων ὑμῶν ὑπακοήν (II Cor. 7:15)
the obedience *of all of you*

2. *Objective Genitive.* If the word in the genitive receives the action implied by the noun of action, it functions as the object of the verbal idea contained in the noun of action and is, therefore, an objective genitive. In some instances the objective genitive appears in an interpretative translation as the direct object

of the verbal idea, in others as the object of a preposition such as about, against, concerning, in, to, towards.

τὸ μαρτύριον τοῦ Χριστοῦ ἐβεβαιώθη ἐν ὑμῖν. (I Cor. 1:6)
The testimony *about Christ* was confirmed among you.

ἔχετε πίστιν θεοῦ. (Mark 11:22)
Have faith *in God.*

ἡ δὲ τοῦ πνεύματος βλασφημία οὐκ ἀφεθήσεται. (Matt. 12:31)
But blasphemy *against the Spirit* shall not be forgiven.

διὰ τὸν φόβον τῶν Ἰουδαίων (John 7:13)
because of fear *of the Jews*

δεῖ . . . μάρτυρα τῆς ἀναστάσεως αὐτοῦ σὺν ἡμῖν γενέσθαι ἕνα τούτων. (Acts 1:22)
One of these must become a witness *to* his *resurrection* with us.

Note: *Only the context can determine whether a genitive which modifies a noun of action is subjective or objective. In other words, a decision must be made on the basis of exegesis rather than a rule of grammar. Sometimes a decision is difficult. Take, for example, the expression* τὸ κήρυγμα Ἰησοῦ Χριστοῦ *in Rom. 16:25. Is* Ἰησοῦ Χριστοῦ *a subjective genitive: that which Jesus Christ preached? Dana and Mantey think so. Or is it an objective genitive: the preaching about Jesus Christ? Robertson in his* Word Pictures *says it is.*

Genitive of Apposition

If the word in the genitive is identical with the word it modifies, it is a genitive of apposition. Indeed, this use is sometimes called the genitive of identity. It is also sometimes called the genitive of content and the genitive of definition or explanation. What some grammarians call the genitive of material is included in this category. One should carefully note that the word with which the genitive is in apposition may or may not be in the genitive case. At this point the genitive of apposition differs from ordinary apposition where the words involved must be in the same case. A test for this use of the genitive is the ability to use some such expression as "consisting of," "namely," "filled with," or "made of" in the translation. This category employs the substantive without a preposition.

σημεῖον ἔλαβεν περιτομῆς. (Rom. 4:11)
He received a sign *of circumcision.*

ἐὰν ἡ ἐπίγειος ἡμῶν οἰκία τοῦ σκήνους καταλυθῇ. . . . (II Cor. 5:1)
If our earthly house *consisting of this tent* should be destroyed. . . .

. . . ὁ δοὺς ἡμῖν τὸν ἀρραβῶνα τοῦ πνεύματος. (II Cor. 5:5)
. . . who has given to us the guarantee *of the Spirit.*

πόλεις Σοδόμων καὶ Γομόρρας (II Pet. 2:6)
the cities *of Sodom* and *Gomorra.*

. . . ἐποικοδομηθέντες ἐπὶ τῷ θεμελίῳ τῶν ἀποστόλων καὶ προφητῶν. (Eph. 2:20)
. . . having been built upon a foundation *which consists of the apostles* and *prophets.*

Genitive Absolute

This construction involves the use of a noun or a pronoun and a participle, both of which are in the genitive case, and neither of which has any grammatical relationship to the main clause. The noun in the genitive produces the action expressed by the participle and in English translation could be looked upon as its subject, but it is different from the subject of the main verb. Therefore, the noun or pronoun in the genitive and the participle in the genitive stand apart from the remainder of the sentence. They are absolute. Occasionally the noun or pronoun in the genitive will be omitted as in the fifth example below. It is necessary to understand the subject of the participle in that case. This construction could also be treated as an ablative. It employs the substantive without a preposition.

χρονίζοντος τοῦ νυμφίου ἐνύσταξαν πᾶσαι καὶ ἐκάθευδον. (Matt. 25:5)
While the bridegroom tarried, all slumbered and slept.

εἰσελθόντος αὐτοῦ εἰς οἶκον οἱ μαθηταὶ αὐτοῦ κατ᾽ ἰδίαν ἐπηρώτων αὐτόν. . . . (Mark 9:28)

When he entered into the house, his disciples asked him privately. . . .

τοῦ Ἰησοῦ γεννηθέντος ἐν Βηθλέεμ . . . ἰδοὺ μάγοι ἀπὸ ἀνατολῶν παρεγένοντο. (Matt. 2:1)
When Jesus was born in Bethlehem, behold wise men came from the east.

καταβαινόντων αὐτῶν ἐκ τοῦ ὄρους ἐνετείλατο αὐτοῖς ὁ Ἰησοῦς λέγων . . . . (Matt. 17:9)
While they were coming down from the mountain, Jesus commanded them saying . . . .

καὶ ἐλθόντων πρὸς τὸν ὄχλον προσῆλθεν αὐτῷ ἄνθρωπος . . . . (Matt. 17:14)
And *when (they) came* to the crowd, a man came to him . . . .

Genitive of Advantage

This use of the genitive indicates the person or thing on behalf of whom or on the behalf of which something is done. It is similar to the dative of advantage (see below page 33). This category employs:

(1)   The Substantive without a Preposition.

. . . ἵνα ὁ θεὸς ἀνοίξῃ ἡμῖν θύραν τοῦ λόγου. (Col. 4:3)
. . . in order that God may open to us a door *for the word.*

. . . ἐπὶ εὐεργεσίᾳ ἀνθρώπου ἀσθενοῦς, . . . (Acts 4:9)
. . . concerning a good work *for a sick man,* . . .

(2)   The Substantive with the Preposition περί.

. . . ἔχω τὴν περὶ σοῦ μνείαν ἐν ταῖς δεήσεσίν μου . . . . (II Tim. 1:3)
. . . I pray *for you* . . . .

. . . ἐν πάσῃ προσκαρτερήσει καὶ δεήσει περὶ πάντων τῶν ἁγίων . . . . (Eph. 6:18)
. . . with all perseverence and prayer *for all the saints* . . . .

(3)   The Substantive with the Preposition πρός.

τοῦτο πρὸς τῆς ὑμετέρας σωτηρίας ὑπάρχει. (Acts 27:34)

This is *in the interest of your health.*

Note: *This is the only use of* πρός *with the genitive in the New Testament.*

(4) The Substantive with the Preposition ὑπέρ.

... δεήσει περὶ πάντων τῶν ἁγίων, καὶ ὑπὲρ ἐμοῦ, ... (Eph. 6:18-19)
... prayer for all the saints and *for me, ...*

Χριστὸς ἡμᾶς ἐξηγόρασεν ἐκ τῆς κατάρας τοῦ νόμου γενόμενος ὑπὲρ ἡμῶν κατάρα. (Gal. 3:13)
Christ redeemed us from the curse of the law by means of becoming a curse *for us.*

Note: ὑπέρ *may convey the idea of substitution. The preceding example could be translated:* ... in our place.

Genitive of Association

The instrumental is the usual case for expressing the idea of association (see below page 47). Association is expressed in the genitive case only by the substantive with the preposition μετά. It is difficult to see any difference in this use of μετά with the genitive and the use of σύν with the instrumental.

οὐκέτι μετ' αὐτοῦ περιεπάτουν. (John 6:66)
They no longer walked *with him.*

ἦν μετὰ τῶν θηρίων. (Mark 1:13)
He was *with the wild beasts.*

Genitive of Attendant Circumstances

A substantive in the genitive with μετά may indicate emotional reactions or phenomena which accompany the action of the verb.

... δεξάμενοι τὸν λόγον ἐν θλίψει πολλῇ μετὰ χαρᾶς πνεύματος ἁγίου. (I Thess. 1:6)
... having received the word in much affliction (but also) *with joy* inspired by the Holy Spirit.

ὄψονται τὸν υἱὸν τοῦ ἀνθρώπου ἐρχόμενον ἐπὶ τῶν νεφελῶν τοῦ οὐρανοῦ μετὰ δυνάμεως καὶ δόξης πολλῆς. (Matt. 24:30)

They shall see the Son of Man coming upon the clouds of heaven *with power* and *great glory.*

Genitive of Oaths

The genitive with κατά may be used with a verb of swearing to indicate the person by whom one swears. Compare the accusative with oaths (see below page 57).

ἐξορκίζω σε κατὰ τοῦ θεοῦ. (Matt. 26:63)
I adjure you *by God.*

ἄνθρωποι κατὰ τοῦ μείζονος ὀμνύουσιν. (Heb. 6:16)
Men swear *by a greater person.*

Genitive of Root Idea or Genitive of Direct Object

Some verbs have a root idea (i.e. a meaning) which is so closely related to the root idea of the genitive (i.e. description, definition) that they take their direct object in the genitive rather than in the accusative case. Therefore, a genitive which functions as the direct object of a verb is a genitive of root idea. This category employs the substantive without a preposition.

ἤκουσεν συμφωνίας καὶ χορῶν. (Luke 15:25)
He heard *music* and *dancing.*

ἀργυρίου ἢ χρυσίου ἢ ἱματισμοῦ οὐδενὸς ἐπεθύμησα. (Acts 20:33)
I coveted the *silver* or *gold* or *garment* of no man.

ἀκούσας δὲ ὅτι Ἀρχέλαος βασιλεύει τῆς Ἰουδαίας ἀντὶ τοῦ πατρὸς αὐτοῦ Ἡρῴδου ἐφοβήθη ἐκεῖ ἀπελθεῖν. (Matt. 2:22)
And when he heard that Archelaus was ruling *Judea* instead of his father Herod he was afraid to go there.

ἐπεὶ οὖν τὰ παιδία κεκοινώνηκεν αἵματος καὶ σαρκός, καὶ αὐτὸς παραπλησίως μετέσχεν τῶν αὐτῶν. (Heb. 2:14)
Since therefore the children have partaken of *blood* and *flesh,* he himself in like manner also shared *the same things.*

καλοῦ ἔργου ἐπιθυμεῖ. (I Tim. 3:1)
He desires *a good work.*

THE ABLATIVE

The ablative case is used to express the idea of separation. It indicates such things as point of departure, source, origin.

Inasmuch as both the genitive and the ablative employ the same case form, one must first decide whether a word in the second inflected form is genitive or ablative. This can usually be done by asking whether the use of the word reflects kind, description, definition—in which case the word is genitive—or separation—in which case the word is ablative.

The ablative has the following uses.

Ablative of Separation

The word in the ablative denotes that from which something is separated. In a five-case system this category would be known as the genitive of separation. It employs:

(1) The Substantive without a Preposition.

οὐ γάρ ἐστιν διαστολὴ Ἰουδαίου τε καὶ Ἕλληνος. (Rom. 10:12)
For there is no distinction *between Jew* and *Greek.*

διάκρισιν καλοῦ τε καὶ κακοῦ (Heb. 5:14)
discernment *between good* and *evil*

ἀπεστερημένων τῆς ἀληθείας (I Tim. 6:5)
deprived *of the truth*

ἐκώλυσεν αὐτοὺς τοῦ βουλήματος. (Acts 27:43)
He hindered them *from (carrying out) their plan.*

ἀπέχεσθαι εἰδωλοθύτων καὶ αἵματος καὶ πνικτῶν καὶ πορνείας
(Acts 15:29)
to abstain *from things sacrificed to idols, from blood, from things strangled,* and *from immorality.*

(2) The Substantive with the Preposition ἀπό.

βάλε ἀπὸ σοῦ. (Matt. 5:29)
Throw (it) *away from you.*

οὐδείς αἴρει αὐτὴν ἀπ᾽ ἐμοῦ. (John 10:18)

No man can take it *away from me.*

(3) The Substantive with the Preposition ἐκ.

οὐκ ἐρωτῶ ἵνα ἄρῃς αὐτοὺς ἐκ τοῦ κόσμου ἀλλ' ἵνα τηρήσῃς αὐτοὺς ἐκ τοῦ πονηροῦ. (John 17:15)
I do not ask that you take them *out of the world* but that you keep them *away from the evil one.*

ἐὰν ὑψωθῶ ἐκ τῆς γῆς, πάντας ἑλκύσω πρὸς ἐμαυτόν. (John 12:32)
If I be lifted up *from the earth,* I will draw all men to me.

(4) The Substantive with the Preposition πρό.

φύλακες πρὸ τῆς θύρας ἐτήρουν τὴν φυλακήν. (Acts 12:6)
Sentries (standing) *before the gate* were guarding the prison.

ἐδίωξαν τοὺς προφήτας τοὺς πρὸ ὑμῶν. (Matt. 5:12)
They persecuted the prophets who were *before you.*

Note: *The example in Acts 12:6 indicates place, that in Matt. 5:12 time. Other prepositions, which are used with the ablative, both proper and adverbial, also indicate place and time. It must not be thought, however, that the ablative indicates place and time in the same way as does the genitive. In the genitive it is usually kind of place and kind of time which is indicated. In the ablative the idea of separation is always present.*

(5) The Substantive with Adverbial Prepositions.

ἄνευ	(Matt. 10:29; I Pet. 3:1)
ἀπέναντι	(Matt. 27:24; Acts 3:16)
ἄτερ	(Luke 22:6, 35)
ἐκτός	(Acts 26:22; I Cor. 6:18)
ἔμπροσθεν	(Matt. 5:24; John 1:15)
ἔξω	(Matt. 10:14; Acts 16:13)
ἔξωθεν	(Rev. 11:2; 14:20)
ἐπέκεινα	(Acts 7:43 only)
μεταξύ	(Matt. 18:15; Rom. 2:15)
ὄπισθεν	(Matt. 15:23; Luke 23:26)
ὀπίσω	(Matt. 3:11; 4:19)
ὀψέ	(Matt. 28:1—but this use may be genitive of time)

παρεκτός	(Matt. 5:32; Acts 26:29)
πέραν	(Matt. 4:15; John 1:28)
πλήν	(Acts 15:28; 27:22)
ὑπεράνω	(Eph. 4:10; Heb. 9:5)
ὑπερέκεινα	(II Cor. 10:16 only)
ὑποκάτω	(Mark 6:11; 7:28)
χωρίς	(Matt. 13:34; 14:21)

Ablative of Source

If the word in the ablative is the source of the substantive it modifies, it is an ablative of source. It is admittedly a fine line which distinguishes separation and source. One must attempt to determine where the greater emphasis is. In a five-case system this category would be known as the genitive of source. It employs:

(1) The Substantive without a Preposition.

. . .περιμένειν τὴν ἐπαγγελίαν τοῦ πατρὸς ἣν ἠκούσατέ μου. (Acts 1:4)
. . .to await the promise *of the Father* which you have heard *from me.*

Note: *By the nature of the case there is a very close relationship between the subjective genitive and the ablative of source. That which is produced by a person owes its source to that person. Therefore, it is sometimes difficult to decide whether a word is a subjective genitive or an ablative of source. Such is the case with* πατρός *above. It should be remembered that the subjective genitive is always used with a noun of action. Such is not so with the ablative of source.* ἐπαγγελίαν *is certainly a noun of action. Therefore,* πατρός *is probably a subjective genitive. Another test is to ask whether the emphasis is on description or separation.*

. . . ἵνα ἡ ὑπερβολὴ τῆς δυνάμεως ᾖ τοῦ θεοῦ καὶ μὴ ἐξ ἡμῶν. (II Cor. 4:7)
. . . so that the greatness of the power may be *from God* and not from us.

. . . διὰ τῆς παρακλήσεως τῶν γραφῶν. (Rom. 15:4)
. . . through the consolation *from the Scriptures.*

πᾶσα προφητεία γραφῆς <u>ἰδίας ἐπιλύσεως</u> οὐ γίνεται. (II Pet. 1:20)
No prophecy of Scripture is (a matter) *of private interpretation*.

(2) The Substantive with the Preposition ἀπό.

οἴδαμεν ὅτι <u>ἀπὸ θεοῦ</u> ἐλήλυθας διδάσκαλος. (John 3:2)
We know that you are a teacher who has come *from God*.

Ἰησοῦν . . . τὸν <u>ἀπὸ Ναζαρέτ</u> (John 1:45)
Jesus the one *from Nazareth*

(3) The Substantive with the Preposition ἐκ.

οὐκ εἰσὶν <u>ἐκ τοῦ κόσμου</u> καθὼς ἐγὼ οὐκ εἰμὶ <u>ἐκ τοῦ κόσμου</u>. (John 17:14)
They are not *from the world* just as I am not *from the world*.

ἰδοὺ φωνὴ <u>ἐκ τῶν οὐρανῶν</u> λέγουσα . . . . (Matt. 3:17)
Behold a voice *from heaven* saying . . . .

(4) The Substantive with the Preposition κατά.

ἔβαλεν <u>κατ' αὐτῆς</u> ἄνεμος τυφωνικός. (Acts 27:14)
A fierce wind swept *down from it* (Crete).

ὥρμησεν ἡ ἀγέλη <u>κατὰ τοῦ κρημνοῦ</u>. (Mark 5:13)
The herd rushed *down from the cliff.*

(5) The Substantive with the Preposition παρά.

ἐξῆλθον <u>παρὰ τοῦ πατρός</u>. (John 16:28)
I went out *from the Father.*

πεπλήρωμαι δεξάμενος <u>παρὰ Ἐπαφροδίτου</u> τὰ <u>παρ' ὑμῶν</u>. (Phil. 4:18)
I am full because I have received *from Epaphroditus* the things *from you.*

(6) The Substantive with an Adverbial Preposition.

ἔξωθεν (Mark 7:15 only)

Ablative of Agency

The word in the ablative indicates the personal agent who performs the action expressed by a verb in the passive voice or by a verbal adjective. In a five-case system this category would be known as the genitive of agency. It employs:

(1) The Substantive without a Preposition.

δεῦτε, οἱ εὐλογημένοι τοῦ πατρός μου. (Matt. 25:34)
Come, you who have been blessed *by my Father.*

λαλοῦμεν οὐκ ἐν διδακτοῖς ἀνθρωπίνης σοφίας λόγοις ἀλλ' ἐν διδακτοῖς πνεύματος. (I Cor. 2:13)
We speak not with words taught by human wisdom but with (words) taught *by the Spirit.*

ἀγαπητοῖς θεοῦ (Rom. 1:7)
beloved *by God*

γεννητοῖς γυναικῶν (Matt. 11:11)
those born *of women*

κλητοὶ Ἰησοῦ Χριστοῦ (Rom. 1:6)
called *by Jesus Christ*

(2) The Substantive with the Preposition ἀπό.

μηδεὶς πειραζόμενος λεγέτω ὅτι Ἀπὸ θεοῦ πειράζομαι. (James 1:13)
Let no one who is being tempted say, I am being tempted *by God.*

ἡ γυνὴ ἔφυγεν εἰς τὴν ἔρημον, ὅπου ἔχει ἐκεῖ τόπον ἡτοιμασμένον ἀπὸ τοῦ θεοῦ. (Rev. 12:6)
The woman fled to the wilderness where (there was) a place which had been prepared *by God.*

(3) The Substantive with the Preposition διά.

. . . ἵνα σωθῇ ὁ κόσμος δι' αὐτοῦ. (John 3:17)
. . . so that the world might be saved *through him.*

Παῦλος ἀπόστολος, οὐκ ἀπ' ἀνθρώπων οὐδὲ δι' ἀνθρώπου ἀλλὰ διὰ Ἰησοῦ Χριστοῦ. (Gal. 1:1)
Paul an apostle, not from men neither *through a man* but *through Jesus Christ.*

(4) The Substantive with the Preposition ἐκ.

. . . εἰ μὴ ὁ λυπούμενος ἐξ ἐμοῦ. (II Cor. 2:2)

... except the one who is made sorrowful *by me.*

πᾶς ὁ πιστεύων ... ἐκ τοῦ θεοῦ γεγέννηται. (I John 5:1)
Everyone who believes ... has been begotten *by God.*

(5) The Substantive with the Preposition παρά.

παρὰ κυρίου ἐγένετο αὕτη. (Matt. 21:42)
This was done *by the Lord.*

ἔσται τελείωσις τοῖς λελαλημένοις αὐτῇ παρὰ κυρίου. (Luke 1:45)
There shall be a completion of the things which have been spoken to her *by the Lord.*

(6) The Substantive with the Preposition ὑπό.

τοῦτο ὅλον γέγονεν ἵνα πληρωθῇ τὸ ῥηθὲν ὑπὸ κυρίου διὰ τοῦ προφήτου. (Matt. 1:22)
All this came about so that the thing spoken *by the Lord* through the prophet might be fulfilled.

Note the difference between direct agency expressed by ὑπό and intermediate or secondary agency expressed by διά.

ἐβαπτίζοντο ἐν τῷ Ἰορδάνῃ ποταμῷ ὑπ᾽ αὐτοῦ. (Matt. 3:6)
They were being baptized in the Jordan River *by him.*

Ablative of Means

Occasionally the ablative is used to indicate the impersonal means used in producing the action of a verb or verbal adjective. The verb may be in any voice. The instrumental is the usual case for expressing means. This category employs:

(1) The Substantive without a Preposition.

λαλοῦμεν οὐκ ἐν διδακτοῖς ἀνθρωπίνης σοφίας λόγοις (I Cor. 2:13)
We do not speak with words taught *by human wisdom.*

Note: *The above is the only example known to the present writers of the substantive alone being used to express means. It is also possible to explain the use as a subjective genitive.*

(2) The Substantive with the Preposition διά.

εἶπεν διὰ παραβολῆς. (Luke 8:4)
He spoke *by using a parable.*

τῇ χάριτί ἐστε σεσῳσμένοι διὰ πίστεως. (Eph. 2:8)
You have been saved by means of grace *through faith.*

(3) The Substantive with the Preposition ἐκ.

ἐσκοτώθη ὁ ἥλιος καὶ ὁ ἀὴρ ἐκ τοῦ καπνοῦ τοῦ φρέατος.
(Rev. 9:2)
The sun and the air were darkened *by the smoke* from the pit.

σοὶ δείξω ἐκ τῶν ἔργων μου τὴν πίστιν. (James 2:18)
I will show you my faith *by means of* my *works.*

(4) The Substantive with the Preposition ὑπό.

τὸ πλοῖον καλύπτεσθαι ὑπὸ τῶν κυμάτων. (Matt. 8:24)
The boat was being engulfed *by the waves.*

τί ἐξήλθατε εἰς τὴν ἔρημον θεάσασθαι; κάλαμον ὑπὸ ἀνέμου
σαλευόμενον; (Matt. 11:7)
What did you go out into the wilderness to see, a reed swayed *by the wind?*

Ablative of Comparison

If a word in the ablative is the basis on which a comparison is made, it is an ablative of comparison. A test for this use is the ability to use the word "than" in the translation of the word in the ablative. In a five-case system this category would be known as the genitive of comparison. It employs:

(1) The Substantive without a Preposition.

ὁ ὀπίσω μου ἐρχόμενος ἰσχυρότερός μού ἐστιν. (Matt. 3:11).
The one who comes behind me is greater *than I.*

πολλῶν στρουθίων διαφέρετε. (Luke 12:7)
You are of more value *than many sparrows.*

μείζων ἐστὶν ὁ θεὸς τῆς καρδίας ἡμῶν. (I Jo. 3:20)
God is greater *than our hearts.*

περισσότερόν ἐστιν πάντων τῶν ὁλοκαυτωμάτων καὶ θυσιῶν.
(Mk. 12:33)

(This) is more *than all whole burnt offerings* and *sacrifices.*

τὸ περισσὸν τούτων ἐκ τοῦ πονηροῦ ἐστιν. (Matt. 5:37)
That which is more *than these* is from the evil one.

(2) The Substantive with an Adverbial Preposition.

ὑπερεκπερισσοῦ (Eph. 3:20 only)

Ablative of Cause

The ablative is sometimes used to indicate the reason for an action. The instrumental is more frequently used for this purpose. In a five-case system this category would be known as the genitive of cause. It employs:

(1) The Substantive with the Preposition ἀντί.

ἔσῃ σιωπῶν..., ἀνθ᾽ ὧν οὐκ ἐπίστευσας. (Luke 1:20)
You shall be silent *because* you did not believe.

Note: *The expression* ἀνθ᾽ ὧν *is the equivalent of a subordinating conjunction. (See also Luke 12:3; 19:44; Acts 12:23).*

ἀντὶ τούτου καταλείψει ἄνθρωπος τὸν πατέρα καὶ τὴν μητέρα.... (Eph. 5:31)
For this reason a man shall leave father and mother....

(2) The Substantive with the Preposition ἀπό.

ἔτι ἀπιστούντων αὐτῶν ἀπὸ τῆς χαρᾶς.... (Luke 24:41)
While they still disbelieved *because of joy....*

οὐκέτι αὐτὸ ἑλκύσαι ἴσχυον ἀπὸ τοῦ πλήθους τῶν ἰχθύων. (John 21:6)
(They were) no longer able to drag it *because of the multitude* of fish.

(3) The Substantive with the Proposition ἐκ.

ἐμασῶντο τὰς γλώσσας αὐτῶν ἐκ τοῦ πόνου. (Rev. 16:10)
They gnawed their tongues *because of the pain.*

ὁ ᾽Ιησοῦς κεκοπιακὼς ἐκ τῆς ὁδοιπορίας ἐκαθέζετο οὕτως ἐπὶ τῇ πηγῇ. (John 4:6)
Jesus, because he was weary as *a result of the journey,* sat down beside the well.

(4) The Substantive with Adverbial Prepositions.

ἕνεκα, ἕνεκεν, εἵνεκεν (Luke 4:18; Acts 19:32)
χάριν (Gal. 3:19; I Jo. 3:12)

Ablative of Rank

This rare use of the ablative expresses the idea of separation in terms of rank, order, or precedence. In a five-case system it would presumably be called the genitive of rank. It employs:

(1) The Substantive with the Preposition πρό.

πρὸ πάντων, ἀδελφοί μου, μὴ ὀμνύετε. (James 5:12)
Above all, my brothers, do not swear.

πρὸ πάντων τὴν εἰς ἑαυτοὺς ἀγάπην ἐκτενῆ ἔχοντες. . . .
(I Pet. 4:8)
Above all having fervent love among yourselves. . . .

(2) The Substantive with an Adverbial Preposition.

ἔμπροσθεν (John 1:15, 30—but these uses could be ablatives of separation)

Ablative of Opposition

Other eight-case grammarians describe this use of substantives in the second inflected form as genitive. Opposition and hostility, however, certainly imply separation, the basic idea of the ablative. This category employs:

(1) The Substantive with the Preposition κατά.

ἦλθον διχάσαι ἄνθρωπον κατὰ τοῦ πατρὸς αὐτοῦ καὶ θυγατέρα κατὰ τῆς μητρὸς αὐτῆς καὶ νύμφην κατὰ τῆς πενθερᾶς αὐτῆς. (Matt. 10:35)
I came to turn a man *against* his *father,* a daughter *against* her *mother,* and a bride *against* her *mother-in-law.*

ὁ μὴ ὢν μετ᾽ ἐμοῦ κατ᾽ ἐμοῦ ἐστιν. (Luke 11:23)
The one who is not with me is *against me.*

(2) The Substantive with an Adverbial Preposition.

ἀπέναντι (Acts 17:7 only)

Ablative of Purpose

On rare occasions the ablative may be used to express purpose. Such purpose is always expressed in terms of removing something, and this use could be included in the ablative of separation. In a five-case system this use would presumably be called the genitive of purpose or else be included in the genitive of separation. It employs:

(1) The Substantive with the Preposition περί.

ὁ θεὸς τὸν ἑαυτοῦ υἱὸν πέμψας ἐν ὁμοιώματι σαρκὸς ἁμαρτίας καὶ περὶ ἁμαρτίας κατέκρινεν τὴν ἁμαρτίαν. (Rom. 8:3)
God condemned sin when he sent his own Son in the likeness of sinful flesh and *for the purpose of taking away* sin.

οὐκέτι προσφορὰ περὶ ἁμαρτίας. (Heb. 10:18)
(There is) no longer a sacrifice *to take away sin.*

(2) The Substantive with an Adverbial Preposition.

ἕνεκεν (II Cor. 7:12 [3rd occurrence] only)

Ablative of Exchange

The ablative with the preposition ἀντί may express the ideas of exchange, substitution, or succession. Such terms as "for," "in place of," "instead of," "in behalf of," and "in exchange for" may be used in the translation.

Ἀρχέλαος βασιλεύει τῆς Ἰουδαίας ἀντὶ τοῦ πατρὸς αὐτοῦ Ἡρῴδου. (Matt. 2:22)
Archelaus was ruling Judea *in the place of* his *father Herod.*

ἠκούσατε ὅτι ἐρρέθη, ὀφθαλμὸν ἀντὶ ὀφθαλμοῦ καὶ ὀδόντα ἀντὶ ὀδόντος. (Matt. 5:38)
You have heard that it was said, an eye *in exchange for an eye* and a tooth *in exchange for a tooth.*

Partitive Ablative

If a word in the ablative indicates the whole of which the word it modifies is a part, it is a partitive ablative. This use might also be called (more accurately?) the ablative of the whole or the ablative of the divided whole. In a five-case system, it is called the partitive genitive. Indeed, many eight-case grammarians also classify it as genitive. The fact that the part is derived from and in some sense is separated from the whole and the fact that the use is found with the prepositions ἀπό and ἐκ, which are always used with the ablative, make it probable that it should be treated as ablative. It employs:

(1) The Substantive without a Preposition

τὸ τρίτον τῆς γῆς κατεκάη, καὶ τὸ τρίτον τῶν δένδρων κατεκάη. (Rev. 8:7)
A third *of the earth* was burned, and a third *of the trees* was burned.

ἐμβὰς εἰς ἓν τῶν πλοίων. . . . (Luke 5:3)
Having embarked in one *of the boats.* . . .

. . . ἵνα βάψῃ τὸ ἄκρον τοῦ δακτύλου αὐτοῦ ὕδατος. (Luke 16:24)
. . . so that he might dip the tip *of* his *finger* in water.

οἱ λοιποὶ τῶν ἀνθρώπων (Luke 18:11)
the remainder *of men*

τοὺς πτωχοὺς τῶν ἁγίων (Rom. 15:26)
the poor *among the saints*

(2) The Substantive with the Preposition ἀπό.

ἐκλεξάμενος ἀπ' αὐτῶν δώδεκα (Luke 6:13)
having chosen twelve *from among them*

. . . ἵνα παρὰ τῶν γεωργῶν λάβῃ ἀπὸ τῶν καρπῶν. (Mark 12:2)
. . . so that he might receive from the tenants *some of the fruits.*

(3) The Substantive with the Preposition ἐκ.

μή τις ἐκ τῶν ἀρχόντων ἐπίστευσεν εἰς αὐτὸν ἢ ἐκ τῶν Φαρισαίων; (John 7:48)
Have any *of the rulers* believed on him or (any) *of the Pharisees?*

οὐδεὶς ἐξ αὐτῶν ἀπώλετο. (John 17:12)
Not one *of them* has perished.

THE DATIVE

The root idea of the dative is that of personal interest. Such personal interest involves either advantage or disadvantage. It should be noted that the dative is ordinarily used in connection with persons rather than things, although something which has been personified may employ the dative. It should also be noted that in an eight-case system prepositions rarely are used with the dative. The dative has the following uses.

Dative of Indirect Object

The indirect object of a verb indicates to whom or for whom something is done, i.e. the person in whose interest the action is performed. By the nature of the case therefore the indirect object in a Greek sentence is expressed in the dative case. This is the most common use of the dative, although the idea of personal interest is not as strong as in the dative of advantage and disadvantage (below). This category employs:

(1) The Substantive without a Preposition.

ἔγραψα ὑμῖν ἐν τῇ ἐπιστολῇ. . . . (I Cor. 5:9)
I wrote *to you* in my letter. . . .

ἐλάλησεν αὐτοῖς πολλὰ ἐν παραβολαῖς. (Matt. 13:3)
He spoke many things *to them* in parables.

πάντα ἀποδώσω σοι. (Matt. 18:26)
I will repay all things *to you.*

ὑμῖν . . . ἀπέστειλεν αὐτόν. (Acts 3:26)
He sent him *to you.*

προσέφερον αὐτῷ παιδία. (Mark 10:13)
They were bringing children *to him.*

(2) The Substantive with the Preposition ἐν.

οὕτως ἐν ταῖς ἐκκλησίαις πάσαις διατάσσομαι. (I Cor. 7:17)
In this way I give instructions *to all the churches.*

σοφίαν λαλοῦμεν ἐν τοῖς τελείοις. (I Cor. 2:6)
We speak wisdom *to those who are mature.*

(3) The Substantive with the Preposition ἐπί.

μακροθύμησον ἐπ' ἐμοί. (Matt. 18:26)
Be merciful *to me.*

προσέχετε ἑαυτοῖς ἐπὶ τοῖς ἀνθρώποις τούτοις τί μέλλετε πράσσειν. (Acts 5:35)
Take heed to yourselves what you are going to do *to these men*.

Dative of Advantage and Dative of Disadvantage

This category is often referred to by the Latin terms *dativus commodi* and *dativus incommodi*. In these uses of the dative the idea of personal interest is most apparent. The dative of advantage indicates the person for whose benefit something is done. The word "for" will ordinarily be used in the translation. The dative of disadvantage indicates the person who will be adversely affected as a result of the action. The word "against" will often be used in the translation. What some grammarians call the ethical dative should be included in this category.

The datives of advantage and disadvantage are specialized uses of the dative of indirect object. All datives of advantage or disadvantage are in fact indirect objects, and all indirect objects to a greater or lesser degree express advantage or disadvantage. Therefore some grammarians do not provide a separate category for the datives of advantage and disadvantage and include them in the category dative of indirect object. If, however, separate categories are to be maintained, the three may be distinguished as follows. The dative of indirect object emphasizes *to* whom something is done, the dative of advantage *for* whom, the dative of disadvantage *against* whom.

1. *Dative of Advantage.* This category employs:

(1) The Substantive without a Preposition.

τὴν πόλιν τὴν ἁγίαν Ἰερουσαλὴμ καινὴν εἶδον . . . ἡτοιμασμένην ὡς νύμφην κεκοσμημένην τῷ ἀνδρὶ αὐτῆς. (Rev. 21:2)
I saw the holy city, the new Jerusalem, . . . having been prepared as a bride who had been adorned *for* her *husband*.

εἴτε ἐξέστημεν, θεῷ· εἴτε σωφρονοῦμεν, ὑμῖν. (II Cor. 5:13)
If we are insane (it is) *for God;* if we are sober (it is) *for you*.

. . . ἵνα οἱ ζῶντες μηκέτι ἑαυτοῖς ζῶσιν ἀλλὰ τῷ ὑπὲρ αὐτῶν ἀποθανόντι καὶ ἐγερθέντι. (II Cor. 5:15)

... so that the ones who live will no longer live *for themselves* but *for the one who died* and *who was raised* for them.

ἐλεύθερος ὢν ἐκ πάντων π̱α̱σ̱ι̱ν̱ ἐμαυτὸ ν ἐδούλωσα. (I Cor. 9:19)
Although I was free from all men, I enslaved myself *for all men.*

ἔκρινα ἐ̱μ̱α̱υ̱τ̱ῷ̱ τοῦτο. (II Cor. 2:1)
I determined this *for myself.*

(2) The Substantive with the Preposition ἐν.

καλὸν ἔργον ἠργάσατο ἐ̱ν̱ ἐ̱μ̱ο̱ί̱. (Mark 14:6)
She has done a good thing *for me.*

(3) The Substantive with the Preposition ἐπί.

τὴν ὑπερβάλλουσαν χάριν τοῦ θεοῦ ἐ̱φ̱' ὑ̱μ̱ῖ̱ν̱ (II Cor. 9:14)
the abounding grace of God *to you*

ἐθεώρουν τὰ σημεῖα ἃ ἐποίει ἐ̱π̱ὶ̱ τ̱ῶ̱ν̱ ἀ̱σ̱θ̱ε̱ν̱ο̱ύ̱ν̱τ̱ω̱ν̱. (John 6:2)
They saw the signs which he was doing *for the sick.*

2. *Dative of Disadvantage.* This category employs:

(1) The Substantive without a Preposition.

μαρτυρεῖτε ἑ̱α̱υ̱τ̱ο̱ῖ̱ς̱ ὅτι υἱοί ἐστε τῶν φονευσάντων τοὺς προφήτας. (Matt. 23:31)
You are bearing witness *against yourselves* that you are sons of the ones who killed the prophets.

καὶ τὸν κονιορτὸν τὸν κολληθέντα ... εἰς τοὺς πόδας ἀπομασσόμεθα ὑ̱μ̱ῖ̱ν̱. (Luke 10:11)
Even the dust which sticks to our feet we are wiping off *against you.*

ἡ Ἡρῳδιὰς ἐνεῖχεν α̱ὐ̱τ̱ῷ̱. (Mark 6:19)
Herodias had a grudge *against him.*

μετανόησον οὖν· εἰ δὲ μή, ἔρχομαί σ̱ο̱ι̱ ταχύ. (Rev. 2:16)
Repent therefore; and if (you do) not, I will come *against you* quickly.

γενηθήτω ἡ τράπεζα αὐτῶν εἰς παγίδα ... α̱ὐ̱τ̱ο̱ῖ̱ς̱. (Rom. 11:9)
Let their table become a snare ... *against them.*

(2) The Substantive with the Preposition ἐν.

ἐποίησαν ἐν αὐτῷ ὅσα ἠθέλησαν. (Matt. 17:12)
They did *with him* whatever they pleased.

ἐν τοῖς ἀπολλυμένοις ἐστὶν κεκαλυμμένον. (II Cor. 4:3)
It is hidden *from those who are perishing.*

(3) The Substantive with the Preposition ἐπί.

τρεῖς ἐπὶ δυσὶν καὶ δύο ἐπὶ τρισίν (Luke 12:52)
three *against two* and two *against three*

τῆς θλίψεως τῆς γενομένης ἐπὶ Στεφάνῳ (Acts 11:19)
the persecution which came *upon Stephen*

Dative of Possession

The word in the dative indicates personal interest in terms of ownership. It indicates the person to whom something belongs and therefore it might more accurately be called the dative of the possessor. The possessive pronouns "his" or "her" will ordinarily be used in the translation. This category employs the substantive without a preposition.

εἰσῆλθεν κατὰ τὸ εἰωθὸς αὐτῷ ἐν τῇ ἡμέρᾳ τῶν σαββάτων εἰς τὴν συναγωγήν. (Luke 4:16)
On the Sabbath day he entered into the synagogue according to *his* custom.

ἐγένετο ἄνθρωπος ἀπεσταλμένος παρὰ θεοῦ, ὄνομα αὐτῷ Ἰωάννης. (John 1:6)
A man appeared who had been sent from God. *His* name (was) John.

διὰ τί . . . οἱ σοὶ μαθηταὶ οὐ νηστεύουσιν; (Mark 2:18)
Why do not *your* disciples fast?

μονογενής μοί ἐστιν. (Luke 9:38)
He is *my* only son.

πάντες οὗτοι ἐκ τοῦ περισσεύοντος αὐτοῖς ἔβαλον εἰς τὰ δῶρα. (Luke 21:4)
All these cast into the offerings box out of *their* excess.

Dative of Reference or Dative of Respect

This dative may be used in connection with things as well as persons. The idea of personal interest is weakened to mere reference. Much like the accusative it limits (or extends) the action or state of the verb to a person or thing. A test for this use is whether the words "with reference to" or "concerning" or "about" can be used in the translation. This category employs:

(1) The Substantive without a Preposition.

ὀφειλέται ἐσμέν, οὐ τῇ σαρκὶ τοῦ κατὰ σάρκα ζῆν. (Rom. 8:12)
We are debtors, not *to the flesh* to live acording to flesh.

μὴ μεριμνᾶτε τῇ ψυχῇ ὑμῶν. (Matt. 6:25)
Be not anxious *about* your *life*.

σὺ τίς εἶ ὁ κρίνων ἀλλότριον οἰκέτην; τῷ ἰδίῳ κυρίῳ στήκει ἢ πίπτει. (Rom. 14:4)
Who are you who judges another's servant? *Before his own master* he stands or falls.

τελεσθήσεται πάντα τὰ γεγραμμένα διὰ τῶν προφητῶν τῷ υἱῷ τοῦ ἀνθρώπου. (Luke 18:31)
All things which have been written by the prophets *about the Son* of Man will be fulfilled.

πάντα μοι ἔξεστιν. (I Cor. 6:12)
All things are lawful *to me*.

(2) The Substantive with the Preposition ἐν.

μέλλει κρίνειν τὴν οἰκουμένην ἐν δικαιοσύνῃ. (Acts 17:31)
He is going to judge the world *with reference to righteousness*.

οὐκ οἴδατε ἐν Ἠλίᾳ τί λέγει ἡ γραφή; (Rom. 11:2)
Do you not know what the Scripture says *about Elijah?*

(3) The Substantive with the Preposition ἐπί.

παρεκλήθημεν, ἀδελφοί, ἐφ' ὑμῖν. (I Thess. 3:7)
We have been encouraged *about you,* brothers.

ἐφ' ὑμῖν χαίρω. (Rom. 16:19)

I am happy *about you.*

Dative of Root Idea or Dative of Direct Object

Some verbs have a root idea which is so closely related to that of the dative that they take their direct object in the dative rather than the accusative case. Therefore a dative which functions as the direct object of a verb is a dative of direct object. This category employs:

(1) The Substantive without a Preposition.

δουλεύω νόμῳ θεοῦ. (Rom. 7:25)
I serve God's *law.*

οἱ ἐν σαρκὶ ὄντες θεῷ ἀρέσαι οὐ δύνανται. (Rom. 8:8)
Those who are in the flesh are not able to please *God.*

ἰδοὺ τοσαῦτα ἔτη δουλεύω σοι. . . . (Luke 15:29)
Behold these many years I serve *you.* . . .

κύριε, βοήθει μοι. (Matt. 15:25)
Lord, help *me.*

ὁ ἀπειθῶν τῷ υἱῷ οὐκ ὄψεται ζωήν. (John 3:36)
The one who does not believe *the son* shall not see life.

(2) The Substantive with the Preposition ἐν.

πᾶς ὅστις ὁμολογήσει ἐν ἐμοὶ ἔμπροσθεν τῶν ἀνθρώπων, ὁμολογήσω κἀγὼ ἐν αὐτῷ ἔμπροσθεν τοῦ πατρός μου. (Matt. 10:32; cf. Luke 12:8)
Everyone who shall confess *me* before men, I will also confess *him* before my Father.

Note: *The above could also be explained as datives of reference: will make a confession* about. . . .

THE LOCATIVE

As clearly implied by its name, the locative case indicates location, place, position. A preposition such as in, on, at, among, during, by, upon, or beside is usually employed in translating the locative into English. The locative is used as follows.

Locative of Place

The word in the locative denotes a particular spot or area. (On the relationship of the locative of place to the adverbial genitive of place, see above page 12.)

In a five-case system this category would be known as the dative of place. It employs:

(1) The Substantive without a Preposition.

καὶ περιβλεψάμενος τοὺς περὶ αὐτὸν κύκλῳ καθημένους λέγει
... (Mark 3:34)
And when he had looked around on those who were sitting around him *in a circle* he said ...

... τῶν ἐπερχομένων τῇ οἰκουμένῃ ... (Luke 21:26)
... of things that are coming *upon the world* ...

ἐπέθηκαν αὐτοῦ τῇ κεφαλῇ. (John 19:2)
They put it *upon* his *head.*

τοῦτον ὁ θεὸς ἀρχηγὸν καὶ σωτῆρα ὕψωσεν τῇ δεξιᾷ αὐτοῦ.
(Acts 5:31)
God exalted this man *to* his *right hand* (to be) a ruler and a saviour.

λῃσταῖς περιέπεσεν. (Luke 10:30)
He fell *among thieves.*

(2) The Substantive with the Preposition ἐν.

εἶδεν ἄλλους ἑστῶτας ἐν τῇ ἀγορᾷ ἀργούς. (Matt. 20:3)
He saw others standing idle *in the market place.*

ἐν τῷ κόσμῳ ἦν. (John 1:10)
He was *in the world.*

(3) The Substantive with the Preposition ἐπί.

δός μοι ... ἐπὶ πίνακι τὴν κεφαλὴν Ἰωάννου. (Matt. 14:8)
Give me the head of John *on a plate.*

γινώσκετε ὅτι ἐγγύς ἐστιν ἐπὶ θύραις. (Matt. 24:33)

Know that it is near (even) *at the gates.*

(4) The Substantive with the Preposition παρά.

ἐπιλαβόμενος παιδίον ἔστησεν αὐτὸ <u>παρ' ἑαυτῷ</u>. (Luke 9:47)
Having taken a child he placed it *beside himself.*

<u>παρ' αὐτῷ</u> ἔμειναν. (John 1:39)
They remained *with him.*

(5) The substantive with the Preposition πρός.

θεωρεῖ δύο ἀγγέλους . . . ἕνα <u>πρὸς τῇ κεφαλῇ</u> καὶ ἕνα <u>πρὸς τοῖς ποσίν</u>. (John 20:12)
She saw two angels, one *at the head* and one *at the feet.*

ἦν ἐκεῖ <u>πρὸς τῷ ὄρει</u> ἀγέλη χοίρων. (Mark 5:11)
There was a herd of pigs there *on the mountain.*

(6) The Substantive with an Adverbial Preposition.

ἐγγύς (Acts 9:38; 27:8)

Locative of Time

The word in the locative indicates a particular point in time. Something is located within a succession of events. The emphasis is upon chronology. (For the relationship of the locative of time to the adverbial genitive of time, the instrumental of time and the adverbial accusative of measure, see above page 10.)

In a five-case system this category would be known as the dative of time. It employs:

(1) The Substantive without a Preposition.

ἀμὴν λέγω σοι ὅτι σὺ σήμερον <u>ταύτῃ τῇ νυκτὶ</u> πρὶν ἢ δὶς ἀλέκτορα φωνῆσαι τρίς με ἀπαρνήσῃ. (Mark 14:30)
Verily I say to you that today, *this (very) night,* before the cock crows twice you will deny me three times.

<u>τῇ μιᾷ</u> τῶν σαββάτων (Luke 24:1)
on the first (day) of the week

προσεύχεσθε ἵνα μὴ γένηται ἡ φυγὴ ὑμῶν χειμῶνος μηδὲ <u>σαββάτῳ</u>. (Matt. 24:20)

Pray that your flight might not be in winter or *on a sabbath.*

Note: *contrast the adverbial genitive of time* (χειμῶνος) *and the locative of time.*

τῇ τρίτῃ ἡμέρα ἐγερθήσεται. (Matt. 20:19)
On the third day he will be raised.

τετάρτῃ φυλακῇ τῆς νυκτός (Matt. 14:25)
during the third watch of the night

τῇ ἑορτῇ τοῦ πάσχα (Luke 2:41)
at (the time of) the Feast of Passover

(2) The Substantive with the Preposition ἐν.

ἀναστήσω αὐτὸν ἐν τῇ ἐσχάτῃ ἡμέρα. (John 6:44)
I will raise him *at the last day.*

ἐθαύμαζον ἐν τῷ χρονίζειν ἐν τῷ ναῷ αὐτόν. (Luke 1:21)
They marvelled *while he tarried* in the temple.

(3) The Substantive with the Preposition ἐπί.

νυνὶ ἅπαξ ἐπὶ συντελείᾳ τῶν αἰώνων . . . πεφανέρωται.
(Heb. 9:26)
Now once *at the end* of the ages he has been manifested.

ἐπὶ τούτῳ ἦλθαν οἱ μαθηταὶ αὐτοῦ. (John 4:27)
At this (point) his disciples came.

Locative of Sphere

This is a metaphorical use of the locative in figurative expressions. The location is in a logical sphere rather than in space or time.

In a five-case system this category is usually included in the dative of place. It employs:

(1) The Substantive without a Preposition.

μὴ παιδία γίνεσθε ταῖς φρεσίν, ἀλλὰ τῇ κακίᾳ νηπιάζετε. (I Cor. 14:20)
Do not be children in your minds, but *in the sphere of evil* be infantile.

Note: *It is uncertain whether* ταῖς φρεσίν *is a locative of place or a locative of sphere.*

μακάριοι οἱ πτωχοὶ τῷ πνεύματι. (Matt. 5:3)
Blessed (are) the poor *in spirit.*

Note: πνεύματι *could also be a dative of reference, as can most locatives with adjectives.*

σχήματι εὑρεθεὶς ὡς ἄνθρωπος (Phil. 2:7)
having been found *in appearance* as a man

θανατωθεὶς μὲν σαρκὶ ζῳοποιηθεὶς δὲ πνεύματι. (I Pet. 3:18)
having been put to death in the flesh but made alive *in the spirit.*

τοῖς ἔθεσιν περιπατεῖν (Acts 21:21)
to walk *in the customs*

(2) The Substantive with the Preposition ἐν.

μάρτυς μού ἐστιν ὁ θεός, ᾧ λατρεύω ἐν τῷ πνεύματί μου ἐν τῷ εὐαγγελίῳ. (Rom. 1:9)
God is my witness, whom I serve with my spirit *in the domain of the gospel.*

ὅσοι ἐν νόμῳ ἥμαρτον, διὰ νόμου κριθήσονται. (Rom. 2:12)
As many as have sinned *within the context of law* will be judged by the law.

(3) The Substantive with the Preposition ἐπί.

... τινας τοὺς πεποιθότας ἐφ᾿ ἑαυτοῖς ... (Luke 18:9)
... certain ones who trusted *in themselves* ...

ἡ σάρξ μου κατασκηνώσει ἐπ᾿ ἐλπίδι. (Acts 2:26)
My flesh shall dwell *in hope.*

(4) The Substantive with the Preposition παρά.

οὐ γάρ ἐστιν προσωπολημψία παρὰ τῷ θεῷ. (Rom. 2:11)
There is no favoritism *with God.*

μὴ γίνεσθε φρόνιμοι παρ᾿ ἑαυτοῖς. (Rom. 12:16)
Do not become conceited *in your own estimation.*

(5) The Substantive with an Adverbial Preposition.

παραπλήσιον (Phil. 2:27)

THE INSTRUMENTAL

The basic idea expressed by the instrumental case is that of means or instrument. The word in the instrumental indicates that by which or with which the action of the verb is carried out.

Inasmuch as the dative, the locative, and the instrumental employ the same case form, the third inflected form, one must first decide the case of a word in the third inflected form before its exact syntax can be determined. This can be done by determining whether the emphasis is upon personal interest (dative), location (locative), or means (instrumental).

The instrumental case has the following uses.

Instrumental of Means

This is the most common, the simplest, and most obvious use of the case. Compare the preceding comments about the case in general. It should also be noted that the instrumental of means always involves impersonal means, never personal agency. Personal agency is expressed by the ablative of agency, with or without ὑπό, and rarely by the instrumental of agency (below). A test for this use is the ability to use the words "by means of" or simply "by" in the translation. The preposition "with" may also be used to translate this use of the instrumental.

In a five-case system this category would be known as the dative of means. It employs:

(1) The Substantive without a Preposition.

. . . διὰ τὸ αὐτὸν πολλάκις πέδαις καὶ ἁλύσεσιν δεδέσθαι. (Mark 5:4)
. . . because he had often been bound *by fetters* and *chains.*

ἔτιλλον οἱ μαθηταὶ αὐτοῦ καὶ ἤσθιον τοὺς στάχυας ψώχοντες ταῖς χερσίν. (Luke 6:1)
His disciples were picking and eating the ears of corn, rubbing (them) *with their hands.*

οὐ φθαρτοῖς, ἀργυρίῳ ἢ χρυσίῳ ἐλυτρώθητε ... ἀλλὰ τιμίῳ αἵματι ... Χριστοῦ. (I Pet. 1:18-19)
You were ransomed not *with corruptible things* (such as) *silver* or *gold* but *with the precious blood* of Christ.

ἀνεῖλεν ᾽Ιάκωβον ... μαχαίρῃ. (Acts 12:2)
He killed James ... *with (the) sword.*

τοῖς δάκρυσιν ἤρξατο βρέχειν τοὺς πόδας αὐτοῦ καὶ ταῖς θριξὶν τῆς κεφαλῆς αὐτῆς ἐξέμασσεν ... καὶ ἤλειφεν τῷ μύρῳ. (Luke 7:38)
She began to wet his feet *with* her *tears,* and she wiped them *with the hairs* of her head, and she anointed him *with ointment.*

(2) The Substantive with the Preposition ἐν.

ἐδόθη αὐτοῖς ἐξουσία ... ἀποκτεῖναι ἐν ῥομφαίᾳ καὶ ἐν λιμῷ καὶ ἐν θανάτῳ. (Rev. 6:8)
Authority was given to them to kill *with the sword, with famine,* and *with death.*

ἐν τούτῳ γινώσκομεν ὅτι ἐγνώκαμεν αὐτόν. (I Jo. 2:3)
By this means we know that we have come to know him.

Instrumental of Cause

The word in the instrumental indicates what caused the action of the verb to be performed. The reference may be to an external cause and thus an occasion or to an internal cause and thus a motive. The instrumental of means indicates intermediary means, the instrumental of cause the original factor which produced the action. A test for this use is the ability to use the word "because" in the translation.

In a five-case system this category would be known as the dative of cause. It employs:

(1) The Substantive without a Preposition.

ἠλεήθητε τῇ τούτων ἀπειθείᾳ (Rom. 11:30)
You have received mercy *because of the disobedience* of these.

ἐγὼ λιμῷ ὧδε ἀπόλλυμαι. (Luke 15:17)
I am perishing here *because of famine.*

τῇ ἀπιστίᾳ ἐξεκλάσθησαν. (Rom. 11:20)
They were broken off *because of unbelief.*

...ἵνα τῷ σταυρῷ τοῦ Χριστοῦ μὴ διώκωνται. (Gal. 6:12)
...so that they may not be persecuted *on account of the cross*
of Christ.

τινὲς τῇ συνηθείᾳ... ἐσθίουσιν. (I Cor. 8:7)
Some eat *because of habit.*

(2) The Substantive with the Preposition ἐν.

ἐδόξαζον ἐν ἐμοὶ τὸν θεόν. (Gal. 1:24)
They glorified God *because of me.*

δοκοῦσιν ὅτι ἐν τῇ πολυλογίᾳ αὐτῶν εἰσακουσθήσονται.
(Matt. 6:7)
They think that they will be heard *because of* their *many words.*

(3) The Substantive with the Preposition ἐπί.

ἐξεπλήσσοντο ἐπὶ τῇ διδαχῇ αὐτοῦ. (Mark 1:22)
They were astonished *because of* his *teaching.*

ἐθαύμαζον ἐπὶ τοῖς λόγοις. (Luke 4:22)
They marveled *because of his words.*

Instrumental of Manner

The word in the instrumental indicates the manner in which
the action of the verb is carried out. It indicates a circumstance
which accompanies the action of the verb.

In a five-case system this category would be known as the
dative of manner or the dative of accompanying circumstance.
It employs:

(1) The Substantive without a Preposition.

παρεκάλει πάντας τῇ προθέσει τῆς καρδίας προσμένειν τῷ
κυρίῳ. (Acts 11:23)
He was exhorting all to remain faithful to the Lord *with purpose*
of heart.

εἰ ἐγὼ χάριτι μετέχω . . . . (I Cor. 10:30)
If I partake *with gratitude* . . . .

δείραντες ἡμᾶς <u>δημοσίᾳ</u>... ἔβαλαν εἰς φυλακήν· καὶ νῦν <u>λάθρα</u> ἡμᾶς ἐκβάλλουσιν; (Acts 16:37)
After they beat us *publicly* they threw (us) into prison; and will they now cast us out *secretly?*

παντὶ τρόπῳ, εἴτε προφάσει εἴτε ἀληθείᾳ.... (Phil. 1:18)
In every way, whether *in pretense* or *in truth....*

<u>ἐπιθυμίᾳ</u> ἐπεθύμησα τοῦτο τὸ πάσχα φαγεῖν μεθ' ὑμῶν. (Luke 22:15)
With (great) desire I have desired to eat this passover with you.

(2) The Substantive with the Preposition ἐν.

τὸ εὐαγγέλιον ἡμῶν οὐκ ἐγενήθη εἰς ὑμᾶς <u>ἐν λόγῳ</u> μόνον ἀλλὰ καὶ <u>ἐν δυνάμει</u> καὶ <u>ἐν πνεύματι ἁγίῳ</u> καὶ <u>ἐν πληροφορίᾳ πολλῇ</u>. (I Thess. 1:5)
Our gospel did not come to you *in word* only but *in power, in the Holy Spirit,* and *with much conviction.*

αὐτὸς ὁ κύριος <u>ἐν κελεύσματι</u>, <u>ἐν φωνῇ</u> ἀρχαγγέλου καὶ <u>ἐν σάλπιγγι θεοῦ</u>, καταβήσεται ἀπ' οὐρανοῦ. (I Thess. 4:16)
The Lord himself will descend from heaven *with a shout, with the voice* of an archangel, *and with the trumpet* of God.

Instrumental of Measure

The word in the instrumental indicates two points in time or space or the logical sphere which are separated by means of an interval. Unless ἑτέρᾳ ὁδῷ in James 2:25 is an example, the instrumental of measure does not occur in the New Testament with expressions of place. It occasionally occurs in comparative phrases which indicate degree of difference, as may be seen in the last two examples of the use of the substantive without a preposition below. It frequently occurs in expressions of time. Some grammarians even provide a separate category for these uses and call it the instrumental of time. It is admittedly a fine line which separates the locative of time and an expression of time in the instrumental. The locative, however, indicates a definite point in time, the instrumental two points separated by an interval of time. The first three examples below involve the instrumental in an expression of time.

In a five-case system the three kinds of expressions which are here included in the instrumental of measure would be placed in the following categories: dative of place, dative of measure (or degree) of difference, and dative of time. This category employs:

(1) The Substantive without a Preposition.

χρόνῳ ἱκανῷ οὐκ ἐνεδύσατο ἱμάτιον. (Luke 8:27)
For a long time he had worn no garment.

. . . κατὰ ἀποκάλυψιν μυστηρίου χρόνοις αἰωνίοις σεσιγημένου. (Rom. 16:25)
. . . according to the revelation of the mystery which he had kept secret *during the eternal ages.*

τεσσεράκοντα καὶ ἓξ ἔτεσιν οἰκοδομήθη ὁ ναὸς οὗτος. (John 2:20)
This temple was built *during (a period of) forty-six years.*

ὁ δὲ πολλῷ μᾶλλον ἔκραζεν. (Mark 10:48)
But he cried out *much* more.

. . . τοσούτῳ κρείττων γενόμενος τῶν ἀγγέλων . . . (Heb. 1:4)
. . . having become *so much* better than the angels . . .

(2) The Substantive with the Preposition ἐν.

Ἰωσὴφ μετεκαλέσατο Ἰακὼβ τὸν πατέρα αὐτοῦ καὶ πᾶσαν τὴν συγγένειαν ἐν ψυχαῖς ἑβδομήκοντα πέντε. (Acts 7:14)
Joseph called Jacob his father and all his relatives *amounting to seventy-five persons.*

ἔφερεν ἐν τριάκοντα καὶ ἐν ἑξήκοντα καὶ ἐν ἑκατόν. (Mark 4:8 variant reading)
It brought forth *thirtyfold, sixtyfold,* and a *hundredfold.*

(3) The Substantive with the Preposition σύν.

σὺν πᾶσιν τούτοις τρίτην ταύτην ἡμέραν ἄγει ἀφ' οὗ ταῦτα ἐγένετο. (Luke 24:21)
In addition to all these things it has been three days since these things happened.

Instrumental of Association

The word in the instrumental indicates the person(s) or thing(s) which accompany or take part in the action of the verb. For some at least, it is difficult to see how the idea of association is related to that of means and as a result to see the justification for including this use in the instrumental case. Some of those who feel this difficulty use the term associative-instrumental case, which seems to imply that one case includes two ideas. But if case is determined by use rather than form, should there not be nine Greek cases just as some think there were in Sanskrit? Others justify the inclusion of the idea of association in the instrumental case by explaining that the second party furnishes the means by which association takes place.

In a five-case system this category would be known as the dative of association or dative of accompaniment or comitative dative. It employs:

(1) The Substantive without a Preposition.

ἐντυγχάνει τῷ θεῷ κατὰ τοῦ Ἰσραήλ. (Rom. 11:2)
He pleads *with God* against Israel.

. . . ἵνα καὶ ἡμεῖς ὑμῖν συμβασιλεύσωμεν. (I Cor. 4:8)
. . . so that we might also reign *with you.*

τίς μετοχὴ δικαιοσύνῃ καὶ ἀνομίᾳ; (II Cor. 6:14)
What fellowship (has) *righteousness* and *lawlessness?*

οὗτος . . . συνεσθίει αὐτοῖς. (Luke 15:2)
This man . . . eats *with them.*

ὡμίλει αὐτῷ. (Acts 24:26)
He conversed *with him.*

(2) The Substantive with the Preposition ἐν.

ἦλθεν κύριος ἐν ἁγίαις μυριάσιν αὐτοῦ. (Jude 14)
The Lord came *with* his *holy myriads.*

. . . ἐν πᾶσιν ἀναλαβόντες τὸν θυρεὸν τῆς πίστεως. (Eph. 6:16)
. . . *with all these* taking the shield of faith.

(3) The Substantive with the Preposition παρά.

ἐρωτᾷ αὐτὸν Φαρισαῖος ὅπως ἀριστήσῃ παρ' αὐτῷ. (Luke 11:37)
A Pharisee asked him to eat breakfast *with him*.

παρὰ ἁμαρτωλῷ ἀνδρὶ εἰσῆλθεν καταλῦσαι. (Luke 19:7)
He has gone in to lodge *with a man who is a sinner*.

(4) The Substantive with the Preposition σύν.

ὁ Πέτρος καὶ οἱ σὺν αὐτῷ ἦσαν βεβαρημένοι ὕπνῳ. (Luke 9:32)
Peter and the ones *with him* were heavy with sleep.

οἱ μὲν ἦσαν σὺν τοῖς Ἰουδαίοις οἱ δὲ σὺν τοῖς ἀποστόλοις.
(Acts 14:4)
Some sided *with the Jews,* others *with the apostles*.

(5) The Substantive with an Adverbial Preposition.

ἅμα (Matt. 13:29; cf. I Thess. 4:17; 5:10)

Instrumental of Agency

On rare occasions the instrumental is used to express personal agency rather than impersonal means. In such instances the verb is in the middle or passive voice.

In a five-case system this category would be known as the dative of agent. It employs:

(1) The Substantive without a Preposition.

οὐδὲν ἄξιον θανάτου ἐστὶν πεπραγμένον αὐτῷ. (Luke 23:15)
Nothing worthy of death has been done *by him*.

εἰ πνεύματι ἄγεσθε, οὐκ ἐστὲ ὑπὸ νόμον. (Gal. 5:18)
If you are being led *by the Spirit,* you are not under law.

ᾧ τις ἥττηται, τούτῳ δεδούλωται. (II Pet. 2:19)
By whom anyone has been defeated, he has become enslaved *by this man*.

Note: *If, however,* ᾧ *and* τούτῳ *are neuter, their syntax will be instrumental of means.* τούτῳ *could also be interpreted as dative of indirect object.*

ὤφθη ἀγγέλοις. (I Tim. 3:16)
He was seen *by angels.*

πρὸς τὸ θεαθῆναι αὐτοῖς (Matt. 6:1)
to be seen *by them*

... Γαμαλιήλ, νομοδιδάσκαλος τίμιος παντὶ τῷ λαῷ. ...
(Acts 5:34)
... Gamaliel, a teacher of the law held in honor *by all people* ...

(2) The Substantive with the Preposition ἐν.

οὗτος οὐκ ἐκβάλλει τὰ δαιμόνια εἰμὴ ἐν τῷ Βεελζεβούλ.
(Matt. 12:24)
This man does not cast out demons except *by Beelzebul.*

μέλλει κρίνειν τὴν οἰκουμένην ἐν δικαιοσύνῃ ἐν ἀνδρὶ ᾧ
ὥρισεν. (Acts 17:31)
He is going to judge the world in righteousness *by a man* whom
he has appointed.

THE ACCUSATIVE

The basic ideas expressed by the accusative are those of
extension and limitation. The accusative indicates how and to
what the action of the verb is extended. It indicates the limit of
that extension. It answers the question, How far? It limits the
action of the verb as to content, scope, extent, direction, duration, and end.

The genitive also limits the meaning of words. For the most
part, however, the genitive limits nouns whereas the accusative limits verbs. The genitive limits as to kind, the accusative
as to extent.

The accusative is used as follows.

Accusative of Direct Object

The direct object is a substantive which directly and immediately receives the action of a transitive verb. If a word in the
accusative functions in this way it is an accusative of direct
object. As has been seen, some verbs take their direct object in

the genitive or dative. This category employs the substantive without a preposition.

εἶδεν ἄλλους δύο ἀδελφούς. (Matt. 4:21)
He saw *two other brothers.*

ἐδίδασκεν τοὺς ὄχλους. (Luke 5:3)
He was teaching *the multitudes.*

ὁ θεὸς ἐξελέξατο τοὺς πτωχούς. (James 2:5)
God chose *the poor.*

ἐκκλεῖσαι ὑμᾶς θέλουσιν. (Gal. 4:17)
They wish to exclude *you.*

ἐδέξαντο αὐτὸν . . . πάντα ἑωρακότες ὅσα ἐποίησεν. (John 4:45)
They received *him* because they saw *all the things which* he did.

Cognate Accusative

Although most grammarians provide a separate category for this use of the accusative, it is really a special kind of direct object. The cognate accusative is a direct object which has the same root or at least contains the same idea as the verb of which it is the direct object. The cognate accusative functions as an internal object of a verb, whereas what is usually called the direct object is an external object. This category employs the substantive without a preposition.

ἐφοβήθησαν φόβον μέγαν. (Mark 4:41)
They feared *a great fear.*

ποιμάνατε τὸ ἐν ὑμῖν ποίμνιον τοῦ θεοῦ. (I Pet. 5:2)
Shepherd *the flock* of God which is among you.

ἐάν τις ἴδῃ τὸν ἀδελφὸν αὐτοῦ ἁμαρτάνοντα ἁμαρτίαν μὴ πρὸς θάνατον . . . . (I Jo. 5:16)
If anyone should see his brother sinning *a sin* which is not unto death . . . .

ἐχάρησαν χαρὰν μεγάλην. (Matt. 2:10)
They rejoiced *with great joy.*

Note: χαράν *is also an adverbial accusative of manner.*

τὴν δικαίαν κρίσιν κρίνετε. (John 7:24)
Judge *the righteous judgement.*

μὴ φοβούμεναι μηδεμίαν πτόησιν. (I Pet. 3:6)
not fearing *any terror.*

Double Accusative

Although most grammarians provide for it a separate category, the double accusative could also properly be looked upon as a subdivision of the accusative of direct object. Some verbs require two objects to complete their meaning, and these objects are referred to as double accusatives. This category employs the substantive without a preposition.

1. *Personal and Impersonal Objects.* Some verbs will have a personal and an impersonal object, both of which should be identified as a double accusative without further description.

πάλιν χρείαν ἔχετε τοῦ διδάσκειν ὑμᾶς τινὰ τὰ στοιχεῖα τῆς ἀρχῆς τῶν λογίων τοῦ θεοῦ. (Heb. 5:12)
You still have need for someone to teach *you the fundamentals* of the beginning of the oracles of God.

ἤρξατο διδάσκειν αὐτοὺς πολλά. (Mark 6:34)
He began to teach *them many things.*

ἐξέδυσαν αὐτὸν τὴν χλαμύδα καὶ ἐνέδυσαν αὐτὸν τὰ ἱμάτια αὐτοῦ. (Matt. 27:31)
They stripped *him* (of) *the cloak,* and they clothed *him* (with) his own *garments.*

2. *Primary and Secondary Objects.* Other verbs have a direct or primary object and a predicate or secondary object. Both objects may be identified as a double accusative without further description, or the primary object may be identified as the direct object, the secondary as the double accusative. The secondary object is in apposition with the primary object, and it would be possible therefore to supply the verb "to be" in order to connect the two objects. The secondary object would be the one which follows the verb "to be" (understood).

εἶχον Ἰωάννην ὑπηρέτην. (Acts 13:5)

They had *John* (as) *an assistant.*

ὑπόδειγμα λάβετε . . . τοὺς προφήτας. (James 5:10)
Take the *prophets* (as) *an example.*

ὑμεῖς αὐτὸν ἐποιήσατε σπήλαιον λῃστῶν. (Luke 19:46)
You have made *it* (into) *a den* of thieves.

Adverbial Accusative

As the name implies, the adverbial accusative functions like an adverb, i.e. it modifies a verb rather than serving as its object. Indeed, most adverbs ending in -ov were originally the accusative of a second declension noun.

1. *Adverbial Accusative of Measure.* The substantive indicates how far the action of the verb extends. Indeed, some grammarians call this category the accusative of extent of time and space. It must be admitted, however, that the idea of extension is not very prominent in some instances, especially where prepositions are involved. In such instances the accusative indicates time and place in much the same way as does the locative (see above pages 38-40). Such looseness in use of the cases is typical of the Hellenistic period. A specialized use of the adverbial accusative of measure is found when the prepositions ἀνά and κατά convey the distributive idea (how many to each one?). This category employs:

(1) The Substantive without a Preposition.

τί ὧδε ἑστήκατε ὅλην τὴν ἡμέραν ἀργοί; (Matt. 20:6)
Why are you standing here idle *all day?*

ἐληλακότες οὖν ὡς σταδίους εἴκοσι πέντε ἢ τριάκοντα θεωροῦσιν τὸν Ἰησοῦν. (John 6:19)
Therefore when they had rowed about *twenty-five* or *thirty stadia,* they saw Jesus.

εἶδον τὰ ἔργα μου τεσσαράκοντα ἔτη. (Heb. 3:9-10)
They saw my works *for forty years.*

προελθὼν μικρὸν ἔπεσεν ἐπὶ πρόσωπον αὐτοῦ. (Matt. 26:39)
And when he had gone forward *a little way,* he fell on his face.

οὐκ ἀφίστατο τοῦ ἱεροῦ νηστείαις καὶ δεήσεσιν λατρεύουσα
<u>νύκτα καὶ ἡμέραν</u>. (Luke 2:37)
She did not leave the temple but served (God) *during the night*
and *during the day* by fasting and praying.

Note: *Contrast the adverbial genitive of time (see above page
10) in the following.*

ὁ θεὸς οὐ μὴ ποιήσῃ τὴν ἐκδίκησιν τῶν ἐκλεκτῶν αὐτοῦ τῶν
βοώντων αὐτῷ <u>ἡμέρας</u> καὶ <u>νυκτός</u>; (Luke 18:7)
Will not God make a vindication of his elect who cry to him *by
day* and *by night?*

(2) The Substantive with the Preposition ἀνά.

ἦλθεν . . . <u>ἀνὰ μέσον</u> τῶν ὁρίων Δεκαπόλεως. (Mark 7:31)
He went *through the center* of the region of Decapolis.

ἀπέστειλεν αὐτοὺς <u>ἀνὰ δύο δύο</u>. (Luke 10:1)
He sent them *in pairs.*

Note: *The above example expresses the distributive idea. See
also I Cor. 14:27.*

(3) The Substantive with the Preposition εἰς.

<u>εἰς ἔθνη</u> μακρὰν ἐξαποστελῶ σε. (Acts 22:21)
I will send you far away *unto the Gentiles.*

<u>εἰς τὸν αἰῶνα</u> (Matt. 21:19 etc.)
forever

(4) The Substantive with the Preposition ἐπί.

ἦλθεν πρὸς αὐτοὺς περιπατῶν <u>ἐπὶ τὴν θάλασσαν</u>. (Matt. 14:25)
He came to them walking *upon the sea.*

τοῦτο ἐποίει <u>ἐπὶ πολλὰς ἡμέρας</u>. (Acts 16:18)
She was doing this *for many days.*

(5) The Substantive with the Preposition κατά.

μηδένα <u>κατὰ τὴν ὁδὸν</u> ἀσπάσησθε. (Luke 10:4)
Greet no one *along the road.*

δύνασθε καθ' ἕνα πάντες προφητεύειν. (I Cor. 14:31)
All of you can prophesy *one at a time*.

Note: *The above is an example of the distributive idea. See also Mark 6:40.*

(6) The Substantive with the Preposition μετά.

μετὰ ταῦτα ἐξῆλθεν. (Luke 5:27)
After these things he went out.

μετὰ τὸ δεύτερον καταπέτασμα σκηνή. (Heb. 9:3)
Behind the second curtain (there was) a tent.

(7) The Substantive with the Preposition παρά.

ὁ ’Ιησοῦς ἦλθεν παρὰ τὴν θάλασσαν. (Matt. 15:29)
Jesus went along *beside the sea.*

ἔπεσεν παρὰ τὴν ὁδόν. (Mark 4:4)
(Some) fell *beside the road.*

(8) The Substantive with the Preposition περί.

σκάψω περὶ αὐτήν. (Luke 13:8)
I shall dig *around it.*

περὶ τετάρτην φυλακὴν τῆς νυκτὸς ἔρχεται πρὸς αὐτούς. (Mark 6:48)
About the fourth watch of the night he came to them.

(9) The Substantive with the Preposition πρός.

ὁ λόγος ἦν πρὸς τὸν θεόν.(John 1:1)
The Word was *with God.*

. . . οἳ πρὸς καιρὸν πιστεύουσιν. (Luke 8:13)
. . . who believe *for a while.*

(10) The Substantive with the Preposition ὑπό.

οὐδὲ καίουσιν λύχνον καὶ τιθέασιν αὐτὸν ὑπὸ τὸν μόδιον. (Matt. 5:15)
Neither do they light a lamp and put it *under a basket.*

εἰσῆλθον ὑπὸ τὸν ὄρθρον εἰς τὸ ἱερόν. (Acts 5:21)
They entered into the temple *about dawn.*

2. *Adverbial Accusative of Manner.* The word in the accusative indicates how the action of the verb takes place. This category also includes the accusatives used with passive verbs as in the third and fourth examples under the substantive without a preposition. All such accusatives will not fit neatly into this category because many indicate more than the manner of the action of the verb (see τὴν ὁδόν in Acts 18:25 and ἅς in II Thess. 2:15). This category employs:

(1) The Substantive without a Preposition.

... ὡς Σόδομα καὶ Γόμορρα καὶ αἱ περὶ αὐτὰς πόλεις, <u>τὸν ὅμοιον τρόπον</u> τούτοις ἐκπορνεύσασαι ... (Jude 7)
... as Sodom and Gomorra and the cities around them, which committed immorality *in the same manner* as these ...

κατακλίνατε αὐτοὺς <u>κλισίας</u> ὡσεὶ ἀνὰ πεντήκοντα. (Luke 9:14)
Make them sit down *in groups* of about fifty.

ἐνεδιδύσκετο <u>πορφύραν</u> καὶ <u>βύσσον</u>. (Luke 16:19)
He was clothed *with purple* and *fine linen*.

ἐκαυματίσθησαν οἱ ἄνθρωποι <u>καῦμα μέγα</u>. (Rev. 16:9)
Men were burned *with a great fire*.

<u>τὰ ἐνόντα</u> δότε ἐλεημοσύνην. (Luke 11:41)
Give alms *from the heart*.

Note: τὰ ἐνόντα *(pres. act. part. acc. neut. pl. of* ἔνειμι*) could also be a double accusative: Give the inward things as alms.*

(2) The Substantive with the Preposition εἰς.

οὐκ <u>εἰς κενὸν</u> ἔδραμον οὐδὲ <u>εἰς κενὸν</u> ἐκοπίασα. (Phil. 2:16)
I have not run *in vain* or labored *in vain*.

ὕπαγε <u>εἰς εἰρήνην</u>. (Mark 5:34)
Go *in peace*.

3. *Adverbial Accusative of Reference or Adverbial Accusative of Respect.* The word in the accusative answers the question, What does the action of the verb relate to? This category includes those uses of the accusative which indicate standard or rule of measurement, which idea is most evident with the prepositions κατά and πρός. A special use of the adverbial accusa-

tive of reference is in connection with a substantive which produces the action expressed by an infinitive, which substantive
appears in English translation as the "subject" of the infinitive.
(Technically infinite verb forms do not have subjects). The last
two examples below of use of the substantive without a preposition represent instances of this use. This category employs:

(1) The Substantive without a Preposition.

πᾶς ὁ ἀγωνιζόμενος πάντα ἐγκρατεύεται. (I Cor. 9:25)
Everyone who strives exercises self-control *with reference to
all things.*

ἀληθεύοντες ἐν ἀγάπῃ αὐξήσωμεν εἰς αὐτὸν τὰ πάντα.
(Eph. 4:15)
Speaking the truth in love let us grow up unto him *with reference
to all things.*

. . . ἵνα ἐλεήμων γένηται καὶ πιστὸς ἀρχιερεὺς τὰ πρὸς τὸν
θεόν. (Heb. 2:17)
. . . so that he might become a merciful and faithful high priest
with reference to the things pertaining to God.

πάλιν χρείαν ἔχετε τοῦ διδάσκειν ὑμᾶς τινά. (Heb. 5:12)
You still have a need *for someone* to teach you.

πρὶν ἀλέκτορα φωνῆσαι δὶς τρὶς με ἀπαρνήσῃ. (Mark 14:72)
Before *the cock* crows twice you will deny me three times.

(2) The Substantive with the Preposition εἰς.

ἕκαστος ἡμῶν τῷ πλησίον ἀρεσκέτω εἰς τὸ ἀγαθόν. (Rom. 15:2)
Let each one of us please his neighbor *with reference to what
is good.*

θέλω ὑμᾶς σοφοὺς εἶναι εἰς τὸ ἀγαθόν, ἀκεραίους δὲ εἰς τὸ
κακόν. (Rom. 16:19)
I want you to be experts *about good* but simpletons *about evil.*

(3) The Substantive with the Preposition κατά.

Χριστὸς ἀπέθανεν ὑπὲρ τῶν ἁμαρτιῶν ἡμῶν κατὰ τὰς γραφάς.
(I Cor. 15:3)
Christ died for our sins *in accordance with the Scriptures.*

τῷ ἐργαζομένῳ ὁ μισθὸς οὐ λογίζεται <u>κατὰ χάριν</u> ἀλλὰ <u>κατὰ ὀφείλημα</u>. (Rom. 4:4)
Reward is not given to one who works *on the basis of grace* but *on the basis of debt.*

(4) The Substantive with the Preposition περί.

τοῦτον ἐλπίζω πέμψαι ὡς ἂν ἀφίδω τὰ <u>περὶ ἐμὲ</u> ἐξαυτῆς. (Phil. 2:23)
I hope to send this man as soon as I shall evaluate the things *affecting me.*

ἡ Μάρθα περιεσπᾶτο <u>περὶ πολλὴν διακονίαν</u>. (Luke 10:40)
Martha was preoccupied *with the many details of serving.*

(5) The Substantive with the Preposition πρός.

<u>πρὸς ἡμᾶς</u> τὴν παραβολὴν ταύτην λέγεις ἢ καὶ <u>πρὸς πάντας</u>; (Luke 12:41)
Are you telling this parable *with reference to us* (only) or *with reference to all men?*

τοὺς πάντας ἡμᾶς φανερωθῆναι δεῖ ἔμπροσθεν τοῦ βήματος τοῦ Χριστοῦ, ἵνα κομίσηται ἕκαστος τὰ διὰ τοῦ σώματος <u>πρὸς ἃ</u> ἔπραξεν. (II Cor. 5:10)
We must all appear before the judgment bar of Christ so that each man may receive the things (he did) through his body *in accordance with what* he did.

Accusative with Oaths

Although most grammarians provide a separate category for this use of the accusative, it could very well be treated as an adverbial accusative of reference. This construction involves a verb which contains the idea of swearing, (usually) an accusative of direct object, and a word in the accusative indicating the person or thing by whom or by which one swears. The latter is the accusative with an oath. The word "by" will ordinarily be used in the translation. This category employs the substantive without a preposition.

ὁρκίζω ὑμᾶς <u>τὸν Ἰησοῦν</u>. (Acts 19:13)
I adjure you *by Jesus.*

ἐνορκίζω ὑμᾶς τὸν κύριον. (I Thess. 5:27)
I adjure you *by the Lord.*

μὴ ὀμνύετε, μήτε τὸν οὐρανὸν μήτε τὴν γῆν μήτε ἄλλον τινὰ
ὅρκον. (James 5:12)
Do not swear, neither *by heaven* neither *by the earth* neither *by
any other oath.*

διαμαρτύρομαι ἐνώπιον τοῦ θεοῦ καὶ Χριστοῦ ᾽Ιησοῦ . . . καὶ
τὴν ἐπιφάνειαν αὐτοῦ καὶ τὴν βασιλείαν αὐτοῦ. (II Tim. 4:1)
I solemnly charge (you) before God and Christ Jesus and *by* his
appearing and *Kingdom.*

Accusative Absolute

There is some doubt about the need for this category. The
accusative in an absolute construction is rare in the New Testament and other Hellenistic Greek. There are however several examples in the New Testament where a noun or
pronoun in the accusative is the subject of the action of a participle also in the accusative and grammatically unrelated to
the subject of the main clause. The first two examples below
seem to be clear examples. In the other three the pronoun
(ὑμᾶς and ἡμᾶς) is repeated or understood in the main clause.
However, it is not the subject of the main clause and is therefore related only loosely. This category employs the substantive without a preposition.

. . . μάλιστα γνώστην ὄντα σε πάντων τῶν κατὰ ᾽Ιουδαίους
ἐθῶν τε καὶ ζητημάτων. (Acts 26:3)
. . . especially *since you are an expert* about all the customs and
controversies of the Jews.

. . . ἵνα ὁ θεὸς . . . δώῃ ὑμῖν πνεῦμα σοφίας καὶ ἀποκαλύψεως ἐν
ἐπιγνώσει αὐτοῦ, πεφωτισμένους τοὺς ὀφθαλμοὺς τῆς καρδίας
. . . (Eph. 1:17-18)
. . . so that God might give to you a spirit of wisdom and revelation in full knowledge of him, *the eyes* of your heart *being
opened* . . .

καὶ ὑμᾶς ὄντας νεκροὺς τοῖς παραπτώμασιν . . . καὶ ὄντας ἡμᾶς
νεκροὺς τοῖς παραπτώμασιν συνεζωοποίησεν τῷ Χριστῷ.
(Eph. 2:1, 5)

And although *you were* dead in trespasses . . . and *we were* dead in trespasses, (God) made (us) alive together in Christ.

καθώς ἐστιν δίκαιον ἐμοὶ τοῦτο φρονεῖν ὑπὲρ πάντων ὑμῶν . . . συγκοινωνούς μου . . . πάντας ὑμᾶς ὄντας. (Phil. 1:7)
Thus it is right for me to think this way about all of you . . . since *you are all* sharers with me.

Accusative of Purpose

A substantive in the accusative may indicate the aim or purpose of the action of the main verb in much the same way as does ἵνα with the subjunctive (see below page 120). This category employs:

(1) The Substantive with the Preposition εἰς.

οὗτος ἦλθεν εἰς μαρτυρίαν. (John 1:7)
This man came *for the purpose of bearing witness.*

ὁ υἱὸς τοῦ ἀνθρώπου παραδίδοται εἰς τὸ σταυρωθῆναι. (Matt. 26:2)
The Son of Man is going to be betrayed *so that he may be crucified.*

(2) The Substantive with the Preposition πρός.

αὐτὸς ἦν ὁ πρὸς τὴν ἐλεημοσύνην καθήμενος ἐπὶ τῇ Ὡραίᾳ Πύλῃ τοῦ ἱεροῦ. (Acts 3:10)
He was the one who was placed at the Beautiful Gate of the temple *so that he could beg.*

πάντα τὰ ἔργα αὐτῶν ποιοῦσιν πρὸς τὸ θεαθῆναι τοῖς ἀνθρώποις. (Matt. 23:5)
They do all their works *for the purpose of being seen* by men.

Accusative of Result

This category indicates what takes place as a result of the action of the main verb. It employs the substantive with the preposition εἰς.

ὡς δι' ἑνὸς παραπτώματος εἰς πάντας ἀνθρώπους εἰς κατάκριμα, οὕτως καὶ δι' ἑνὸς δικαιώματος εἰς πάντας ἀνθρώπους εἰς δικαίωσιν ζωῆς. (Rom. 5:18)

Just as the sinful act of one man *resulted in condemnation* extending to all men, so also the righteous act of one man *resulted in* life-giving *acquittal* extending to all men.

Note: εἰς πάντας ἀνθρώπους *is an adverbial accusative of measure.*

τοῦτο προσεύχομαι, ἵνα ἡ ἀγάπη ὑμῶν ἔτι μᾶλλον καὶ μᾶλλον περισσεύῃ ... , <u>εἰς τὸ δοκιμάζειν</u> ὑμᾶς τὰ διαφέροντα. (Phil. 1:9-10)
This I pray, that your love may abound more and more (and) *as a result* you *may test* the things which are important.

Accusative of Cause

The substantive indicates the ground or reason for the action. It answers the question, Why? This category employs:

(1) The Substantive with the Preposition διά.

χαρᾷ χαίρει <u>διὰ τὴν φωνὴν</u> τοῦ νυμφίου. (John 3:29)
He rejoices with great joy *because of the voice* of the bridegroom.

Ἰησοῦς οὐκ ἐπίστευεν αὐτὸν αὐτοῖς <u>διὰ τὸ</u> αὐτὸν γινώσκειν πάντας. (John 2:24)
Jesus did not commit himself to them *because* he *knew* all men.

(2) The Substantive with the Preposition εἰς.

ὑμᾶς βαπτίζω ἐν ὕδατι <u>εἰς μετάνοιαν</u>. (Matt. 3:11)
I baptize you in water *because of (your) repentance.*

μετανοήσατε... , καὶ βαπτισθήτω ἕκαστος ὑμῶν... <u>εἰς ἄφεσιν</u> τῶν ἁμαρτιῶν ὑμῶν. (Acts 2:38)
Repent, and let each one of you be baptized *because of the remission* of your sins.

Accusative of Possession

This rare use employs the substantive with the preposition κατά.

... ὡς καί τινες τῶν <u>καθ᾽ ὑμᾶς</u> ποιητῶν εἰρήκασιν. (Acts 17:28)
... as also certain of *your own* poets have said.

... γνώστην ὄντα σε πάντων τῶν <u>κατὰ Ἰουδαίους</u> ἐθῶν. (Acts 26:3)

. . . because you are an expert with reference to all of the customs *of the Jews.*

Accusative of Comparison

This category employs:

(1) The Substantive with the Preposition παρά.

δοκεῖτε ὅτι οἱ Γαλιλαῖοι οὗτοι ἁμαρτωλοὶ <u>παρὰ πάντας τοὺς Γαλιλαίους</u> ἐγένοντο; (Luke 13:2)
Do you think that these Galileans were *greater* sinners *than all (the other) Galileans?*

ἐλάτρευσαν τῇ κτίσει <u>παρὰ τὸν κτίσαντα.</u> (Rom. 1:25)
They served the creature *more than the creator.*

(2) The Substantive with the Preposition πρός.

λογίζομαι ὅτι οὐκ ἄξια τὰ παθήματα τοῦ νῦν καιροῦ <u>πρὸς τὴν μέλλουσαν δόξαν.</u> (Rom. 8:18)
I consider that the sufferings of the present time (are) not worthy of being compared *with the coming glory.*

(3) The Substantive with the Preposition ὑπέρ.

ὁ φιλῶν πατέρα ἢ μητέρα <u>ὑπὲρ ἐμὲ</u> οὐκ ἔστιν μου ἄξιος. (Matt. 10:37)
The one who loves father or mother *more than me* is not worthy of me.

οὐκ ἔστιν μαθητὴς <u>ὑπὲρ τὸν διδάσκαλον.</u> (Matt. 10:24)
The disciple is not *greater than this teacher.*

Note: ὑπέρ *always expresses comparison in terms of that which is greater.*

Accusative of Relationship

This designation is an attempt to avoid multiplying categories and to group together several uses of the accusative which at best have only a little in common. These uses are found only with the prepositions which are listed below, each of which has its own distinctive meaning. It is possible, however, to combine these uses into a single category because all of them express one of two antithetical ideas. On the one hand this category expresses the idea of advantage, benefit, favorable disposition, support, or friendly relationship. On the other hand this category expresses the idea of disadvantage, detriment, unfavorable disposition, opposition, or hostile relationship. Also included under the substantive used with πρός is an example in which the idea of speaking or communicating something to someone is evident. This is the use of πρός and the accusative which is very close to the dative of indirect object. Perhaps these ideas do have enough in common to justify combining them. This category employs:

(1) The Substantive with the Preposition διά.

τὸ σάββατον διὰ τὸν ἄνθρωπον ἐγένετο καὶ οὐχ ὁ ἄνθρωπος διὰ τὸ σάββατον. (Mark 2:27)
The Sabbath was made *for man's benefit,* not man *for the Sabbath's benefit.*

εἰσὶν εὐνοῦχοι οἵτινες εὐνούχισαν ἑαυτοὺς διὰ τὴν βασιλείαν τῶν οὐρανῶν. (Matt. 19:12)
There are eunuchs who castrated themselves *for the sake of the Kingdom* of heaven.

(2) The Substantive with the Preposition εἰς.

περὶ τῆς λογείας τῆς εἰς τοὺς ἁγίους . . . (I Cor. 16:1)
Concerning the offering *for the saints* . . .

πᾶς ὃς ἐρεῖ λόγον εἰς τὸν υἱὸν τοῦ ἀνθρώπου, ἀφεθήσεται αὐτῷ. (Luke 12:10)
Everyone who shall speak a word *against the Son* of man, it shall be forgiven to him.

(3) The Substantive with the Preposition ἐπί.

σπλαγχνίζομαι ἐπὶ τὸν ὄχλον. (Matt. 15:32)
I have compassion *upon the crowd.*

ὡς ἐπὶ λῃστὴν ἐξήλθατε; (Matt. 26:55)
Have you come out as *against a thief?*

(4) The Substantive with the Preposition παρά.

παρὰ τὸν νόμον ἀναπείθει οὗτος τοὺς ἀνθρώπους σέβεσθαι τὸν θεόν. (Acts 18:13)

This man is urging men to worship God *contrary to the law.*

παρακαλῶ ὑμᾶς, ἀδελφοί, σκοπεῖν τοὺς τὰς διχοστασίας καὶ τὰ σκάνδαλα παρὰ τὴν διδαχὴν ἣν ὑμεῖς ἐμάθετε ποιοῦντας. (Rom. 16:17)
I beseech you, brothers, take note of the ones who create divisions and problems *contrary to the teaching* which you have learned.

(5) The Substantive with the Preposition πρός.

μακροθυμεῖτε πρὸς πάντας. (I Thess. 5:14)
Be patient *with all men.*

οὐκ ἔστιν ἡμῖν ἡ πάλη πρὸς αἷμα καὶ σάρκα, ἀλλὰ πρὸς τὰς ἀρχάς, πρὸς τὰς ἐξουσίας . . . (Eph. 6:12)
Our struggle is not *against blood* and *flesh* but *against rulers, against authorities . . .*

. . . καὶ τῆς διαθήκης ἧς διέθετο ὁ θεὸς πρὸς τοὺς πατέρας ὑμῶν, λέγων πρὸς ᾿Αβραάμ, Καὶ ἐν τῷ σπέρματί σου . . . (Acts 3:25)
. . . and of the covenant which God made *with* our *fathers,* saying *to Abraham,* "And to your seed . . ."

Predicate Accusative

A predicate accusative follows the verb "to be." A predicate accusative may be one member of a double accusative (see above page 51), in which case the verb must be understood. This use of the accusative should be referred to as a double accusative. The present category is limited to the substantive with the preposition εἰς. Sometimes the verb is expressed; sometimes it is not. The present category also expresses the idea of equivalence. It could be translated with the word "as" or with the verb "to be."

ἔσομαι ὑμῖν εἰς πατέρα. (II Cor. 6:18)
I shall be *a father* to you.

ἔσονται οἱ δύο εἰς σάρκα μίαν. (Matt. 19:5)
The two shall be *one flesh.*

THE VOCATIVE

Some grammarians deny the vocative the status of a case because it does not enter into relationship with other elements in a sentence and because it has but a single use. The fact that some vocatives have a separate case form and the fact that the vocative does have a distinctive function would nevertheless seem to justify treating it as a case. The vocative indicates the person or thing being addressed. In edited texts it is usually set off by the use of a comma.

Κύριε, πρὸς τίνα ἀπελευσόμεθα; (John 6:68)
Lord, to whom shall we go?

τὸ λοιπόν, ἀδελφοί μου, χαίρετε ἐν κυρίῳ. (Phil. 3:1)
Finally, my *brothers,* rejoice in the Lord.

πάτερ, ἐλήλυθεν ἡ ὥρα. (John 17:1)
Father, the hour has come.

ἄνδρες ἀδελφοὶ καὶ πατέρες, ἀκούσατέ μου. (Acts 22:1)
Men, brothers, and *fathers,* hear me.

διὸ ἀναπολόγητος εἶ, ὦ ἄνθρωπε πᾶς ὁ κρίνων. (Rom. 2:1)
Therefore you are without excuse, *O man who judges.*

In a few instances a word of address has what appears to be a nominative form. Some grammarians refer to this use as the nominative used as a vocative. It is best simply to treat these as true vocatives and to consider the form rather than the usage to be irregular. Inasmuch as the nominative and vocative always have the same form in the plural and often have the same form in the singular it is easy to see how a vocative sometimes appears in what seems to be a nominative form.

ναὶ, ὁ πατήρ, ὅτι οὕτως εὐδοκία ἐγένετο ἔμπροσθέν σου. (Matt. 11:26)
Yes, *Father,* for so it was pleasing to you.

As in the above example, the article often has the effect of converting a nominative form into a vocative.

APPENDIX: PREPOSITIONS

The function of prepositions already has been discussed (see above page 2). The use of the various prepositions with each of the oblique cases also has been given (see above pages 10-63). It remains only to list the prepositions and summarize their use.

Proper Prepositions

		Pages
ἀνά	Adverbial Accusative of Measure	53
ἀντί	Ablative of Cause	28
	Ablative of Exchange	30
ἀπό	Ablative of Separation	21
	Ablative of Source	24
	Ablative of Agency	25
	Ablative of Cause	28
	Partitive Ablative	31
διά	Adverbial Genitive of Time	10
	Adverbial Genitive of Place	12
	Ablative of Agency	25
	Ablative of Means	26
	Accusative of Cause	60
	Accusative of Relationship	62
εἰς	Adverbial Accusative of Measure	53
	Adverbial Accusative of Manner	55
	Adverbial Accusative of Reference	56
	Accusative of Purpose	59
	Accusative of Result	59
	Accusative of Cause	60
	Accusative of Relationship	62
	Predicate Accusative	63
ἐκ	Ablative of Separation	22
	Ablative of Source	24
	Ablative of Agency	25
	Ablative of Means	27
	Ablative of Cause	28
	Partitive Ablative	31

ἐν

Dative of Indirect Object   32
Dative of Advantage   34
Dative of Disadvantage   35
Dative of Reference   36
Dative of Root Idea   37
Locative of Place   38
Locative of Time   40
Locative of Sphere   41
Instrumental of Means   43
Instrumental of Cause   44
Instrumental of Manner   45
Instrumental of Measure   46
Instrumental of Association   47
Instrumental of Agency   49

ἐπί

Adverbial Genitive of Time   11
Adverbial Genitive of Place   13
Dative of Indirect Object   32
Dative of Advantage   34
Dative of Disadvantage   35
Dative of Reference   36
Locative of Place   38
Locative of Time   40
Locative of Sphere   41
Instrumental of Cause   44
Adverbial Accusative of Measure   53
Accusative of Relationship   62

κατά

Adverbial Genitive of Place   13
Genitive with Oaths   20
Ablative of Source   24
Ablative of Opposition   29
Adverbial Accusative of Measure   53
Adverbial Accusative of Reference   56
Accusative of Possession   60

μετά

Genitive of Association   19
Genitive of Attendant
  Circumstances   19
Adverbial Accusative of Measure   54

παρά	Ablative of Source	24
	Ablative of Agency	26
	Locative of Place	39
	Locative of Sphere	41
	Instrumental of Association	47
	Adverbial Accusative of Measure	54
	Accusative of Comparison	61
	Accusative of Relationship	62
περί	Adverbial Genitive of Reference	14
	Genitive of Advantage	18
	Ablative of Purpose	30
	Adverbial Accusative of Measure	54
	Adverbial Accusative of Reference	57
πρό	Ablative of Separation	22
	Ablative of Rank	29
πρός	Genitive of Advantage	18
	Locative of Place	39
	Adverbial Accusative of Measure	54
	Adverbial Accusative of Reference	57
	Accusative of Purpose	59
	Accusative of Comparison	61
	Accusative of Relationship	63
σύν	Instrumental of Measure	46
	Instrumental of Association	48
ὑπέρ	Adverbial Genitive of Reference	14
	Genitive of Advantage	19
	Accusative of Comparison	61
ὑπό	Ablative of Agency	26
	Ablative of Means	27
	Adverbial Accusative of Measure	54

Adverbial Prepositions

ἅμα	Instrumental of Association	48
ἄνευ	Ablative of Separation	22
ἄντικρυς	Adverbial Genitive of Place	13

ἀντιπέρα	Adverbial Genitive of Place	13
ἀπέναντι	Ablative of Separation	22
	Ablative of Opposition	29
ἄτερ	Ablative of Separation	22
ἄχρι	Adverbial Genitive of Time	11
	Adverbial Genitive of Measure	12
	Adverbial Genitive of Place	13
ἐγγύς	Adverbial Genitive of Place	13
	Locative of Place	39
ἐκτός	Ablative of Separation	22
ἔμπροσθεν	Ablative of Separation	22
	Ablative of Rank	29
ἔναντι	Adverbial Genitive of Place	13
ἐναντίον	Adverbial Genitive of Place	13
ἔνεκα, ἔνεκεν, εἵνεκεν	Ablative of Cause	29
	Ablative of Purpose	30
ἐντός	Adverbial Genitive of Place	13
ἐνώπιον	Adverbial Genitive of Place	13
ἔξω	Ablative of Separation	22
ἔξωθεν	Ablative of Separation	22
	Ablative of Source	24
ἐπάνω	Adverbial Genitive of Place	13
ἐπέκεινα	Ablative of Separation	22
ἔσω	Adverbial Genitive of Place	13
ἕως	Adverbial Genitive of Time	11
	Adverbial Genitive of Measure	12
	Adverbial Genitive of Place	13
κατέναντι	Adverbial Genitive of Place	13
κατενώπιον	Adverbial Genitive of Place	13

κυκλόθεν	Adverbial Genitive of Place	13
κύκλῳ	Adverbial Genitive of Place	13
μέσον	Adverbial Genitive of Place	13
μεταξύ	Ablative of Separation	22
μέχρι(ς)	Adverbial Genitive of Time	11
	Adverbial Genitive of Measure	12
	Adverbial Genitive of Place	14
ὄπισθεν	Ablative of Separation	22
ὀπίσω	Ablative of Separation	22
ὀψέ	Adverbial Genitive of Time	11
	Ablative of Separation	22
παραπλήσιον	Locative of Sphere	42
παρεκτός	Ablative of Separation	23
πέραν	Ablative of Separation	23
πλήν	Ablative of Separation	23
πλησίον	Adverbial Genitive of Place	14
ὑπεράνω	Ablative of Separation	23
ὑπερέκεινα	Ablative of Separation	23
ὑπερεκπερισσοῦ	Ablative of Comparison	28
ὑποκάτω	Ablative of Separation	23
χάριν	Ablative of Cause	29
χωρίς	Ablative of Separation	23

KINDS

As indicated above on page 1, nouns, adjectives, the article, pronouns, and in certain instances infinitives and participles are substantives. The syntax of the infinitive and participle will be discussed below on pages 132-152. In this section something will be said about the use of nouns, adjectives, the article, and pronouns.

NOUN

The English word noun is derived from the Latin word *nomen* which means a name. A noun is a word which names or designates a person, thing, or quality. It is an appelation applied to a person, thing, or quality. The previous discussion of case, gender, and number is sufficient to show the way in which nouns are used.

ADJECTIVE

The word adjective is derived from a Latin verb which means to add something. The idea seems to be that an adjective is a word which is added to a noun in order to modify or distinguish or further describe it. As a matter of fact nouns and adjectives seem to have had a common origin. This fact explains why they are declined so much alike. The close relationship is further seen in the fact that adjectives may be used in the place of nouns. Nevertheless the Greek adjective has developed in its use to the point where it is correct to treat it as a separate part of speech. Adjectives exist in three degrees: positive, comparative, and superlative. Numbers are adjectives. There is a special class of Greek adjectives which are known as verbal adjectives because they express action. They are comprised of a verb stem and the ending -τος. Adjectives are used in the following ways.

Attributively

The attributive adjective modifies a noun by ascribing a quality to it, by giving an incidental description of it. The attributive adjective follows the article if there is one in the construction. The adjective agrees with the noun it modifies in case, gender, and number.

... ἀπὸ τῆς πρώτης ἡμέρας ἄχρι τοῦ νῦν. (Phil. 1:5)
... from the *first* day until now.

ὁ ποιμὴν ὁ καλός (John 10:11)
the *good* shepherd

ζωὴν αἰώνιον (Matt. 25:46)
eternal life

τὸν καλὸν οἶνον (John 2:10)
the *good* wine

τετρακισχίλιοι ἄνδρες (Matt. 15:38)
four thousand men

Predicatively

The predicate adjective modifies a noun by making an important additional statement about it. A linking verb may or may not be found in the text, but if not it must be understood. The predicative adjective is never immediately preceded by an article. It agrees in case, gender, and number with the noun about which it makes the assertion.

τὸ φρέαρ ἐστὶν βαθύ. (John 4:11)
The well is *deep.*

ὁ ποιήσας με ὑγιῆ ἐκεῖνός μοι εἶπεν... (John 5:11)
The one who made me *well* said to me...

μακάριοι οἱ πτωχοὶ τῷ πνεύματι. (Matt. 5:3)
Blessed (are) the poor in spirit.

τί με λέγεις ἀγαθόν; (Mark 10:18)
Why do you say that I (am) *good?*

... οὐχ ἵνα ἡμεῖς δόκιμοι φανῶμεν... (II Cor. 13:7)
... not so that we may appear (to be) *approved*...

Substantivally

The adjective may be used as a pure substantive, i.e. just like a noun is used, in place of a noun. The adjective will immediately follow the article if there is one in the construction. Indeed, this use could be looked upon as a subdivision of the attributive use of the adjective. The case, gender, and number are determined by use in the sentence.

τυφλοὶ ἀναβλέπουσιν καὶ χωλοὶ περιπατοῦσιν, λεπροὶ καθαρίζονται καὶ κωφοὶ ἀκούουσιν, καὶ νεκροὶ ἐγείρονται καὶ πτωχοὶ εὐαγγελίζονται. (Matt. 11:5)
Blind men see and lame men walk, lepers are cleansed and deaf men hear, and dead men are raised and poor men are being evangelized.

εἰ τῷ τοῦ ἑνὸς παραπτώματι οἱ πολλοὶ ἀπέθανον . . . (Rom. 5:15)
If by the sin of the one man many died . . .

ῥῦσαι ἡμᾶς ἀπὸ τοῦ πονηροῦ. (Matt. 6:13)
Deliver us from the evil one.

. . . καὶ εἴπωσιν πᾶν πονηρὸν καθ' ὑμῶν . . . (Matt. 5:11)
. . . and say every evil thing against you . . .

Adverbially

Sometimes the adjective modifies the verbal idea rather than a noun and is therefore used like an adverb. The adverbial adjective will usually be in the accusative case (cf. the adverbial accusative above pages 52-57).

προβὰς ὀλίγον εἶδεν Ἰάκωβον. (Mark 1:19)
When he had gone forward a little he saw James.

. . . τὸν τόπον ὅπου ἦν Ἰωάννης τὸ πρῶτον βαπτίζων. (John 10:40)
. . . the place where John was baptizing at first.

μόνον ἀκούοντες ἦσαν . . . (Gal. 1:23)
Only they kept on hearing . . .

μικρὸν καὶ οὐ θεωρεῖτέ με. (John 16:19)
In a little while you will no longer see me.

τίς ἡ ὠφέλεια τῆς περιτομῆς; πολὺ κατὰ πάντα τρόπον. πρῶτον μὲν γὰρ ὅτι ἐπιστεύθησαν τὰ λόγια τοῦ θεοῦ. (Rom. 3:1-2)
What (is) the advantage of circumcision? Much in every way. First, they were entrusted with the oracles of God.

Note: πρῶτον has been used so often adverbially that most lexicons list it separately as an adverb.

ARTICLE

The basic function of the Greek article is to point out, to draw attention to, to identify, to make definite, to define, to limit. Generally, though not always, substantives with the article are definite or generic, while those without the article are indefinite or qualitative. It would probably be an accurate summary statement to say that the presence of the article emphasizes identity, the absence of the article quality. There is great variety in the use of the Greek article. There are many special uses. The variety of usage is so great that an exhaustive treatment is impossible, but the following are the most important uses. Three examples will be given of each. Most of the examples involve the use of the article with a noun, but the article is used in much the same way with adjectives, participles, pronouns, adverbs, and prepositional phrases. The unique use of the article with infinitives is best considered in connection with the study of the infinitive (see below pages 132-143). The article is used:

To Identify or Denote Persons or Things and to Distinguish Them from All Others

This of course is the basic, fundamental use of the article, and it is quite similar to the use of the English article.

ἀνέβη εἰς τὸ ὄρος. (Matt. 5:1)
He went up to *the* mountain.

ἱλάσθητί μοι τῷ ἁμαρτωλῷ. (Luke 18:13)
Be merciful to me *the* sinner.

ὁρκίζω ὑμᾶς τὸν Ἰησοῦν ὃν Παῦλος κηρύσσει. (Acts 19:13)
I adjure you by *the particular* Jesus whom Paul is preaching.

Note: *See below the use of the article with proper names.*

To Indicate That a Substantive is Monadic

A substantive is monadic when it is the only such thing there is. An article is not always used with monadic nouns, however.

οὕτως ἠγάπησεν ὁ θεὸς τὸν κόσμον. (John 3:16)
God so loved *the* world.

τὸ ἔργον κυρίου ἐργάζεται ὡς κἀγώ. (I Cor. 16:10)
He does *the* work of the Lord just as I do.

ὁ ἄνωθεν ἐρχόμενος ἐπάνω πάντων ἐστίν.... ὁ ἐκ τοῦ
οὐρανοῦ ἐρχόμενος ἐπάνω πάντων ἐστίν. (John 3:31)
The one who comes from above is above all. *The* one who comes
from heaven is above all.

To Denote Previous Reference

The article calls attention to a substantive which has been
previously mentioned and which may be defined or identified
or understood by recollection of the previous reference. The
initial reference may or may not have the article. This use is
sometimes referred to as the anaphoric use.

τότε Ἡρῴδης λάθρᾳ καλέσας τοὺς μάγους ... (Matt. 2:7; the
previous reference to the wise men is in v. 1)
Then Herod having secretly called *the* wise men ...

ἔλαβεν τοὺς ἄρτους ... καὶ ἐκ τῶν ὀψαρίων. (John 6:11; the
previous reference to the bread and fish is in v. 9)
He took *the* bread and some of *the* fish.

μετὰ τὰς δύο ἡμέρας ἐξῆλθεν. (John 4:43; the previous reference to the two days is in v. 40)
After *the* two days he went away.

To Distinguish One Quality from Another

The effect of this use is to objectify or personify an abstract
noun. English does not use an article with abstract nouns unless
there has been previous reference to the noun. Therefore the
Greek article with an abstract noun will not be translated.
Greek does not always use the article with abstract nouns, however, as for example χάριν ἀντὶ χάριτος in John 1:16.

ἡ ἀγάπη μακροθυμεῖ, χρηστεύεται ἡ ἀγάπη. (I Cor. 13:4)
Love is patient; love is kind.

ἡ χάρις καὶ ἡ ἀλήθεια διὰ Ἰησοῦ Χριστοῦ ἐγένετο. (John 1:17)
Grace and truth came through Jesus Christ.

ἀπόδοτε πᾶσιν τὰς ὀφειλάς, τῷ τὸν φόρον τὸν φόρον, τῷ τὸ τέλος τὸ τέλος, τῷ τὸν φόβον τὸν φόβον, τῷ τὴν τιμὴν τὴν τιμήν. (Rom. 13:7)
Give to all men their dues, taxes to whom taxes (are due), revenue to whom revenue (is due), fear to whom fear (is due), honor to whom honor (is due).

To Call Special Attention to a Proper Name

Theoretically a proper name should not need an article because it is by its very nature quite definite. English uses no article with proper names. Sometimes, however, Greek writers do attach the article to proper names to emphasize them.

μὴ παρενοχλεῖν τοῖς ἀπὸ τῶν ἐθνῶν ἐπιστρέφουσιν ἐπὶ τὸν θεόν. (Acts 15:19)
We should not impose difficulties upon the Gentiles who are turning to God.

ἐν τῷ τὸν Ἀπολλῶ εἶναι ἐν Κορίνθῳ... (Acts 19:1)
While Apollos was in Corinth...

Note: *The article* τὸν *also denotes previous reference. See 18:24ff.*

ἦλθεν ὁ Ἰησοῦς εἰς τὴν Γαλιλαίαν. (Mark 1:14)
Jesus came into Galilee.

To Distinguish One class or Group from Another, to Indicate that a Substantive is Typical or Representative of Its Class or Group

This use of the article is often referred to as the generic use. This use of the (definite) article may be translated as though the article were indefinite. Sometimes it may be best to translate a singular noun which is generic as though it were plural.

ἄξιος ὁ ἐργάτης τοῦ μισθοῦ αὐτοῦ. (Luke 10:7)
A laborer is worthy of his wages.

δεῖ τὸν ἐπίσκοπον ἀνεπίλημπτον εἶναι. (I Tim. 3:2)
A bishop must be irreproachable.

ἔστω σοι ὥσπερ ὁ ἐθνικὸς καὶ ὁ τελώνης. (Matt. 18:17)
Let him be to you like Gentiles and tax collectors.

To Indicate the Relationship of Substantives Connected by καί

Sharp's rule states: if two substantives are connected by καί and both have the article, they refer to different persons or things (third and fourth examples below); if the first has an article and the second does not, the second refers to the same person or thing as the first (first and second examples below). Of course the rule could also be applied to a series of three or more.

τοῦ μεγάλου θεοῦ καὶ σωτῆρος ἡμῶν 'Ιησοῦ Χριστοῦ (Titus 2:13)
our great God and Savior Jesus Christ

ἦλθον οἱ ὑπηρέται πρὸς τοὺς ἀρχιερεῖς καὶ Φαρισαίους. (John 7:45)
The officers came to *the* chief priests and Pharisees.

Note: *The implication is that the chief priests and Pharisees comprised a single group at this juncture.*

ὅταν εἰσφέρωσιν ὑμᾶς ἐπὶ τὰς συναγωγὰς καὶ τὰς ἀρχὰς καὶ τὰς ἐξουσίας ... (Luke 12:11)
Whenever they bring you before synagogues and before rulers and before authorities ...

ὁ Πιλᾶτος εἶπεν πρὸς τοὺς ἀρχιερεῖς καὶ τοὺς ὄχλους ... (Luke 23:4)
Pilate said to *the* priests and to *the* crowd ...

To Express the Idea of a Pronoun

1. *A Demonstrative Pronoun.* ὁ, ἡ, τό was originally a demonstrative pronoun. In the evolution of the language it became the article, but even then it retained a demonstrative force. Sometimes the demonstrative force is so strong that the words "this" or "that," if singular, or "these" or "those," if plural, will appear in the translation (first and second examples below). In other instances, where the article in the nominative refers to a person or persons previously mentioned in an oblique case, it will be translated as though it were a personal pronoun: "he," "she," or

"they" depending on its gender and number (third and fourth examples below).

ἀσπάζονται ὑμᾶς οἱ ἀπὸ τῆς Ἰταλίας. (Heb. 13:24)
Those from Italy greet you.

αἱ δυμάμεις ἐνεργοῦσιν ἐν αὐτῷ. (Matt. 14:2)
These miraculous powers are active in him.

ὁ δὲ φησιν . . . (Matt. 13:29; ὁ refers to ἀνθρώπῳ in v. 24)
But *he* said . . .

οἱ δὲ εἶπαν . . . (Matt. 2:5; οἱ refers to αὐτῶν in v. 4)
But *they* said . . .

2. *An Alternative Pronoun.* When both μέν and δέ are preceded by an article, the construction has the force of an alternative pronoun and will be translated "one" . . . "another," if singular, "some" . . . "others,"if plural.

ἕκαστος ἴδιον ἔχει χάρισμα ἐκ θεοῦ, ὁ μὲν οὕτως, ὁ δὲ οὕτως. (I Cor. 7:7)
Each person has his own gift from God, *one* this kind, *another* that kind.

οἱ μὲν ἦσαν σὺν τοῖς Ἰουδαίοις οἱ δὲ σὺν τοῖς ἀποστόλοις. (Acts 14:4)
Some sided with the Jews, *others* with the apostles.

ἔδωκεν τοὺς μὲν ἀποστόλους, τοὺς δὲ προφήτας, τοὺς δὲ εὐαγγελιστάς, τοὺς δὲ ποιμένας καὶ διδασκάλους. (Eph. 4:11)
He gave *some* apostles, *others* prophets, *others* evangelists, *others* pastors and teachers.

3. *A Possessive Pronoun.* If the idea of possession is obvious, the article alone without a pronoun is sufficient to convey the idea.

συνεπέμψαμεν μετ' αὐτοῦ τὸν ἀδελφόν. (II Cor. 8:18)
We sent with him *his* brother.

οὐ ἀπέστειλεν ὁ θεὸς τὸν υἱὸν . . . ἵνα κρίνῃ τὸν κόσμον. (John 3:17)
God did not send *his* Son to condemn the world.

οἱ ἄνδρες, ἀγαπᾶτε τὰς γυναῖκας. (Eph. 5:25)
Husbands, love *your* wives.

4. *A Relative Pronoun.* The repetition of the article in a phrase which modifies a substantive which itself has an article usually has the force of a relative pronoun. In Rev. 1:4, 8 and 11:17 a single article has relative force.

τοῦτό ἐστιν τὸ αἷμά μου τῆς διαθήκης τὸ περὶ πολλῶν ἐκχυννόμενον εἰς ἄφεσιν ἁμαρτιῶν. (Matt. 26:28)
This is my blood of the covenant *which* is poured out for many for the remission of sins.

. . . πίστει τῇ ἐν Χριστῷ 'Ιησοῦ (I Tim. 3:13)
. . . the faith *which* is in Christ Jesus

. . . εἰρήνη ἀπὸ ὁ ὢν καὶ ὁ ἦν καὶ ὁ ἐρχόμενος. (Rev. 1:4)
. . . peace from the one who is and *the one who* was and the one who is to come.

Note: *The first and third instances of ὁ could be looked upon as having relative force, but there the relative idea is provided by the substantival use of the participle.*

To Distinguish the Subject Nominative from
the Predicate Nominative in a Sentence
Containing a Linking Verb

The substantive with the article will be the subject, the one without the predicate nominative. If both have the article they are interchangeable. If one of the substantives is a pronoun, it will be the subject even if the other has an article.

ἔρημός ἐστιν ὁ τόπος. (Mark 6:35)
This place is a desert.

ὁ θεὸς ἀγάπη ἐστίν. (I Jo. 4:8)
God is love.

θεὸς ἦν ὁ λόγος. (John 1:1)
The Word was God.

To Indicate that a Nominative is
Being Used as a Vocative

ἔλεγον, Χαῖρε, ὁ βασιλεὺς τῶν Ἰουδαίων. (John 19:3)
They began to say, Hail, King of the Jews.

εἶπεν αὐτῷ, Ὁ κύριός μου καὶ ὁ θεός μου. (John 20:28)
He said to him, My Lord and my God!

ναί, ὁ πατήρ, ὅτι . . . (Matt. 11:26)
Yes, Father, because . . .

To Indicate Grammatical Relationships

The article frequently indicates the function of indeclinable nouns, prepositional phrases, adjectival clauses, and modifiers. In many instances this article cannot be translated into English because English does not have similar structures.

τὸ τῆς δόξης καὶ τὸ τοῦ θεοῦ πνεῦμα ἐφ᾽ ὑμᾶς ἀναπαύεται. (I Pet. 4:14)
The Spirit of glory and *the* Spirit of God rests upon you.

Note: *The articles relate the modifiers* τῆς δόξης *and* τοῦ θεοῦ *to* πνεῦμα.

εὑρίσκει Φίλιππος τὸν Ναθαναήλ. (John 1:45)
Philip found Nathaniel.

ἀνάδειξον ὃν ἐξελέξω ἐκ τούτων τῶν δύο ἕνα. (Acts 1:24)
Show which one of these two you have chosen.

To Take the Place of a Noun

When the article stands with words which modify or phrases which serve as modifiers, it takes the place of a noun. Which noun is supplied is determined by the context and the gender of the article.

. . . μηδὲ τὰ ἐν τῷ κόσμῳ. (I Jo. 2:15)
. . . neither *the (things)* in the world.

οἱ τοῦ Χριστοῦ Ἰησοῦ . . . (Gal. 5:24)
The (followers) of Christ Jesus . . .

λέγει τοῖς ἐκεῖ. (Matt. 26:71)
He spoke *to (some people)* there.

PRONOUN

The word pronoun is derived from two Latin words, the preposition *pro* which means for and the noun *nomen* which means name. A pronoun therefore is a word which stands for or in the place of or instead of a noun. Pronouns are used to prevent the monotony which would result from unnecessary repetition of nouns. Inasmuch as pronouns take the place of nouns, they are used in much the same way as nouns are used. It is unnecessary therefore to provide separate syntactical categories for them. The syntax of the case of pronouns is like that of nouns. Where either the pronoun or its antecedent has been attracted to the case of the other, it should be treated as though it had retained its own case. Note for example the following sentence:

ὑμεῖς ἐστε οἱ υἱοὶ τῶν προφητῶν καὶ τῆς διαθήκης ἧς διέθετο ὁ θεὸς πρὸς τοὺς πατέρας ὑμῶν. (Acts 3:25)
You are sons of the prophets and of the covenant *which* God gave to your fathers.

The syntax of the case of ἧς should be described as follows. ἧς is in the genitive case due to attraction to διαθήκης. It functions as the direct object of διέθετο and therefore as though it were an accusative of direct object.

PART II
THE VERB

A verb is usually defined as a word which expresses action or state of being. Such a definition is inadequate, however, because some nouns and some adjectives also express action (see above pages 15-16, 70). Therefore a definition of a verb should include its characteristics (below). Also it is necessary to distinguish between finite and infinite verbs (see below pages 131-132). The word "verb" properly applies only to the former, though in common usage it is often loosely applied to the latter as well.

CHARACTERISTICS

Finite verbs possess the following characteristics: tense, voice, mood, person, and number. Infinite verbs have only tense and voice. The participle also has number, but this characteristic is due to its relationship to the substantive rather than to the verb.

TENSE

Tense is that quality of a finite or infinite verb which indicates the kind of action expressed by the verb. The action may be linear, durative, progressive, continuous, incomplete. Such action may be illustrated by a continuous line (_____). Or the action may be punctiliar, momentary, instantaneous, unlimited, indefinite, undefined, simple. Such action is looked upon as merely occurring, and there is no reference to its beginning, continuation, or completion. Such action is sometimes called point action and therefore may be illustrated by a dot (.).

Or the action may be perfective, completed, existing. Perfective action implies a state of being which resulted from a past, completed action. The completed action has produced a permanent result. Such action may be illustrated by a dot and a line (. _____). Kind of action is often referred to by the German word *Aktionsart*. Technically *Aktionsart* refers to the kind of action inherent in a verb root. Some verbs have a root meaning which permits the expression of only one kind of action, and for this reason such roots are not used in certain tenses. Other verbs of course have a root meaning which permits the expression of different kinds of action. Kind of action was originally expressed by the verb root alone, and it was later that it came to be expressed also by tense. In common usage therefore the term *Aktionsart* applies to the kind of action expressed both by the verb root and by tense.

Only in the indicative mood does tense also indicate time of action: present, past, or future. Even in the indicative mood time of action is secondary to kind of action. Therefore the term tense (from the Latin *tempus*, time) is not a very accurate designation for that quality of the Greek verb which describes the action itself, but the term is the common designation and will likely continue to be used.

The syntax of tense is best observed in the indicative mood. For this reason all of the following examples employ a finite verb in the indicative. Most, but not all, of the following uses of the various tenses also appear in the other moods and in the infinite forms.

PRESENT TENSE

It is often said that the present tense expresses linear action. This is almost always true in the subjunctive, optative, and imperative moods and in the infinitive and the participle. It is usually true in the indicative mood, but some presents express punctiliar action and a few even express perfective action. Only in the indicative mood does the present tense also indicate time of action, action which takes place in the present.

The following uses of the present express linear action.

Descriptive Present

This category is sometimes referred to as the progressive present of description. This use of the present describes what is now actually taking place. It might even be called the pictorial present. It depicts an action in progress.

κύριε, σῶσον, ἀπολλύμεθα. (Matt. 8:25)
Lord, save (us). We *are perishing.*

ἐν ᾧ ἔρχομαι ἐγὼ ἄλλος πρὸ ἐμοῦ καταβαίνει. (John 5:7)
While I *am coming* another *goes down* before me.

θαυμάζω ὅτι οὕτως ταχέως μετατίθεσθε ἀπὸ τοῦ καλέσαντος ὑμᾶς. (Gal. 1:6)
I *marvel* that so quickly you have turned away from the one who called you.

ὅλη συγχύννεται Ἰερουσαλήμ. (Acts 21:31)
All Jerusalem *is rioting.*

ἡ σκοτία παράγεται καὶ τὸ φῶς τὸ ἀληθινὸν ἤδη φαίνει. (I Jo. 2:8)
The darkness *is passing away* and the true light already *is shining.*

Durative Present

Some grammarians call this the progressive present. An action or a state of being which began in the past is described as continuing until the present. The past and the present are gathered up in a single affirmation. An adverb of time is often used with this kind of present, but a verb alone is sometimes sufficient as in the final example given below. This use of the Greek present is usually translated by the English present perfect. Although impractical to bring out in English translation, the full meaning is that something has been and still is.

ἰδοὺ τρία ἔτη ἀφ᾽ οὗ ἔρχομαι ζητῶν καρπὸν ἐν ἐτῇ συκῇ ταύτη καὶ οὐχ εὑρίσκω. (Luke 13:7)
Behold, I *have been coming* for three years seeking fruit on this fig tree, and I *have found* none.

ἰδοὺ τοσαῦτα ἔτη δουλεύω σοι. (Luke 15:29)
Behold, all these years I *have served* you.

τοῦτον ἰδὼν ὁ Ἰησοῦς κατακείμενον, καὶ γνοὺς ὅτι πολὺν ἤδη
χρόνον ἔχει, λέγει αὐτῷ, Θέλεις ὑγιὴς γενέσθαι; (John 5:6)
When Jesus saw this man lying (there), and when he realized
that already he *had been* (this way) for a long time, he said to
him, Do you want to be well?

ἀπ᾽ ἀρχῆς μετ᾽ ἐμοῦ ἐστε. (John 15:27)
You *have been* with me from the beginning.

εἴρηκέν μοι, Ἀρκεῖ σοι ἡ χάρις μου· ἡ γὰρ δύναμις ἐν ἀσθενείᾳ
τελεῖται. (II Cor. 12:9)
He said to me, My grace *is sufficient* for you; my power *is made
perfect* in weakness.

Iterative Present

The iterative present depicts an action which is repeated at
various intervals. It might be illustrated by a series of dots
(. . . .) rather than a straight line (_____). Sometimes
the repetition takes the form of a local, as opposed to universal,
custom or practice. It is necessary to distinguish this use from
those statements of universal truth called "gnomic" (see below
page 86).

ἕνεκεν σοῦ θανατούμεθα ὅλην τὴν ἡμέραν. (Rom. 8:36)
For your sake we *are being killed* all day long.

ἕκαστος τὸ ἴδιον δεῖπνον προλαμβάνει ἐν τῷ φαγεῖν. (I
Cor. 11:21)
When you eat each person *makes a practice of going ahead* with
his own meal.

νηστεύω δὶς τοῦ σαββάτου, ἀποδεκατῶ πάντα ὅσα κτῶμαι.
(Luke 18:12)
I *make a practice of fasting* twice each week; I *make a practice of
tithing* all that I *acquire* from time to time.

ὁσάκις ἐὰν ἐσθίητε τὸν ἄρτον τοῦτον καὶ τὸ ποτήριον πίνητε,
τὸν θάνατον τοῦ κυρίου καταγγέλλετε. (I Cor. 11:26)
As often as you eat this bread and drink this cup, you *proclaim*
the death of the Lord.

οὕτως πυκτεύω ὡς οὐκ ἀέρα δέρων· ἀλλὰ ὑπωπιάζω μου τὸ σῶμα καὶ δουλαγωγῶ. (I Cor. 9:26-27)
Thus I *box* but not as one beating the air, but I *repeatedly strike* my body and *subdue* it.

Tendential Present

The present tense is sometimes used to indicate an action being contemplated, or proposed, or attempted but which has not actually taken place. The name is derived from the intention to produce the desired result. Other grammarians call this the conative present or the inchoative present. An auxiliary verb such as "attempt," "try," "go," or "begin" may be used in the translation.

ἐπυνθάνετο παρ' αὐτῶν ποῦ ὁ Χριστὸς γεννᾶται. (Matt. 2:4)
He inquired from them where the Christ *was going to be born.*

κατηργήθητε ἀπὸ Χριστοῦ οἵτινες ἐν νόμῳ δικαιοῦσθε. (Gal. 5:4)
You are cut off from Christ who *are attempting to be justified* by the law.

ὅσοι θέλουσιν εὐπροσωπῆσαι ἐν σαρκί, οὗτοι ἀναγκάζουσιν ὑμᾶς περιτέμνεσθαι. (Gal. 6:12)
As many as want to make a good show in the flesh, these *are trying to compel* you to be circumcised.

(Πέτρος) λέγει αὐτῷ, Κύριε, σύ μου νίπτεις τοὺς πόδας; (John 13:6)
Peter said to him, Lord, *are* you *going to wash* my feet?

ὁ Ἀγρίππας πρὸς τὸν Παῦλον, Ἐν ὀλίγῳ με πείθεις Χριστιανὸν ποιῆσαι. (Acts 26:28)
Agrippa (said) to Paul, By a little (talk) you *are trying to persuade* me to become a Christian.

The following uses of the present tense usually express punctiliar or unlimited action.

Gnomic Present

The gnomic present is used to express a universal truth, a maxim, a commonly accepted fact, a state or condition which perpetually exists, and a very widespread practice or custom.

The time element is remote even in the indicative mood because the action or state or truth is true for all time—the past and future as well as the present. Such words as "always," "ever," and "never" are often used in the translation.

In attempting to determine whether a present which depicts a custom or practice is iterative or gnomic, the following should be taken into consideration. If the custom or practice is local in nature and/or is confined to a comparatively brief period, the present is iterative. If the custom or practice is widespread and/or extends over a comparatively long period of time the present is gnomic. It should also be remembered that the iterative present expresses linear action, the gnomic punctiliar action.

πᾶν δένδρον ἀγαθὸν καρποὺς καλοὺς <u>ποιεῖ</u>, τὸ δὲ σαπρὸν δένδρον καρποὺς πονηροὺς <u>ποιεῖ</u>. (Matt. 7:17)
Every healthy tree *produces* good fruit, and every diseased tree *produces* poor fruit.

ἱλαρὸν δότην <u>ἀγαπᾷ</u> ὁ θεός. (II Cor. 9:7)
God *always loves* a cheerful giver.

ἐκ τῆς Γαλιλαίας προφήτης οὐκ <u>ἐγείρεται</u>. (John 7:52)
No prophet *ever comes* out of Galilee.

ὁ θεὸς ἀπείραστός <u>ἐστιν</u> κακῶν, <u>πειράζει</u> δὲ αὐτὸς οὐδένα. ἕκαστος δὲ <u>πειράζεται</u> ὑπὸ τῆς ἰδίας ἐπιθυμίας ... εἶτα ἡ ἐπιθυμία συλλαβοῦσα <u>τίκτει</u> ἁμαρτίαν, ἡ δὲ ἁμαρτία ἀποτελεσθεῖσα <u>ἀποκύει</u> θάνατον. (James 1:13-15)
God *is* not capable of being tempted by evil, and he himself *tempts* no man. But each person is *tempted* by his own lusts. When lust has conceived it *bears* sin, and sin when it is completed *brings* death.

ἀπ' ἀρχῆς ὁ διάβολος <u>ἁμαρτάνει</u>. (I John 3:8)
The devil *has been sinning* from the beginning.

Historical Present

For the sake of vividness or dramatic effect a writer sometimes imagines that he and/or his readers are present and are witnessing a past event. He narrates the past event as though it were actually taking place. The present tense is used for this purpose. The historical present is frequently found in Mark and John. It is ordinarily translated into English by the simple past tense.

ἐν ταῖς ἡμέραις ἐκείναις παραγίνεται Ἰωάννης ὁ βαπτιστής. (Matt. 3:1)
In those days John the Baptist *appeared*

τῇ ἐπαύριον βλέπει τὸν Ἰησοῦν ἐρχόμενον πρὸς αὐτόν, καὶ λέγει, Ἴδε ὁ ἀμνὸς τοῦ θεοῦ. (John 1:29)
The next day he *saw* Jesus coming to him, and he *said,* Behold the lamb of God.

εἰσπορεύονται εἰς Καφαρναούμ. (Mark 1:21)
They *entered* into Capernaum.

λέγουσιν αὐτῷ περὶ αὐτῆς. (Mark 1:30)
They *spoke* to him about her.

καὶ ἀφέντες τὸν ὄχλον παραλαμβάνουσιν αὐτὸν ὡς ἦν ἐν τῷ πλοίῳ. (Mark 4:36)
And when they had dismissed the crowd they *took* him as he was in the boat.

Futuristic Present

The present tense is sometimes used for confident assertions about what is going to take place in the future. The event, although it has not yet occurred, is looked upon as so certain that it is thought of as already occurring. The futuristic present is often used in prophecies. A test for this use is the ability to translate the Greek present with an English future, though the future will not always be used in the translation.

ὑπάγω καὶ ἔρχομαι πρὸς ὑμᾶς. (John 14:28)
I will go away and *I will come* to you.

πάλιν ἔρχομαι καὶ παραλήμψομαι ὑμᾶς πρὸς ἐμαυτόν. (John 14:3)
I *will come* again and will receive you unto myself.

πρὸς σὲ ποιῶ τὸ πάσχα μετὰ τῶν μαθητῶν μου. (Matt. 26:18)
I *will keep* the Passover at your place with my disciples.

μετὰ τρεῖς ἡμέρας <u>ἐγείρομαι</u>. (Matt. 27:63)
After three days *I will be raised.*

ὁ υἱὸς τοῦ ἀνθρώπου <u>παραδίδοται</u> εἰς χεῖρας ἀνθρώπων.
(Mark 9:31)
The Son of Man *will be delivered* into the hands of men.

Aoristic Present

What is here called the aoristic present and what some grammarians call the specific or effective present involves a simple expression of undefined action in the present time without any of the more developed implications of the gnomic, historical, or futuristic presents. The aoristic present presents the action as a simple event or as a present fact without any reference to its progress. By the nature of the case the verb εἰμί is often an aoristic present.

<u>παραγγέλλω</u> σοι ἐν ὀνόματι ᾽Ιησοῦ Χριστοῦ ἐξελθεῖν ἀπ᾽
αὐτῆς. (Acts 16:18)
I *command* you in the name of Jesus Christ to come out of her.

<u>γνωρίζω</u> ὑμῖν, ἀδελφοί, τὸ εὐαγγέλιον. (Gal. 1:11)
I *declare* to you, brothers, the gospel.

<u>ἐπιτρέπεταί</u> σοι περὶ σεαυτοῦ λέγειν. (Acts 26:1)
You *are permitted* to speak for yourself.

τέκνον, <u>ἀφίενταί</u> σου αἱ ἁμαρτίαι. (Mark 2:5)
Son, your sins *are forgiven.*

αὐτοὶ ὑμεῖς μοι <u>μαρτυρεῖτε</u> ὅτι εἶπον . . . (John 3:28)
You, yourselves, *bear witness* for me that I said . . .

The following use of the present tense expresses perfective action.

Perfective Present

This use emphasizes the present reality of something which came into being in the past. The perfective present is not limited to verbs whose stem expresses perfective *Aktionsart,* (e.g. ἥκω, ἀδικέω, ἀπέχω, πείθω, etc.). Context as well as root meaning can produce the perfective idea of existing results, as may be seen in the last two examples cited below.

The perfective present admittedly has something in common with the durative present (above). The durative present, however, emphasizes the fact that the action is still in progress, the perfective present the result or state of being of the action.

ὁ ἀδελφός σου ἥκει. (Luke 15:27)
Your brother *has come.* (Or, Your brother *is here.*)

τίς ἐστιν οὗτος περὶ οὗ ἀκούω τοιαῦτα; (Luke 9:9)
Who is this person about whom I *have heard* these things?

ἀπέχουσιν τὸν μισθὸν αὐτῶν. (Matt. 6:2)
They *have received* their reward.

οἱ τὴν οἰκουμένην ἀναστατώσαντες οὗτοι καὶ ἐνθάδε πάρεισιν. (Acts 17:6)
These (are) the ones who have turned the world upside down, and (now) they *have come* here.

θαυμάζω ὅτι οὕτως ταχέως μετατίθεσθε ἀπὸ τοῦ καλέσαντος ὑμᾶς. (Gal. 1:6)
I marvel that so quickly you *have turned away* from the one who called you.

Note: *It is also possible to interpret* μετατίθεσθε *as a descriptive present (You are turning away).*

ἕκαστος τὸ ἴδιον δεῖπνον προλαμβάνει ἐν τῷ φαγεῖν, καὶ ὃς μὲν πεινᾷ, ὃς δὲ μεθύει. (I Cor. 11:21)
When you eat each person makes a practice of going ahead with his own meal, and as a result some *are hungry* and some *are drunk.*

IMPERFECT TENSE

The imperfect tense appears only in the indicative mood and always expresses linear action. In all but a few instances such action takes place in the past time. The imperfect is one of three tenses which have an augment in the indicative mood, and the augment itself indicates past time. The imperfect is closely related to the present. This relationship is seen in the fact that both are built upon the first principal part, both express linear action—the imperfect always, the present usually—and both have certain syntactical usages in common. On the other hand, the imperfect also has something in common with the aorist indicative in that both usually refer to past time in the indicative mood, and both are sometimes translated in the same way. The imperfect has the following uses.

Descriptive Imperfect

This use of the imperfect describes what was actually taking place at some point in the past. The action is described as having been in progress. Compare this with the descriptive present on page 84 above.

ἐδίωκον τὴν ἐκκλησίαν τοῦ θεοῦ καὶ ἐπόρθουν αὐτήν. (Gal. 1:13)
I was persecuting the church of God and *attempting to destroy* it.

Note: ἐπόρθουν *could also be interpreted as a tendential imperfect (see below). It does in this instance describe Paul's activity over a period of time in the past.*

ὁ ᾽Ιησοῦς ἐπορεύετο σὺν αὐτοῖς. (Luke 7:6)
Jesus *was going* with them.

αὐτὸς δὲ ἐκάθευδεν. (Matt. 8:24)
But he himself *was sleeping.*

ὁ ᾽Ιησοῦς ἐσιώπα. (Matt. 26:63)
Jesus *was silent.*

ἤσθιον, ἔπινον, ἐγάμουν, ἐγαμίζοντο, ἄχρι ἧς ἡμέρας εἰσῆλθεν Νῶε εἰς τὴν κιβωτόν. (Luke 17:27)
They *were eating,* they *were drinking,* they *were marrying,* they *were giving in marriage* until the day Noah entered into the ark.

Durative Imperfect

Other grammarians refer to this use as the progressive imperfect, the imperfect of prolonged action, the simultaneous imperfect, and the progressive imperfect of duration. An act which began in the past is depicted as having continued over a period of time up to some undefined point. Presumably the action has been completed, else the present tense would have been used, but there is no attempt to indicate the completion of the action, else the pluperfect tense would have been used. The term simultaneous imperfect is helpful because this use of the imperfect often refers to a parallel event, to an event which took place at the same time as some other event in the context. The progressive form of the English present perfect (has/have been _____ing) may be used to translate this idiom. But the word in the imperfect may also denote an action which preceded the other action in the context. In such a case the progressive form of the English past perfect (had been _____ing) may be used in the translation. The emphasis is upon the fact that the action endured through a period of time. Often words will be used which indicate a period of time (see examples 3, 4, and 5).

τί ὅτι ἐζητεῖτέ με; (Luke 2:49)
Why *have* you *been seeking* me?

Note: *Jesus's parents sought him over a period of three days—thus the appropriateness of the term durative imperfect. And they sought him at the same time he was discoursing with the doctors of the law—thus the appropriateness of the term simultaneous imperfect.*

ἐγὼ ἐφύτευσα, ᾿Απολλῶς ἐπότισεν, ἀλλὰ ὁ θεὸς ηὔξανεν. (I Cor. 3:6)
I planted, Apollos watered, but God *caused it to grow.*

οὐκ ἐντολὴν καινὴν γράφω ὑμῖν, ἀλλ᾿ ἐντολὴν παλαιάν ἣν εἴχετε ἀπ᾿ ἀρχῆς. (I Jo. 2:7)
I am not writing a new commandment to you but an old commandment which you *have had* from the beginning.

ἐνεκοπτόμην τὰ πολλὰ τοῦ ἐλθεῖν πρὸς ὑμᾶς. (Rom. 15:22)
Many times I *have been hindered* from coming to you.

χρονίζοντος τοῦ νυμφίου ἐνύσταξαν πᾶσαι καὶ ἐκάθευδον. (Matt. 25:5)
While the bridegroom was tarrying all fell asleep and *kept on sleeping.*

Iterative Imperfect

This imperfect emphasizes the repetition of the action. Sometimes the repetition takes the form of a practice or custom. Such expressions as "kept on" and "used to" may be used in the translation. (Compare this use with the iterative present, above page 85.)

κατὰ ἑορτὴν ἐπέλυεν αὐτοῖς ἕνα δέσμιον. (Mark 15:6)
At the feast he *used to make a practice of releasing* one prisoner to them.

ἔπινον ἐκ πνευματικῆς ἀκολουθούσης πέτρας. (I Cor. 10:4)
They *used to drink* from a spiritual rock which followed (them).

ἐν τῷ μεταξὺ ἠρώτων αὐτὸν οἱ μαθηταὶ . . . (John 4:31)
In the meantime his disciples *repeatedly asked* him . . .

ἤρχοντο πρὸς αὐτὸν καὶ ἔλεγον, Χαῖρε, ὁ βασιλεὺς τῶν Ἰουδαίων. (John 19:3)
They *kept on coming* to him and *kept on saying,* Hail, King of the Jews.

τὶς ἀνὴρ χωλὸς ἐκ κοιλίας μητρὸς αὐτοῦ ὑπάρχων ἐβαστάζετο, ὃν ἐτίθουν καθ᾽ ἡμέραν πρὸς τὴν θύραν τοῦ ἱεροῦ. (Acts 3:2)
A certain man who was lame from his mother's womb, *used to be carried* (and) *placed* each day at the gate of the temple.

Tendential Imperfect

The action is presented as having been attempted but not having been accomplished. Thus the action is incomplete or interrupted. The words "was/were going," "was/were trying," "endeavor," or "attempt" may be used in the translation. Some grammarians call this the conative imperfect.

ὁ Ἰωάννης διεκώλυεν αὐτόν. (Matt. 3:14)
John *was attempting to prevent* him.

τῇ τε ἐπιούσῃ ἡμέρᾳ ὤφθη αὐτοῖς μαχομένοις καὶ συνήλλασσεν αὐτούς. (Acts 7:26)
The next day he appeared to them who had been fighting and *attempted to reconcile* them.

αὐτοὺς ἠνάγκαζον βλασφημεῖν. (Acts 26:11)
I *attempted to compel* them to blaspheme.

τὸν μονογενῆ προσέφερεν ὁ τὰς ἐπαγγελίας ἀναδεξάμενος.
(Heb. 11:17)
The one who had received the promise *was going to sacrifice* his
only son.

ἐδίδουν αὐτῷ ἐσμυρνισμένον οἶνον, ὃς δὲ οὐκ ἔλαβεν.
(Mark 15:23)
They *were trying to give* spiced wine to him, but he would not
take (it).

Voluntative Imperfect

Some grammarians prefer to call this the desiderative imperfect, others the potential imperfect. Whatever the name, it
expresses a present desire, wish, or disposition. The imperfect
rather than the present is used when there is a need to express
the desire as politely and inoffensively as possible or when there
is a certain amount of hesitation due to the fact that the desire is
impractical or impossible. Inasmuch as both imply a lack of
realization, some grammarians combine this category with the
tendential imperfect. Admittedly, those who attempt to do
something (see first example above) desire that it be done.

ηὐχόμην ἀνάθεμα εἶναι αὐτὸς ἐγὼ ἀπὸ τοῦ Χριστοῦ ὑπὲρ τῶν
ἀδελφῶν μου. (Rom. 9:3)
I *could wish* that I myself were accursed from Christ on behalf of
my brothers.

ἤθελον παρεῖναι πρὸς ὑμᾶς ἄρτι. (Gal. 4:20)
I *could wish* that I were present with you right now.

... ὃν ἐγὼ ἐβουλόμην πρὸς ἐμαυτὸν κατέχειν. (Phm. 13)
... whom I *would prefer* to keep with me.

οὐκ ἔδει καὶ σὲ ἐλεῆσαι τὸν σύνδουλόν σου; (Matt. 18:33)
Should you not *have had* mercy upon your fellow servant?

ἐδύνατο τοῦτο πραθῆναι πολλοῦ καὶ δοθῆναι πτωχοῖς.
(Matt. 26:9)
This (ointment) *could have been* sold for much money and given
to the poor.

Inceptive Perfect

Some grammarians call this use the inchoative imperfect. Emphasis is placed on the beginning of the action. The word "began" is frequently used in the translation. Since both emphasize the beginning of the action some grammarians combine this category with the tendential imperfect.

περιεβλέπετο ἰδεῖν τὴν τοῦτο ποιήσασαν. (Mark 5:32)
He *began to look around* to see the woman who had done this.

ἐξαλλόμενος ἔστη καὶ περιεπάτει. (Acts 3:8)
When he had leaped up he stood and *began to walk.*

ἰδοὺ ἄγγελοι προσῆλθον καὶ διηκόνουν αὐτῷ. (Matt. 4:11)
Behold angels came and *began to minister* to him.

εἰσελθὼν εἰς τὴν συναγωγὴν ἐδίδασκεν. (Mark 1:21)
When he entered into the synagogue he *began to teach.*

τότε ὁ Παῦλος ἐκτείνας τὴν χεῖρα ἀπελογεῖτο. (Acts 26:1)
Then Paul when he had stretched out his hand *began to defend himself.*

FUTURE TENSE

The future tense sometimes expresses punctiliar action, sometimes linear, with punctiliar being the more frequent. The element of time, however, is more important in the future than in other tenses. It primarily expresses future time in the indicative mood. The future infinitive and participle in relation to the main verb also express future time.

Predictive Future

The predictive future represents the simplest, most basic use of the future to affirm that an action will take place or that a state will be.

δώσω τέρατα ἐν τῷ οὐρανῷ ἄνω. (Acts 2:19)
I *will give* wonders in heaven above.

τότε φανήσεται τὸ σημεῖον τοῦ υἱοῦ τοῦ ἀνθρώπου ἐν οὐρανῷ, καὶ τότε κόψονται πᾶσαι αἱ φυλαὶ τῆς γῆς καὶ ὄψονται τὸν υἱὸν τοῦ ἀνθρώπου ἐρχόμενον. (Matt. 24:30)
Then *will appear* the sign of the Son of Man in heaven, and then all the tribes of the earth *will wail,* and they *will see* the Son of Man coming.

αὐτὸς ὑμᾶς βαπτίσει ἐν πνεύματι ἁγίῳ καὶ πυρί. (Matt. 3:11)
He himself *will baptize* you with the Holy Spirit and with fire.

ἀρθήσεται ἀφ' ὑμῶν ἡ βασιλεία τοῦ θεοῦ καὶ δοθήσεται ἔθνει ποιοῦντι τοὺς καρποὺς αὐτῆς. (Matt. 21:43)
The Kingdom of God *will be taken away* from you and *will be given* to a nation which produces its fruits.

ἐκεῖνος ὑμᾶς διδάξει πάντα. (John 14:26)
That one *will teach* you all things.

Progressive Future

Special emphasis is placed upon the progress of the action. Not all grammarians, however, provide a separate category for this use and include the examples of it in other categories, mostly the predictive future. The expression "keep on" or a similar expression may be used in the translation.

οἵτινες ἀπεθάνομεν τῇ ἁμαρτίᾳ, πῶς ἔτι ζήσομεν ἐν αὐτῇ; (Rom. 6:2)
How shall we who have died to sin *keep on living* in it?

Note: ζήσομεν *is also a deliberative future (below).*

πεποίθαμεν . . . ὅτι ἃ παραγγέλλομεν καὶ ποιεῖτε καὶ ποιήσετε. (II Thess. 3:4)
We are persuaded that what we command, you are both doing and *will continue to do.*

ὁ ἐναρξάμενος ἐν ὑμῖν ἔργον ἀγαθὸν ἐπιτελέσει ἄχρι ἡμέρας Χριστοῦ Ἰησοῦ. (Phil. 1:6)
The one who began a good work in you *will keep on perfecting* it until the Day of Christ Jesus.

ἐν ταῖς ἡμέραις ἐκείναις ζητήσουσιν οἱ ἄνθρωποι τὸν θάνατον. (Rev. 9:6)
In those days men *will repeatedly seek* death.

ἀλλὰ καὶ χαρήσομαι. (Phil. 1:18)
But I will also *keep on rejoicing.*

Imperative Future

Sometimes the future tense is used instead of the imperative mood to express a command. Some call this the volitive future. The future used with οὐ or οὐ μὴ is prohibitive (see examples 3 and 5 below).

καλέσεις τὸ ὄνομα αὐτοῦ Ἰησοῦν. (Matt. 1:21)
You *shall call* his name Jesus.

ἠκούσατε ὅτι ἐρρέθη, Ἀγαπήσεις τὸν πλησίον σου καὶ μισήσεις τὸν ἐχθρόν σου. (Matt. 5:43)
You have heard that it was said, You *shall love* your neighbor and *shall hate* your enemy.

οὐ φονεύσεις. (Matt. 5:21)
You *shall* not *kill.*

ἔσεσθε ὑμεῖς τέλειοι. (Matt. 5:48)
You *must be* perfect.

ἁμαρτία ὑμῶν οὐ κυριεύσει. (Rom. 6:14)
Sin *must* not *lord it over* you.

Deliberative Future

The deliberative future is used in questions, real or rhetorical. It is used to consult the judgment of another person. It asks about the possibility, desirability, or necessity of a proposed action. It asks what ought to be done or what can be done. Contrast a question which asks for mere facts.

εἰ ἡ ἀδικία ἡμῶν θεοῦ δικαιοσύνην συνίστησιν, τί ἐροῦμεν; . . . ἐπεὶ πῶς κρινεῖ ὁ θεὸς τὸν κόσμον; (Rom. 3:5-6)
If our unrighteousness magnifies the righteousness of God, what *shall* we *say?* . . . How then *will* God *judge* the world?

ὁ Πέτρος εἶπεν αὐτῷ, Κύριε, ποσάκις ἁμαρτήσει εἰς ἐμὲ ὁ ἀδελφός μου καὶ ἀφήσω αὐτῷ; (Matt. 18:21)
Peter said to him, Lord, how often *shall* my brother *sin* against me and I *shall forgive* him?

Κύριε, εἰ πατάξομεν ἐν μαχαίρῃ; (Luke 22:49)
Lord, *shall* we *strike* with the sword?

τίνι ὁμοιώσω τὴν γενεὰν ταύτην; (Matt. 11:16)
To what *shall* I *compare* this generation?

ἐπεὶ τί ποιήσουσιν οἱ βαπτιζόμενοι ὑπὲρ τῶν νεκρῶν; (I Cor. 15:29)
Then what *will* the ones who are being baptized on behalf of the
dead *do?*

Gnomic Future

The gnomic future states what will always happen, if the
proper conditions are present, or what will always be true under
given circumstances. The following appear to be the only examples cited in the New Testament.

ἕκαστος τὸ ἴδιον φορτίον βαστάσει. (Gal. 6:5)
Each man *shall bear* his own responsibility.

Note: βαστάσει *could also be an imperative future.*

μόλις ὑπὲρ δικαίου τις ἀποθανεῖται. (Rom. 5:7)
Scarcely for a righteous man *will* anyone *die.*

ἀντὶ τούτου καταλείψει ἄνθρωπος τὸν πατέρα καὶ τὴν μητέρα
καὶ προσκολληθήσεται πρὸς τὴν γυναῖκα αὐτοῦ, καὶ ἔσονται οἱ
δύο εἰς σάρκα μίαν. (Eph. 5:31; cf. Matt. 19:5 & I Cor. 6:16)
For this reason a man *will leave* his father and mother and *will
be joined* to his wife, and the two *will be* one flesh.

ἄρα οὖν ζῶντος τοῦ ἀνδρὸς μοιχαλὶς χρηματίσει ἐὰν γένηται
ἀνδρὶ ἑτέρῳ. (Rom. 7:3)
Therefore if she becomes (the wife) of another man while her
husband is still living she *will be called* an adulteress.

AORIST TENSE

The aorist tense expresses punctiliar action. Indeed, the word
ἀόριστος means without limit, unqualified, undefined—which
of course is the significance of punctiliar action. Only in the
indicative mood does the aorist also indicate past time. Past

time is indicated there by the augment. The absence of the augment from the aorist subjunctive, optative, imperative, infinitive, and participle is itself proof that there is no time element present in these moods and infinite verb forms. Even in the indicative, however, a few aorists are timeless.

Constative Aorist

The constative aorist views the action in its entirety with no reference to its beginning, its end, its progress, or its result. The action is simply stated as a fact. It may be used to describe action which took place in a moment (first example). It may collect a series of events into one statement (second example). It may sum up an action of long duration (third and fourth examples) or short duration (fifth example). This kind of aorist is often found in verbs whose roots express linear Aktionsart. Other grammarians call this the indefinite aorist, the historical aorist (in the indicative mood only), the summary aorist, and the complexive aorist.

ἐκτείνας τὴν χεῖρα ἥψατο αὐτοῦ. (Matt. 8:3)
Having stretched out his hand he *touched* him.

κατὰ πίστιν ἀπέθανον οὗτοι πάντες. (Heb. 11:13)
All these *died* in faith.

ἐβασίλευσεν ὁ θάνατος ἀπὸ ᾽Αδὰμ μέχρι Μωϋσέως. (Rom. 5:14)
Death *reigned* from Adam to Moses.

ὁ θεὸς . . . διὰ τὴν πολλὴν ἀγάπην αὐτοῦ ἣν ἠγάπησεν ἡμᾶς . . . (Eph. 2:4)
God because of his great love with which he *loved* us . . .

ἐπέμεινα πρὸς αὐτὸν ἡμέρας δεκαπέντε. (Gal. 1:18)
I *remained* with him fifteen days.

Ingressive Aorist

A slight emphasis is placed on the beginning of the action. The ingressive aorist is often found in verbs whose roots convey the idea of a state or condition, and it indicates entrance into that state or condition. The words "came" or "became" or "began" may be appropriately used in the translation. Other grammarians prefer to use such terms as inceptive aorist and inchoative aorist.

ἐσίγησεν πᾶν τὸ πλῆθος. (Acts 15:12)
All the multitude *began to be silent.*

ἐπύθετο τὴν ὥραν παρ᾽ αὐτῶν ἐν ᾗ κομψότερον ἔσχεν. (John 4:52)
He inquired from them the hour at which he *began to have* improvement.

τοῦτο εἰπὼν ἐκοιμήθη. (Acts 7:60)
Having said this he *fell asleep.*

Χριστὸς ἀπέθανεν καὶ ἔζησεν. (Rom. 14:9)
Christ died and *came to life* (again).

ὁ λόγος σὰρξ ἐγένετο. (John 1:14)
The word *became* flesh.

Culminative Aorist

A slight emphasis is placed on the conclusion or the results of the completed action. This use of the aorist encroaches upon the meaning of the perfect. It is often found in verbs whose roots signify effort or attempt or intention or process, and it indicates the completion or attainment of such things. The culminative aorist is usually translated by the auxiliary "have/has" or "was/were" when it affects a situation in the present, by the auxiliary "had" when the situation is relatively past. Other grammarians call this the resultative, the perfective, or the effective aorist.

ἐπειδήπερ πολλοὶ ἐπεχείρησαν ἀνατάξασθαι διήγησιν . . . (Luke 1:1)
Inasmuch as many *have taken in hand* to draw up a narrative . . .

τί ἔθου ἐν τῇ καρδίᾳ σου τὸ πρᾶγμα τοῦτο; (Acts 5:4)
Why *have* you *devised* this deed in your heart?

κατὰ ἀποκάλυψιν ἐγνωρίσθη μοι τὸ μυστήριον. (Eph. 3:3)
By revelation the mystery *was made known* to me.

ὁ ἑκατοντάρχης . . . ἐκώλυσεν αὐτούς. (Acts 27:43)
The centurion *successfully prevented* them.

ἰδοὺ ἐνίκησεν ὁ λέων ὁ ἐκ τῆς φυλῆς Ἰούδα . . . ἀνοῖξαι τὸ βιβλίον. (Rev. 5:5)
Behold the Lion of the Tribe of Judah *has prevailed* to open the book.

Gnomic Aorist

When a universal truth or a generally accepted fact is stated in the aorist, it is gnomic. Time is of little importance in this use, and the translation into English may employ any appropriate tense to convey the idea of universality.

ἐδικαιώθη ἡ σοφία ἀπὸ πάντων τῶν τέκνων αὐτῆς. (Luke 7:35)
Wisdom *is vindicated* by all her children.

οἱ τοῦ Χριστοῦ Ἰησοῦ τὴν σάρκα ἐσταύρωσαν. (Gal. 5:24)
Those who belong to Christ Jesus *have crucified* the flesh.

ἐὰν μή τις μένῃ ἐν ἐμοί, ἐβλήθη ἔξω ὡς τὸ κλῆμα καὶ ἐξηράνθη. (John 15:6)
Unless a person remains in me, he *is cast* out as a branch and *withers.*

ἀνέτειλεν ὁ ἥλιος σὺν τῷ καύσωνι καὶ ἐξήρανεν τὸν χόρτον, καὶ τὸ ἄνθος αὐτοῦ ἐξέπεσεν καὶ ἡ εὐπρέπεια τοῦ προσώπου αὐτοῦ ἀπώλετο. (James 1:11)
The sun *rises* with its scorching heat and *dries up* the grass, and its flower *falls off* and the beauty of its appearance *perishes.*

πάντες ἥμαρτον καὶ ὑστεροῦνται τῆς δόξης τοῦ θεοῦ. (Rom. 3:23)
All *sin* and fall short of the glory of God.

Note: *This example indicates the difficulty of distinguishing between the gnomic and culminative aorists. If* ἥμαρτον *is culminative then the translation should be "All have sinned . . . ." This example also illustrates the similarity and difference between the gnomic present* (ὑστεροῦνται) *and gnomic aorist.* ὑστεροῦνται *could also be a descriptive present.*

Epistolary Aorist

The epistolary aorist, as the name implies, is most often found in letters where there is a time gap between writing and reading. As a courtesy to the reader, the writer adopts the time perspective of the reader, which is different from his own. He uses the aorist tense to describe an event which is present or future for him but which will be in the past by the time the reader receives the letter. Since there is no such idiom in English, such aorists are usually translated by using the present or future tense.

μηνυθείσης μοι ἐπιβουλῆς εἰς τὸν ἄνδρα ἔσεσθαι, ἐξαυτῆς ἔπεμψα πρὸς σέ. (Acts 23:30)
Because it has become known to me that there is going to be a plot against the man, I *am sending* him to you immediately.

Τυχικὸς ... ὃν ἔπεμψα πρὸς ὑμᾶς (Col. 4:7-8)
Tychicus whom I *am sending* to you.

ἐγὼ Παῦλος ἔγραψα τῇ ἐμῇ χειρί. (Phm. 19)
I, Paul, *write* (this) with my own hand.

σπουδαιότερος ὑπάρχων αὐθαίρετος ἐξῆλθεν πρὸς ὑμᾶς. συνεπέμψαμεν δὲ μετ' αὐτοῦ τὸν ἀδελφόν. (II Cor. 8:17-18)
Because he is so eager he *is going* to you of his own accord. And we *are sending* the brother with him.

ἀναγκαῖον ἡγησάμην 'Επαφρόδιτον ... πέμψαι πρὸς ὑμᾶς. (Phil. 2:25)
I *consider* (it to be) a necessary thing to send Epaphroditus to you.

Dramatic Aorist

This category represents a use of the aorist for emphasis or dramatic effect. Basically it states a present reality with the certainty of a past event. More specifically it describes something which has just happened, the effect of which is felt in the present. Adverbs of time are often used with the dramatic aorist. The present tense is usually used in the translation.

There is some question about the legitimacy of this category. Not all grammars have it. On the one hand it is closely related to the gnomic aorist. The gnomic, however, has more of a universal aspect. On the other hand, it is closely related to the culminative, as a consideration of the above description and that of the culminative aorist will reveal. The dramatic aorist, however, is more forceful and puts more emphasis on recent attainment than the culminative.

οὗτός ἐστιν ὁ υἱός μου ὁ ἀγαπητός, ἐν ᾧ εὐδόκησα. (Matt. 3:17)
This is my beloved son in whom I *am well pleased.*

ὡς μὴ ἐρχομένου δέ μου πρὸς ὑμᾶς ἐφυσιώθησάν τινες. (I Cor. 4:18)
As though I were not coming to you certain ones *have become arrogant.*

ἡ θυγάτηρ μου ἄρτι ἐτελεύτησεν. (Matt. 9:18)
My daughter *has* just *died.*

ἐνέγκατε ἀπὸ τῶν ὀψαρίων ὧν ἐπιάσατε νῦν. (John 21:10)
Bring (some) of the fish which just now you *have caught.*

ἠγέρθη, οὐκ ἔστιν ὧδε. (Mark 16:6)
He *has* just *been raised.* He is not here.

Futuristic Aorist

This category is also called the prophetic aorist or the proleptic aorist by those grammars which include it. It involves the use of the aorist tense to indicate an event which has not in fact happened but which is so certain to happen that it is depicted as though it had already happened.

There is a gnomic element in most futuristic aorists, but the emphasis is not on a universal truth but on a strongly anticipated occurrence.

ἐν τούτῳ ἐδοξάσθη ὁ πατήρ μου. (John 15:8)
By this my Father *will be glorified.*

κατηργήθητε ἀπὸ Χριστοῦ οἵτινες ἐν νόμῳ δικαιοῦσθε, τῆς χάριτος ἐξεπέσατε. (Gal. 5:4)
Those of you who try to be justified by the law *will be cut off* from Christ (and) *will fall* from grace.

πιστεύετε ὅτι ἐλάβετε. (Mark 11:24)
Believe that you *will receive.*

ἐὰν δὲ καὶ γαμήσῃς, οὐχ ἥμαρτες. (I Cor. 7:28)
If you do marry, *you will* not *have sinned.*

ἐάν σου ἀκούσῃ, ἐκέρδησας τὸν ἀδελφόν σου. (Matt. 18:15)
If he hears you, you *will have gained* your brother.

PERFECT TENSE

The perfect tense expresses perfective action. Perfective action involves a present state which has resulted from a past action. The present state is a continuing state; the past action is a completed action. Therefore the perfect combines linear and punctiliar action. The perfect tense has the following uses.

Intensive Perfect

Remember that the perfect conveys the idea of a present state resulting from a past action. This use of the perfect emphasizes the present state of being, the continuing result, the finished product, the fact that a thing is. Some grammarians call this the perfect of existing state. This use approaches the meaning of the present tense. The punctiliar force has been greatly reduced; the linear element is much in ascendency.

οὕτως γέγραπται παθεῖν τὸν Χριστόν. (Luke 24:46)
Thus it *stands written* that the Christ should suffer.

ὁ διακρινόμενος ἔοικεν κλύδωνι θαλάσσης. (James 1:6)
The one who doubts *is like* a wave of the sea.

τὸ στόμα ἡμῶν ἀνέῳγεν πρὸς ὑμᾶς, Κορίνθιοι, ἡ καρδία ἡμῶν πεπλάτυνται. (II Cor. 6:11)
Our mouth *is open* to you, Corinthians, our heart *is enlarged.*

ἰδοὺ ἔστηκα ἐπὶ τὴν θύραν καὶ κρούω. (Rev. 3:20)
Behold, I *stand* at the door and knock.

πέποιθα ἐν κυρίῳ. (Phil. 2:24)
I *am persuaded* in the Lord.

Consummative Perfect

Other grammarians call this the perfect of completed action or the extensive perfect. The emphasis is on the past, completed action. This use approaches the meaning of the aorist tense. The punctiliar element is the more pronounced. This use of the perfect is usually translated with the auxiliary "have/has" plus the past tense of the verb involved. Occasionally the translation may employ the simple past as in the fifth example.

ἡ ἀγάπη τοῦ θεοῦ ἐκκέχυται ἐν ταῖς καρδίαις ἡμῶν. (Rom. 5:5)
The love of God *has been poured out* in our hearts.

ἡ πίστις σου σέσωκέν σε. (Mark 10:52)
Your faith *has made* you *well.*

τὸν λόγον σου τετήρηκαν. (John 17:6)
They *have kept* your word.

ἰδοὺ πεπληρώκατε τὴν Ἰερουσαλὴμ τῆς διδαχῆς ὑμῶν. (Acts 5:28)
Behold, you *have filled* Jerusalem with your teaching.

ὁ πατήρ μου ὃ δέδωκέν μοι πάντων μεῖζόν ἐστιν. (John 10:29)
My Father who *gave* (them) to me is greater than all.

Iterative Perfect

This could be looked upon as a subdivision of the consummative perfect. It, like the consummative use, emphasizes the past action rather than the present state. There is, however, something in the meaning of the word or in the context which indicates that the past action was iterative in nature, i.e. it was repeated, it took place at recurrent intervals.

ὁ πέμψας με πατὴρ ἐκεῖνος μεμαρτύρηκεν περὶ ἐμοῦ. οὔτε φωνὴν αὐτοῦ πώποτε ἀκηκόατε οὔτε εἶδος αὐτοῦ ἑωράκατε. (John 5:37)
The Father who sent me *has repeatedly born witness* concerning me. You *have never once heard* his voice or *seen* his form.

θεὸν οὐδεὶς ἑώρακεν πώποτε. (John 1:18)
No one *has seen* God at any time.

εἰ μὲν οὖν ἀδικῶ καὶ ἄξιον θανάτου <u>πέπραχά</u> τι, οὐ παραιτοῦμαι τὸ ἀποθανεῖν. (Acts 25:11)
If therefore I am a wrongdoer and if I *have done* anything worthy of death, I do not refuse to die.

οὐδενὶ <u>δεδουλεύκαμεν</u> πώποτε. (John 8:33)
We *have never served* any man.

ὃ ἦν ἀπ᾿ ἀρχῆς, ὃ <u>ἀκηκόαμεν</u>, ὃ <u>ἑωράκαμεν</u> τοῖς ὀφθαλμοῖς . . .
(I Jo. 1:1)
That which was from the beginning, which we *have repeatedly heard,* which we *have repeatedly seen* with our eyes . . .

Dramatic Perfect

The perfect, just like the historical present and dramatic aorist, may be used to bring a past event vividly and dramatically into the present. The narrator describes the past event in such a way that his hearers or readers are led to think for a moment that they are present and witnessing it. Like the intensive perfect the emphasis is on the existing state, and the dramatic perfect could be looked upon as a very specialized use of the intensive perfect. The determination that a perfect is a dramatic is most often dependent upon the larger context of a passage. The story itself usually supplies the dramatic element. The perfect tense is linked indiscriminately with other tenses in such stories.

Ἰωάννης μαρτυρεῖ περὶ αὐτοῦ καὶ <u>κέκραγεν</u>. (John 1:15)
John is bearing witness concerning him and *is crying out.*

ἦλθεν καὶ <u>εἴληφεν</u> ἐκ τῆς δεξιᾶς τοῦ καθημένου ἐπὶ τοῦ θρόνου. (Rev. 5:7)
He has come and he *has just taken* (it) from the right hand of the one who is sitting upon the throne.

μέσης νυκτὸς κραυγὴ <u>γέγονεν</u>. (Matt. 25:6)
In the middle of the night there *was* a cry.

ἀπελθὼν <u>πέπρακεν</u> πάντα ὅσα εἶχεν. (Matt. 13:46)
Having gone out he *sold* all that he had.

ἐμαρτύρησεν Ἰωάννης λέγων ὅτι <u>Τεθέαμαι</u> τὸ πνεῦμα καταβαῖνον ὡς περιστερὰν ἐξ οὐρανοῦ. (John 1:32)

John has born witness saying, "I *have just beheld* the Spirit coming down as a dove from heaven.

Gnomic Perfect

The legitimacy of this category is questionable. The distinctive element is the element of custom or generally accepted truth. It is possible to treat all of the examples below as intensive perfects.

γυνὴ δέδεται ἐφ᾽ ὅσον χρόνον ζῇ ὁ ἀνὴρ αὐτῆς. (I Cor. 7:39)
A wife *is bound* as long as her husband is living.

ὃς ἂν τηρῇ αὐτοῦ τὸν λόγον, ἀληθῶς ἐν τούτῳ ἡ ἀγάπη τοῦ θεοῦ τετελείωται. (I Jo. 2:5)
Whoever keeps his word, in this man God's love *is* indeed *perfected.*

ὅστις ὅλον τὸν νόμον τηρήσῃ, πταίσῃ δὲ ἐν ἑνί, γέγονεν πάντων ἔνοχος. (James 2:10)
Whoever keeps the whole law but offends in one thing *is* guilty of all.

ὁ διακρινόμενος ἐὰν φάγῃ κατακέκριται. (Rom. 14:23)
The one who doubts *stands condemned* if he eats.

ὁ μὴ πιστεύων ἤδη κέκριται, ὅτι μὴ πεπίστευκεν. (John 3:18)
The one who does not believe *is* already *judged* because he *has* not *believed.*

Aoristic Perfect

Some grammarians include a category for the perfect in which the perfect seems to have lost completely the element of result. The perfect tense is used when the action seems to be merely stated without reference to a continuing result. This differs from the consummative (above page 105) in that in the consummative the element of result is minor but still present. Other grammarians treat these examples as dramatic perfects.

ἄγγελος αὐτῷ λελάληκεν. (John 12:29)
An angel *spoke* to him.

οὐκ ἔσχηκα ἄνεσιν τῷ πνεύματί μου τῷ μὴ εὑρεῖν με Τίτον. (II Cor. 2:13)
I *had* no rest in my spirit because I did not find Titus.

PLUPERFECT TENSE

The pluperfect tense indicates a past state which had resulted from a previous action. The state of being continued up to some point in the past and then presumably ceased. If it had continued to the present the perfect tense would have been used. The action which preceded the state of being was of course a completed action. Therefore the pluperfect, like the perfect, combines linear and punctiliar action. But the time element is different. The perfect looks back on the past from a standpoint of the present; the pluperfect looks back on the past from the standpoint of the past. In both the completed action is in the past, but in the perfect the state of being continues to the present, in the pluperfect only to some point in the past. Therefore the pluperfect looks upon the action as perfected in relationship to some point in the past. Past time is properly indicated by the augment. The augment does not always appear in the Koine pluperfect.

The close relationship between the perfect and pluperfect can be seen by the fact that both are built upon the fourth and fifth principal parts, both express the same kind of action, and both have similar syntactical uses.

Intensive Pluperfect

The intensive pluperfect emphasizes the abiding results of the past action, i.e. its linear aspect. It is usually translated by the English past tense. It could also be translated by the helping verbs "was/were" plus _____ing.

ᾔδεισαν τὸν Χριστὸν αὐτὸν εἶναι. (Luke 4:41)
They *knew* he was the Christ.

ὁ Πέτρος εἱστήκει πρὸς τῇ θύρᾳ ἔξω. (John 18:16)
Peter *stood* outside at the gate.

εἰ ἐγνώκειτε τί ἐστιν, Ἔλεος θέλω καὶ οὐ θυσίαν, οὐκ ἂν κατεδικάσατε τοὺς ἀναιτίους. (Matt. 12:7)
If you *knew* what this means, "I desire mercy and not sacrifice," you would not have condemned the innocent.

ὡς εἰώθει πάλιν ἐδίδασκεν αὐτούς. (Mark 10:1)
As he *was accustomed* he again taught them.

Consummative Pluperfect

Emphasis is placed on the completed action. The auxiliary "had" will ordinarily be used in the translation. The use is also referred to as the extensive pluperfect and the pluperfect of completed action.

Μαρία . . . , ἀφ' ἧς δαιμόνια ἑπτὰ ἐξεληλύθει . . . (Luke 8:2)
Mary . . . , from whom he *had cast out* seven demons . . .

ὧδε εἰς τοῦτο ἐληλύθει. (Acts 9:21)
He *had come* here for this (purpose).

σκοτία ἤδη ἐγεγόνει καὶ οὔπω ἐληλύθει πρὸς αὐτοὺς ὁ Ἰησοῦς. (John 6:17)
Darkness *had* already *fallen,* and Jesus *had* not yet *come* to them.

οἱ μαθηταὶ αὐτοῦ ἀπεληλύθεισαν εἰς τὴν πόλιν. (John 4:8)
His disciples *had gone away* into the city.

παρέθεντο αὐτοὺς τῷ κυρίῳ εἰς ὃν πεπιστεύκεισαν. (Acts 14:23)
They committed them to the Lord on whom they *had believed.*

VOICE

Voice is that quality of a verb which indicates the relation of the subject to the action or state of being expressed by the verb. Infinite verbs have no subject, and it is somewhat surprising therefore that they have voice. There is, however, something present in the sentence or context which functions as the "subject" of the verbal idea present in the infinitive or participle, and for this reason infinitives and participles have voice. Most if not all of the following categories apply to all of the moods and infinite forms. Some of the examples cited involve a form other than the indicative.

ACTIVE VOICE

The active voice represents the subject as producing the action or, in the case of a linking verb, as existing. There are two uses of the active voice.

Simple Active

The subject itself directly performs the action or is described as existing.

αὐτὸν ἤγαγον καὶ εἰσήγαγον εἰς τὴν οἰκίαν τοῦ ἀρχιερέως. (Luke 22:54)
They *led* and *brought* him into the house of the high priest.

ἐγὼ ἐφύτευσα, ᾿Απολλῶς ἐπότισεν, ἀλλὰ ὁ θεὸς ηὔξανεν. (I Cor. 3:6)
I *planted,* Apollos *watered,* but God caused it to grow.

᾿Ιωάννης ἐβάπτισεν ὕδατι. (Acts 1:5)
John *baptized* with water.

ἐδέξαντο αὐτὸν οἱ Γαλιλαῖοι. (John 4:45)
The Galileans *received* him.

αὕτη ἐστὶν ἡ μαρτυρία τοῦ ᾿Ιωάννου. (John 1:19)
This *is* the witness of John.

Causitive Active

The subject itself does not produce the action but causes it to take place. The subject is indirectly responsible for the action. The word "cause" will often be used in the translation.

ἐγὼ ἐφύτευσα, ᾿Απολλῶς ἐπότισεν, ἀλλὰ ὁ θεὸς ηὔξανεν. (I Cor. 3:6)
I planted, Apollos watered, but God *caused it to grow.*

εἰ βρῶμα σκανδαλίζει τὸν ἀδελφόν μου . . . (I Cor. 8:13)
If meat *makes* my brother *sin . . .*

ἔλαβεν ὁ Πιλᾶτος τὸν ᾿Ιησοῦν καὶ ἐμαστίγωσεν. (John 19:1)
Pilate *had* Jesus *taken* and *flogged.*

περιέτεμεν αὐτὸν διὰ τοὺς Ἰουδαίους. (Acts 16:3)
He *had* him *circumcised* because of the Jews.

κατεκληρονόμησεν τὴν γῆν αὐτῶν. (Acts 13:19)
He *caused* them *to inherit* their land.

Note: *For the purpose of syntax, deponent verbs must be treated as having active voice.*

MIDDLE VOICE

The middle voice represents the subject as participating in the results of the action, as acting in relation to itself, as having personal interest in the action, as being intimately involved in the action. There is no equivalent in English. The middle voice is used in the following ways.

Direct or Reflexive Middle

The subject acts directly upon itself with reflexive force. The word "self" will be the direct object in the translation.

ἐὰν μὴ βαπτίσωνται οὐκ ἐσθίουσιν. (Mark 7:4)
Unless they *wash themselves* they do not eat.

ἵνα ὑμεῖς ὑποτάσσησθε τοῖς τοιούτοις. (I Cor. 16:16)
Submit yourselves to such men.

ὗς λουσαμένη εἰς κυλισμὸν βορβόρου. (II Peter 2:22)
A pig *washes itself* by rolling in the mire.

τίς παρασκευάσεται εἰς πόλεμον; (I Cor. 14:8)
Who *will prepare himself* for battle?

φυλάσσεσθε ἀπὸ πάσης πλεονεξίας. (Luke 12:15)
Keep yourselves from all covetousness.

Indirect or Intensive or Dynamic Middle

The subject acts for itself, with reference to itself, upon something belonging to itself, or by itself. Emphasis is upon the subject producing the action. The word "self" may be used in the translation to intensify the subject or as a kind of indirect object.

εἴτε γλῶσσαι, παύσονται. (I Cor. 13:8)
Wherever (there are) tongues, they will *cease by themselves.*

... ὃν σὺ φυλάσσου. (II Tim. 4:15)
... concerning whom you *yourself must be on guard.*

τί αἱρήσομαι οὐ γνωρίζω. (Phil. 1:22)
I do not know what I *shall choose for myself.*

ὁ Χριστὸς προσελάβετο ὑμᾶς. (Rom. 15:7)
Christ *took* you *unto himself.*

Καίσαρα ἐπικαλοῦμαι. (Acts 25:11)
I *call upon* Caesar *in my behalf.*

Permissive Middle or Causative Middle

The subject permits or causes the action to take place upon itself. The subject indirectly does something to or for itself by means of someone or something else. This use could be looked upon as a subdivision of the indirect middle. Sometimes the words "permit" or "cause" will be used in the translation. Sometimes a passive translation will be used.

ἀνέβη Ἰωσὴφ ἀπὸ τῆς Γαλιλαίας ... εἰς τὴν Ἰουδαίαν ...
ἀπογράψασθαι ... (Luke 2:4-5)
Joseph went up from Galilee ... to Judea ... *to have himself registered.*

εἰ οὐ κατακαλύπτεται γυνή, καὶ κειράσθω· εἰ δὲ αἰσχρὸν γυναικὶ
τὸ κείρασθαι ἢ ξυρᾶσθαι, κατακαλυπτέσθω. (I Cor. 11:6)
If a woman will not veil herself, she *should* also *have her hair cut short,* but if *having her hair cut short* or *shaved off* is shameful for a woman, she should veil herself.

Note: κατακαλύπτεται *and* κατακαλυπτέσθω *are direct middles. The latter could be looked upon as a causative middle, but the idea of obligation comes from the mood rather than the voice.*

ὄφελον ἀποκόψονται οἱ ἀναστατοῦντες ὑμᾶς. (Gal. 5:12)
Oh that the ones who are troubling you *would have themselves castrated!*

βάπτισαι καὶ ἀπόλουσαι τὰς ἁμαρτίας σου. (Acts 22:16)
Permit yourself to be baptized and *have* your sins *washed away.*

Reciprocal Middle

The middle reflects an interchange of action between or among the members of a plural subject. This use could be looked upon as a subdivision of the direct middle.

συνεβουλεύσαντο. (Matt. 26:4)
They conferred with one another.

τὰς πρωτοκλισίας ἐξελέγοντο. (Luke 14:7)
They *chose* the best seats *for themselves.*

Note: ἐξελέγοντο *could also be an indirect middle.*

ἔγραψα ὑμῖν . . . μὴ συναναμίγνυσθαι πόρνοις. (I Cor. 5:9)
I wrote to you not *to imtimately associate* with immoral persons.

Note: συναναμίγνυσθαι *could also be a permissive middle: not to permit yourselves to get mixed up with immoral persons.*

PASSIVE VOICE

The passive voice represents the subject as being acted upon by someone or something else. Therefore the subject receives the action of the verbal idea. Since the subject of passive verbs does not produce the action nor participate in the action or state of being, the agent of the action must be expressed in other ways. The basic grammars usually list ways that this is done. This is, however, not a function of the passive voice and is best treated as part of the syntax of the substantives (see, for example, pages 24-27, 42-43, etc.).

Something should be said at this place about the relationship of the voice of a verb to its nature. When verbs are classified according to their nature they are either transitive or intransitive. A transitive verb is one which makes an incomplete affirmation and requires a direct object to complete its meaning. An intransitive verb makes a complete affirmation by itself and does not require an object to complete the meaning. Verbs in the active or middle voices may be either transitive or intransitive. Verbs in the passive voice are usually intransitive. In some instances, however, a verb in the passive is transitive (e.g. ἐδιδάχθητε in II Thess. 2:15, the direct object of which is ἅς). These facts lead to the conclusion that voice as such has nothing to do with the nature of a verb. Transitive verbs can be used with any voice; intransitive verbs can be used with any voice.

MOOD

Mood—some grammarians prefer the term mode—is that quality of a finite verb which indicates the relation of the action or state of being to reality. (Infinite verbs do not have mood.) By the nature of the case the action may be related to reality in one of two ways: it may be actual or it may be potential. In Greek real action is affirmed by the indicative mood, potential action by the subjunctive, optative, and imperative moods. Note should be taken of the word "affirmed" in the preceding sentence. Mood does not indicate whether or not the action or state is an objective fact. It has to do with the way in which the speaker or writer conceives of the action or state, the way in which he affirms it, the statement he makes about it.

INDICATIVE MOOD

As previously indicated, the indicative mood affirms the reality of the action. It affirms that the action has taken place, or that it is taking place, or that it will take place. Recall that tense indicates time of action as well as kind of action in the indicative mood only. The indicative does not guarantee, however, that the statement is true, only that the speaker or writer affirms that it is true.

Declarative Indicative

This use of the indicative involves a simple statement of fact.

παρακαλῶ ὑμᾶς . . . ἐν κυρίῳ . . . (Eph. 4:1)
I *exhort* you in the Lord . . .

διὰ τοῦτο παρεκλήθημεν. (I Thess. 3:7)
For this reason we *were called.*

εἴδομεν αὐτοῦ τὸν ἀστέρα . . . καὶ ἤλθομεν προσκυνῆσαι αὐτῷ.
(Matt. 2:2)
We *have seen* his star and *have come* to worship him.

ἄλλο ἔπεσεν εἰς τὰς ἀκάνθας, καὶ ἀνέβησαν αἱ ἄκανθαι καὶ
συνέπνιξαν αὐτό, καὶ καρπὸν οὐκ ἔδωκεν. (Mark 4:7)
Other *fell* among the thorns, and the thorns *grew up* and *choked*
it, and it *produced* no fruit.

Interrogative Indicative

The indicative may be used in a simple question which can be
answered by providing factual information.

τίνα λέγουσιν οἱ ἄνθρωποι εἶναι τὸν υἱὸν τοῦ ἀνθρώπου;
(Matt. 16:13)
Who *do* men *say* that the Son of Man is?

ἦλθες ἀπολέσαι ἡμᾶς; (Mark 1:24)
Have you *come* to destroy us?

πιστεύεις τοῦτο; (John 11:26)
Do you *believe* this?

σὺ εἶ ὁ βασιλεὺς τῶν Ἰουδαίων; (Matt. 27:11)
Are you the King of the Jews?

σὺ τίς εἶ; (John 1:19)
Who *are* you?

Potential Indicative

Sometimes the indicative rather than one of the other moods
is used to express potential action.

1. *Potential Indicative Expressing Command.* This is sometimes called the cohortative indicative. A future indicative may
be used to give a command rather than to make a prediction.

ὑμεῖς ὄψεσθε. (Matt. 27:24)
You yourselves *see to it.*

καλέσεις τὸ ὄνομα αὐτοῦ 'Ιωάννην. (Luke 1:13)
You *shall call* his name John.

οὐκ ἐπ' ἄρτῳ μόνῳ ζήσεται ὁ ἄνθρωπος. (Matt. 4:4)
Man *must* not *live* by bread alone.

ἐκκόψεις αὐτήν. (Luke 13:9)
Cut it *down.*

οὐ φονεύσεις. (Matt. 5:21)
You *shall* not *commit murder.*

2. *Potential Indicative Expressing Obligation.* The indicative may be used to express obligation, necessity, propriety, or possibility. This use is most frequent with verbs whose root meaning conveys the idea of obligation. It is by no means limited to the secondary tenses as is sometimes thought, as several of the following examples will show.

ἔδει σε βαλεῖν τὰ ἀργύριά μου τοῖς τραπεζίταις. (Matt. 25:27)
It *should have appeared necessary* to you to have invested my money with the bankers.

ἐν Ἰεροσολύμοις ἐστὶν ὁ τόπος ὅπου προσκυνεῖν δεῖ. (John 4:20)
Jerusalem is the place where it *is necessary* to worship.

ἐγὼ ὤφειλον ὑφ' ὑμῶν συνίστασθαι. (II Cor. 12:11)
I *ought* to have been commended by you.

οὐκ ὀφείλομεν νομίζειν . . . (Acts 17:29)
We *ought* not to think . . .

. . . οὓς ἔδει ἐπὶ σοῦ παρεῖναι. (Acts 24:19)
. . . who *ought* to be here before you.

3. *Potential Indicative Expressing a Wish or Impulse.* Here the indicative is used where we might expect the optative. Most wishes expressed by the indicative are incapable of being realized, or at least there was doubt about the possibility of realization at the time they were originally expressed.

ἐβουλόμην αὐτὸς τοῦ ἀνθρώπου ἀκοῦσαι. (Acts 25:22)
I myself *have been wanting* to hear the man.

ἤθελον παρεῖναι πρὸς ὑμᾶς. (Gal. 4:20)

I *have been wanting* to be present with you.

ὄφελόν γε ἐβασιλεύσατε. (I Cor. 4:8)
O that you *did* in fact *reign!*

ὄφελον ἀποκόψονται οἱ ἀναστατοῦντες ὑμᾶς. (Gal. 5:12)
O that the ones who are troubling you *would get themselves castrated!*

ὄφελον ἀνείχεσθέ μου μικρόν τι ἀφροσύνης. (II Cor. 11:1)
O that you *would endure* a little of my foolishness.

4. *Potential Indicative Expressing a Condition.* A condition contrary to fact is expressed by the indicative of a secondary tense. The protasis is usually introduced by εἰ, and ἄν is ordinarily found in the apodosis.

Note: *An indicative in a first class condition is a declarative indicative.*

ἀπολελύσθαι ἐδύνατο ὁ ἄνθρωπος οὗτος εἰ μὴ ἐπεκέκλητο Καίσαρα. (Acts 26:32)
This man *could have been released* if he *had* not *appealed* to Caesar.

οὗτος εἰ ἦν προφήτης, ἐγίνωσκεν ἄν τίς καὶ ποταπὴ ἡ γυνή. (Luke 7:39)
If this man *were* a prophet, he *would have known* who and what sort of person this woman is.

εἰ ἐκ τοῦ κόσμου ἦτε, ὁ κόσμος ἄν τὸ ἴδιον ἐφίλει. (John 15:19)
If you *were* of the world, the world *would have loved* its own thing.

εἰ ἐν Τύρῳ καὶ Σιδῶνι ἐγένοντο αἱ δυνάμεις αἱ γενόμεναι ἐν ὑμῖν, πάλαι ἄν ἐν σάκκῳ καὶ σποδῷ μετενόησαν. (Matt. 11:21)
If the miracles which have been performed in you *had been performed* in Tyre and Sidon, they *would have repented* in sackcloth and ashes long ago.

εἰ μὴ ἐκολόβωσεν κύριος τὰς ἡμέρας, οὐκ ἄν ἐσώθη πᾶσα σάρξ. (Mark 13:20)
If the Lord *had not shortened* those days, no flesh *would have been saved.*

SUBJUNCTIVE MOOD

The subjunctive expresses action or a state of being which is objectively possible. It is the mood of moderate contingency. It is the mood of probability. It is used for doubtful assertions. By the nature of the case the subjunctive deals with the future. As a result it is closely related to the future indicative, and in some instances a future is used where we might expect a subjunctive. The future, however, indicates what will take place, the subjunctive what may take place.

The Subjunctive in Independent (Main) Clauses

The subjunctive is by no means confined to subordinate clauses as the name seems to suggest.

1. *Hortatory or Volitive Subjunctive.* This construction involves the use of the first person plural to urge others to join with the speaker or writer in a course of action. The words "let us" are used in the translation. (The use of the first person singular in Matt. 7:4 and Luke 6:42 is sometimes put in this category. These verses, however, involve the use of the subjunctive in a subordinate clause.)

δι' ὑπομονῆς τρέχωμεν τὸν προκείμενον ἡμῖν ἀγῶνα. (Heb. 12:1)
Let us run with patience the race which is set before us.

ἀγαπῶμεν ἀλλήλους. (I John 4:7)
Let us love one another.

διέλθωμεν δὴ ἕως Βηθλέεμ καὶ ἴδωμεν τὸ ῥῆμα τοῦτο. (Luke 2:15)
Let us go then to Bethlehem, and *let us see* this thing.

λάχωμεν περὶ αὐτοῦ τίνος ἔσται. (John 19:24)
Let us cast lots for it (to determine) whose it will be.

2. *Subjunctive of Prohibition.* The aorist subjunctive only with μή is used to forbid the initiation of an action. (Contrast the present imperative with μή which is used to stop an action already in progress.) The words "don't ever" may be used in the translation. Prohibition is usually expressed in the second person. Occasionally the third person is used, as in the final example below.

μὴ <u>μεριμνήσητε</u> εἰς τὴν αὔριον. (Matt. 6:34)
Never be anxious about the next day.

μὴ <u>νομίσητε</u> ὅτι ἦλθον καταλῦσαι τὸν νόμον. (Matt. 5:17)
Don't ever get the idea that I came to destroy the law.

μὴ <u>θαυμάσῃς</u> ὅτι εἶπόν σοι, Δεῖ ὑμᾶς γεννηθῆναι ἄνωθεν.
(John 3:7)
Don't be surprised that I said to you, You must be born from above.

μή τις αὐτὸν <u>ἐξουθενήσῃ</u>. (I Cor. 16:11)
Let *not* anyone *dispise* him.

3. *Deliberative Subjunctive.* The deliberative subjunctive is used in interrogative sentences which deal with what is necessary, desirable, or possible. It is not factual information which is desired. (For this purpose the indicative would be used.) The need is for a decision about the proper course of action, concerning which the speaker or writer is uncertain. Sometimes the question is merely rhetorical; sometimes an answer is expected.

<u>δῶμεν</u> ἢ μὴ <u>δῶμεν</u>; (Mark 12:14)
Shall we give or *shall we* not *give?*

τί <u>ποιήσωμεν</u>; (Luke 3:10)
What *shall we do?*

τὸν βασιλέα ὑμῶν <u>σταυρώσω</u>; (John 19:15)
Shall I crucify your King?

μὴ μεριμνήσητε λέγοντες, Τί <u>φάγωμεν</u>; ἤ, Τί <u>πίωμεν</u>; ἤ, Τί <u>περιβαλώμεθα</u>; (Matt. 6:31)
Never be anxious saying, What *shall we eat?* or, What *shall we drink?* or, What *shall we wear?*

4. *Subjunctive of Emphatic Negation.* The aorist subjunctive with the double negative οὐ μή is used to strongly deny that something will happen. The word "never" may be used in the translation.

<u>οὐ μὴ</u> <u>εἰσέλθητε</u> εἰς τὴν βασιλείαν. (Matt. 5:20)
Under no circumstances will you enter into the kingdom.

μὴ κρίνετε, καὶ <u>οὐ μὴ κριθῆτε</u>. (Luke 6:37)
Do not make a practice of judging, and you *will never be judged.*

ὁ ἐρχόμενος πρὸς ἐμὲ <u>οὐ μὴ πεινάσῃ</u>, καὶ ὁ πιστεύων εἰς ἐμὲ
<u>οὐ μὴ διψήσει πώποτε</u>. (John 6:35)
The one who comes to me *will never hunger,* and the one who
believes on me will never thirst.

Note the use of the future διψήσει *where a subjunctive would
be expected.*

πνεύματι περιπατεῖτε καὶ ἐπιθυμίαν σαρκὸς <u>οὐ μὴ τελέσητε</u>.
(Gal. 5:16)
Live in the Spirit and you *will certainly not carry out* the lust of
the flesh.

<u>οὐ μὴ ἀπόλωνται</u> εἰς τὸν αἰῶνα. (John 10:28)
They *shall never perish.*

The Subjunctive in Dependent (Subordinate) Clauses

The subjunctive is used in many different ways in subordinate clauses. The following is an attempt to describe and
illustrate this variety of use. It is not an attempt to deal system-
atically with the subject of clauses (see below page 168). It will
be possible to give only two examples of each use. Of the various
uses of the subjunctive in subordinate clauses, the subjunctive
with ἵνα to express purpose and the subjunctive with ἐάν to
express a probable future condition are by far the most
common.

1. *Purpose (Final) Clauses.* The subjunctive indicates the
purpose of the action of the main verb. The purpose clause is
introduced by ἵνα, ὅπως, or a relative pronoun, or in the case of
negative purpose by ἵνα μή, ὅπως μή, μήποτε, μή πως, or μή
alone. The words "so that," or in the case of negative purpose
"lest" may be used in the translation.

οὗτος ἦλθεν εἰς μαρτυρίαν, ἵνα <u>μαρτυρήσῃ</u> περὶ τοῦ φωτός, ἵνα
πάντες <u>πιστεύσωσιν</u> δι' αὐτοῦ. (John 1:7)
This man came as a witness so that he *might give testimony* concerning the light, so that all men *might believe* through him.

φιλοῦσιν ἐν ταῖς συναγωγαῖς . . . προσεύχεσθαι, ὅπως <u>φανῶσιν</u> τοῖς ἀνθρώποις. (Matt. 6:5)
They love to pray in the synagogues *for the purpose of being seen* by men.

2. *Conditional Clauses.* The subjunctive with ἐάν or ἄν is used in the protasis of a third class condition to express probable future condition. The word "if" will usually appear in the translation of the protasis. See also the use of the subjunctive in relative clauses (below).

ἐὰν μόνον <u>ἅψωμαι</u> τοῦ ἱματίου αὐτοῦ σωθήσομαι. (Matt. 9:21)
If I *can* just *touch* his garment I shall be healed.

ἐὰν <u>ἀποθάνῃ</u> ὁ ἀνήρ, κατήργηται ἀπὸ τοῦ νόμου τοῦ ἀνδρός. (Rom. 7:2)
If her husband *should die,* she is released from the marriage bond.

Note: *The use of εἰ with the subjunctive* θελήσῃ *in Rev. 11:5 is probably a grammatical error which later scribes corrected by different means.*

3. *Result Clauses.* The subjunctive indicates what has resulted from the action of the main verb. Result clauses employing the subjunctive are usually introduced by ἵνα or ἵνα μή. The word "result" can often be used in the translation. Sometimes it is difficult to distinguish between purpose and result. In other instances the distinction is clear. See also the use of the subjunctive in relative clauses (below).

ταῦτα ἀλλήλοις ἀντίκειται, ἵνα μὴ ἃ ἐὰν θέλητε ταῦτα <u>ποιῆτε</u>. (Gal. 5:17)
These things are contrary to one another, (and) *as a result you cannot do* what you wish.

μὴ ἔπταισαν ἵνα <u>πέσωσιν</u>; (Rom. 11:11)
Did they err (and) *as a result were rejected?*

4. *Relative Clauses.* The subjunctive with a relative pronoun and ἄν or ἐάν is used in a third class condition (probable future condition), as in the first example below. The subjunctive with a relative pronoun may be used to express practical result, as in the second example below. In giving the syntax of the subjunc-

tive these uses may be placed in the above categories or in the present category.

ὃς ἐὰν λύσῃ μίαν τῶν ἐντολῶν τούτων τῶν ἐλαχίστων καὶ διδάξῃ οὕτως τοὺς ἀνθρώπους, ἐλάχιστος κληθήσεται ἐν τῇ βασιλείᾳ τῶν οὐρανῶν· ὃς δ' ἂν ποιήσῃ καὶ διδάξῃ, οὗτος μέγας κληθήσεται ἐν τῇ βασιλείᾳ τῶν οὐρανῶν. (Matt. 5:19)
Whoever *shall break* one of the least of these commandments and *shall teach* men so shall be called least in the Kingdom of Heaven, but whoever *shall do* and *teach* will be called great in the Kingdom of Heaven.

ἄξιός ἐστιν ᾧ παρέξῃ τοῦτο. (Luke 7:4)
He is worthy and as a result you *should do* this for him.

5. *Comparative Clauses Where an Element of Contingency Is Present.*

ἐστὶν ἡ βασιλεία τοῦ θεοῦ ὡς ἄνθρωπος βάλῃ τὸν σπόρον ἐπὶ τῆς γῆς. (Mark 4:26)
The Kingdom of God is like a man (who) *scatters* seed on the ground.

ἐγενήθημεν νήπιοι ἐν μέσῳ ὑμῶν, ὡς ἐὰν τροφὸς θάλπῃ τὰ ἑαυτῆς τέκνα. (I Thess. 2:7)
We became gentle among you as if we were a mother (who) *nurses* her own children.

6. *Indefinite Local Clauses Where the Action Is Expected to Take Place in the Future.* The usual construction is an adverb of place, ἄν or ἐάν, and a subjunctive.

ἀκολουθήσω σοι ὅπου ἐὰν ἀπέρχῃ. (Luke 9:57)
I will follow you wherever you *may go.*

ὅπου ἐὰν ᾖ τὸ πτῶμα, ἐκεῖ συναχθήσονται οἱ ἀετοί. (Matt. 24:28)
Wherever *there is* a corpse, there the vultures will be gathered together.

7. *Temporal Clauses.* The subjunctive with ὅταν, ἐπάν, or ἡνίκα (all of which mean "whenever") and with ἕως, ἕως οὗ, ἕως ὅτου, ἄχρι, ἄχρι οὗ, μέχρι(ς), μέχρι(ς) οὗ, or ὡς ἄν (all of which mean "until") is used in clauses where the temporal element is indefinite and implies uncertainty as to realization.

ὅταν ἴδητε πάντα ταῦτα, γινώσκετε ὅτι ἐγγύς ἐστιν. (Matt. 24:33)
Whenever you *see* all these things, know that (the end) is near.

οὐ μὴ παρέλθῃ ἡ γενεὰ αὕτη μέχρις οὗ ταῦτα πάντα γένηται. (Mark 13:30)
This generation will not come to an end until all these things *come to pass.*

8. *Concessive Clauses.* The subjunctive with ἐάν is used to express certain types of concession. Some such expression as "if," "even if," "even though," "although" will be used in the translation.

ἐάν καὶ προλημφθῇ ἄνθρωπος ἔν τινι παραπτώματι, ὑμεῖς οἱ πνευματικοὶ καταρτίζετε τὸν τοιοῦτον. (Gal. 6:1)
Even if a man *is overtaken* in some transgression, you who are spiritual restore him.

καὶ ἐάν κρίνω δὲ ἐγώ, ἡ κρίσις ἡ ἐμὴ ἀληθινή ἐστιν. (John 8:16)
But even if I *should judge,* my judgment is true.

9. *Substantival Clauses.* A substantival clause may function as the subject of a verb, as the predicate nominative, as the object of a verb, or as an appositive. The subjunctive with ἵνα or ὅπως is used in these ways.

(1) As a Subject.

οὐκ ἔστιν θέλημα ἔμπροσθεν τοῦ πατρὸς ὑμῶν τοῦ ἐν οὐρανοῖς ἵνα ἀπόληται ἓν τῶν μικρῶν τούτων. (Matt. 18:14)
That one of these little ones *should perish* is not the will of your Father who is in heaven.

(2) As a Predicate Nominative.

ἐμὸν βρῶμά ἐστιν ἵνα ποιήσω . . . (John 4:34)
My meat is *to do . . .*

(3) As an Object.

εἰπὲ ἵνα οἱ λίθοι οὗτοι ἄρτοι γένωνται. (Matt. 4:3)
Command that these stones *shall become* bread.

(4) As an Appositive.

αὕτη ἐστὶν ἡ ἐντολὴ ἡ ἐμή, ἵνα ἀγαπᾶτε ἀλλήλους. (John 15:12)
This is my commandment, (namely) that you *should love*
one another.

10. *Imperative Clauses.* There seems to have been an idiom
in Hellenistic Greek in which ἵνα with the subjunctive was used
in place of a verb in the imperative mood. Such clauses are usually preceded by verbs of saying, of praying, or of exhortation.

ἡ γυνὴ ἵνα φοβῆται τὸν ἄνδρα. (Eph. 5:33; λέγω is in verse 32.)
A wife *is to respect* her husband.

. . . ἵνα ἐν ταύτῃ τῇ χάριτι περισσεύητε. (II Cor. 8:7)
Abound in this grace.

OPTATIVE MOOD

The optative and subjunctive are closely related. The
optative could be looked upon as a weakened subjunctive. The
subjunctive is the mood of probability, the optative of possibility. The subjunctive expresses action which is objectively possible, the optative that which is subjectively possible. The
optative is a step further removed from reality than the subjunctive. The assertion made by the optative is more doubtful
than that of the subjunctive. It is reduced to the level of a wish.

The Optative in Indpendent (Main) Clauses

1. *Voluntative Optative.* As the name implies, the most common use of the optative is to express a wish or prayer.

τὸ ἀργύριόν σου σὺν σοὶ εἴη εἰς ἀπώλειαν. (Acts 8:20)
May your money *perish* with you.

χάρις ὑμῖν καὶ εἰρήνη πληθυνθείη. (I Pet. 1:2)
May grace and peace *be multiplied* toward you.

ὁ θεὸς τῆς εἰρήνης ἁγιάσαι ὑμᾶς. (I Thess. 5:23)
May the God of peace *sanctify* you.

ὁ θεὸς . . . δῴη ὑμῖν τὸ αὐτὸ φρονεῖν. (Rom. 15:5)
May God *give* to you (the ability) to think the same thing.

μὴ γένοιτο. (Rom. 3:4, etc.)
Let it never *happen!*

2. *Potential or Futuristic Optative.* Both these names are inadequate because all optatives deal with potential action which is future, but there seems to be no better name. The optative with ἄν is used to indicate what would happen if an expressed or implied condition were fulfilled.

ἐνένευον τῷ πατρὶ αὐτοῦ τὸ τί ἂν θέλοι καλεῖσθαι αὐτό. (Luke 1:62)
They motioned to his father as to what he *would have* him called.

πῶς ἂν δυναίμην ἐὰν μή τις ὁδηγήσει με; (Acts 8:31)
How *can* I unless someone will guide me?

διηπόρουν περὶ αὐτῶν τί ἂν γένοιτο τοῦτο. (Acts 5:24)
They were doubting concerning these things, concerning what *would come about* as a result of this.

εὐξαίμην ἂν τῷ θεῷ . . . (Acts 26:29)
I *could wish* to God . . .

διελάλουν πρὸς ἀλλήλους τί ἂν ποιήσαιεν τῷ Ἰησοῦ. (Luke 6:11)
They kept talking to one another about what they *might do* to Jesus.

3. *Deliberative Optative.* This use of the optative involves an indirect, rhetorical question. Indirect statements usually retain the same mood and tense which appeared in the direct statement. Therefore the indirect, rhetorical question often employs the optative because the direct question did so. In some instances, however, an indicative or subjunctive in a direct question is changed to an optative in the indirect report.

ἤρξαντο συζητεῖν πρὸς ἑαυτοὺς τὸ τίς ἄρα εἴη ἐξ αὐτῶν ὁ τοῦτο μέλλων πράσσειν. (Luke 22:23)
They began to inquire among themselves about which of them *might be* the one who was going to do this.

. . . καθ᾽ ἡμέραν ἀνακρίνοντες τὰς γραφὰς εἰ ἔχοι ταῦτα οὕτως.
(Acts 17:11)
. . . examining the Scriptures day after day (to see) whether
these (claims) *might have* substance.

εἰσῆλθεν διαλογισμὸς ἐν αὐτοῖς, τὸ τίς ἂν εἴη μείζων αὐτῶν.
(Luke 9:46)
A discussion arose among them about which of them *was* the
greatest.

προσδοκῶντος τοῦ λαοῦ καὶ διαλογιζομένων . . . περὶ τοῦ
Ἰωάννου, μήποτε αὐτὸς εἴη ὁ Χριστός . . . (Luke 3:15)
While the crowd was expecting and reasoning about John,
whether he *might be* the Christ . . .

The Optative in Dependent (Subordinate) Clauses

Unless one wants to treat indirect statements (above) as
clauses, which is not necessary in the case of either the subjunctive or the optative, the optative appears only in conditional
clauses in the New Testament, namely in the fourth class condition (possible future condition). This construction involves the
use of εἰ with the optative in the protasis, ἄν with the optative in
the apodosis. There is, however, no example in the New Testament of a fourth class condition with both the protasis and
apodosis actually expressed. The following are examples of
fragmentary constructions.

εἰ καὶ πάσχοιτε διὰ δικαιοσύνην, μακάριοι. (I Pet. 3:14)
Even if you *should suffer* because of righteousness, (you will
be) blessed.

κρεῖττον ἀγαθοποιοῦντας, εἰ θέλοι τὸ θέλημα τοῦ θεοῦ,
πάσχειν ἢ κακοποιοῦντας. (I Pet. 3:17)
It is better to suffer as a result of doing good, if the will of God
should will (it), than as a result of doing evil.

τοσαῦτα εἰ τύχοι γένη φωνῶν εἰσιν ἐν κόσμῳ. (I Cor. 14:10)
If it *should happen to be* (this way), there are so many kinds of
sounds in the world.

οὐ τὸ σῶμα τὸ γενησόμενον σπείρεις ἀλλὰ γυμνὸν κόκκον εἰ τύχοι σίτου. (I Cor. 15:37)
You are not sowing the body which is going to come about but a bare grain of wheat, if it *should happen to be* (that).

IMPERATIVE MOOD

The imperative is used to express various kinds of commands. It expresses an action or state of being which is volitionally possible, i.e. action or state which may come about as the result of the exercise of the will. It involves the attempt of one person to exert the force of his will upon the will of another person. This mood is the furthest removed from reality.

Imperative in Independent (Main) Clauses

1. *Imperative of Command.* This use of the imperative makes a direct, positive demand upon the will of another. The idea of authority, right to command, is implied.

εἴσελθε εἰς τὸ ταμεῖόν σου καὶ . . . πρόσευξαι. (Matt. 6:6)
Enter into your private room and . . . *pray.*

πάντοτε χαίρετε, ἀδιαλείπτως προσεύχεσθε, ἐν παντὶ εὐχαριστεῖτε. (I Thess. 5:16-18)
Rejoice always; *pray* without ceasing; *give thanks* for all things.

δέξασθε τὸν ἔμφυτον λόγον. (James 1:21)
Receive the implanted word.

2. *Imperative of Prohibition.* The present imperative with μή is used to stop an action already in progress. (Contrast the aorist subjunctive with μή which forbids the beginning of an action.) The word "stop" may be used in the translation to bring out the full meaning.

μὴ πλανᾶσθε. (I Cor. 6:9)
Stop being deceived.

μὴ θησαυρίζετε ὑμῖν θησαφροὺς ἐπὶ τῆς γῆς. (Matt. 6:19)
Stop accumulating treasures for yourselves on earth.

μὴ οὖν βασιλευέτω ἡ ἁμαρτία. (Rom. 6:12)
Therefore *do not let* sin *continue to rule.*

τὸ πνεῦμα μὴ σβέννυτε, προφητείας μὴ ἐξουθενεῖτε. (I Thess. 5:19-20)
Stop quenching the Spirit; *stop despising* prophecy.

3. *Imperative of Entreaty.* Sometimes the force of the imperative is softened to that of a request. This kind of imperative will frequently appear when a person of subordinate status addresses a person of superior status as for example when one addresses God in prayer. The meaning can be fully expressed by using the word "please" in the translation.

βοήθησον ἡμῖν. (Mark 9:22)
Please help us.

πάτερ ἅγιε, τήρησον αὐτούς. (John 17:11)
Holy Father, *please preserve* them.

τὸν ἄρτον ἡμῶν τὸν ἐπιούσιον δὸς ἡμῖν σήμερον· καὶ ἄφες ἡμῖν τὰ ὀφειλήματα ἡμῶν. (Matt. 6:11-12)
Please give to us each day our necessary food; and *please forgive* us our debt of sin.

ῥῦσαι ἡμᾶς ἀπὸ τοῦ πονηροῦ. (Matt. 6:13)
Please deliver us from the evil one.

4. *Imperative of Permission.* In this instance the imperative is used to give consent to the request or desire of another.

εἶπεν αὐτοῖς, Ὑπάγετε. (Matt. 8:32)
He said to them, You *may go.*

πληρώσατε τὸ μέτρον τῶν πατέρων ὑμῶν. (Matt. 23:32)
You *may bring to completion* the quantity (of guilt) of your fathers.

ὃ θέλει ποιείτω. (I Cor. 7:36)
He *may do* what he wishes.

εἴ τις ὑμῶν λείπεται σοφίας, αἰτείτω παρὰ τοῦ διδόντος θεοῦ πᾶσιν ἁπλῶς . . . αἰτείτω δὲ ἐν πίστει. (James 1:5-6)
If any of you lacks wisdom, he *may ask* from the God who gives to all men liberally, . . . but he must ask in faith.

Note: *It must not be thought that every imperative in the third person is an imperative of permission because the word "let" or "permit" is usually used in the translation. These words are used because of the necessity of employing a periphrastic translation for something which has no English equivalent, not because of the idea of permission in the use of the word. The second instance of* αἰτείτω *in the preceding example is clearly command, not permission. So is* ἔστω *in the statement* ἔστω πᾶς ἄνθρωπος ταχὺς εἰς τὸ ἀκοῦσαι *(James 1:19). Every man must be quick to hear. The syntax of imperatives in the third person is determined by their use in the sentence.*

5. *Imperative of Condition.* The imperative in an independent clause is sometimes the equivalent of a dependent, conditional clause. The usual construction consists of an imperative and either a future or a subjunctive connected by καί. In the following examples the imperative is translated as though it constituted a conditional clause; the usual translation would also be acceptable. Indeed, most of these uses could be included in one of the above categories, and there is some doubt about the necessity of the present category.

λύσατε τὸν ναὸν τοῦτον καὶ ἐν τρισὶν ἡμέραις ἐγερῶ αὐτόν. (John 2:19)
If you destroy this temple, I will rebuild it in three days.

ἀντίστητε τῷ διαβόλῳ, καὶ φεύξεται ἀφ' ὑμῶν· ἐγγίσατε τῷ θεῷ, καὶ ἐγγιεῖ ὑμῖν. (James 4:7-8)
If you resist the devil, he will flee from you; *if you draw near* to God, he will also draw near to you.

μὴ κρίνετε, καὶ οὐ μὴ κριθῆτε· καὶ μὴ καταδικάζετε, καὶ οὐ μὴ καταδικασθῆτε. ἀπολύετε, καὶ ἀπολυθήσεσθε· δίδοτε, καὶ δοθήσεται ὑμῖν. (Luke 6:37-38)
If you do not *judge,* you will not be judged; *if you do* not *condemn,* you will not be condemned; *if you forgive,* you will be forgiven; *if you give,* it will be given to you.

6. *Imperative of Concession.* There are two possible instances in the New Testament where the first of two imperatives connected by καί expresses concession. Again, however,

there is uncertainty about the necessity of the present category.

ὀργίζεσθε καὶ μὴ ἁμαρτάνετε. (Eph. 4:26)
Although you may become angry, you must not sin.

ἐραύνησον καὶ ἴδε ὅτι ἐκ τῆς Γαλιλαίας προφήτης οὐκ ἐγείρεται. (John 7:52)
Although you may search, you will see that no prophet comes from Galilee.

The Imperative in Dependent (Subordinate) Clauses

This use is rare and is apparently found only in relative clauses.

ὁ ἀντίδικος ὑμῶν διάβολος... περιπατεῖ ζητῶν τινα καταπιεῖν· ᾧ ἀντίστητε. (I Pet. 5:8-9)
Your opponent the devil ... is walking around seeking to devour someone, whom you *must oppose.*

ταύτην εἶναι ἀληθῆ χάριν τοῦ θεοῦ· εἰς ἣν στῆτε. (I Pet. 5:12)
This is the true grace of God, in which you *must stand fast.*

μνημονεύετε τῶν ἡγουμένων ὑμῶν..., ὧν ἀναθεωροῦντες τὴν ἔκβασιν τῆς ἀναστροφῆς μιμεῖσθε τὴν πίστιν. (Heb. 13:7)
Remember your leaders, ... whose faith you *must imitate* as a result of beholding the outcome of their conduct.

Ἀλέξανδρος... ὃν καὶ σὺ φυλάσσου. (II Tim. 4:14-15)
Alexander ... against whom you also *must guard for yourself.*

... ὧν ἔστω οὐχ ὁ ἔξωθεν ἐμπλοκῆς τριχῶν ... κόσμος. (I Pet. 3:3)
... the adorning of whom *must* not *be* outward consisting of braided hair.

PERSON

Person is that quality of a verb which indicates the relation of the subject to the action. If the subject is represented as speaking, the verb is in the first person. If the subject is being spoken to, the verb is in the second person. If the subject is being spoken about, the verb is in the third person. Person is determined mechanically by observation of the personal endings of verbs and has no syntax as such.

NUMBER

Number is that quality of a verb which indicates whether the subject is one person or one thing (the singular number) or more than one (the plural number). Classical Greek also had a dual number for a subject consisting of exactly two persons or things. The dual died out during the Koine period, however, and no example of it appears in the New Testament. Number is determined mechanically by observation of the personal endings and has no syntax as such.

KINDS

There are two kinds of verbs—using the term verb loosely in its broad sense. There are finite verbs and infinite verbs.

FINITE

A finite verb is a word which both expresses action or state of being *and* which makes an assertion about the subject of a sentence or clause. Such verbs are called finite because of the limitation imposed upon them by the requirement of a subject. A finite verb and its subject may constitute a complete sentence. In Greek, however, a finite verb has a self-contained, pronominal subject in its personal ending, though a more specific subject may be indicated by using a substantive in the nominative case. Therefore a Greek finite verb by itself may constitute a complete sentence. A finite verb in Greek may further be defined as one which is capable of being conjugated according to tense, voice, mood, person, and number. The preceding discussion and illustration of these characteristics is sufficient to indicate how the verb finite is used in Greek.

INFINITE

Infinite verb forms, namely the infinitive and the participle, express action or state of being, but they make no assertion about the subject of the sentence or clause. Indeed they cannot have a subject. They cannot constitute a complete sentence. They cannot be conjugated. Like finite verbs they have tense, voice, and in a limited sense even number, but unlike finite verbs they have no mood or person. Therefore it is not altogether accurate to refer to infinitives and participles as verbs. Actually an infinitive is a verbal noun, a participle is a verbal adjective. Infinitives and participles are treated as verbs because they employ a verb stem, because they express action, and because they have tense and voice.

INFINITIVE

The infinitive is a verbal noun. As such it has some of the characteristics of a verb and some of the characteristics of a noun. As a verb it has tense and voice, it can take a direct object, and it can be modified by an adverb; but it does not have mood, person, or number, and it cannot have a subject. As a noun it can have case relationships, it can be used with the article and prepositions, it can be modified by adjectives, and it can modify other words in the sentence.

Although infinitives do not have subjects in the same sense that finite verbs do, there is often a word in the construction which indicates who or what produces the action expressed by the infinitive and which is sometimes loosely referred to as the "subject" of the infinitive. Such a word is with few exceptions in the accusative case rather than the nominative (but see Rev. 12:7) and as was indicated above (page 55) is an adverbial accusative of reference. Some grammarians refer to this use as the subject accusative. When the subject of the main verb also produces the action of the infinitive, the infinitive is not often accompanied by an accusative of reference. Such is unnecessary.

The infinitive may be used with or without the article. Only the singular of the neuter article is used, i.e., only the forms τό, τοῦ, and τῷ as appropriate depending on the case function of the infinitive itself. The infinitive itself is treated as though it were an indeclinable neuter noun.

When the infinitive is used with the article it may also be used with a preposition. The following prepositions are used with infinitives in the new Testament: ἀντί (once), διά (33 times), εἰς (72 times), ἐν (55 times), ἕνεκεν (once), ἐκ (once), ἕως (once), μετά (15 times), πρό (9 times), and πρός (12 times). When the articular infinitive is used with a preposition it is impossible to translate it literally. The idea expressed by the infinitive must be rephrased in good English.

The Verbal Infinitive

The name "verbal" does not fit this category as well as the name "substantival" fits the next category. In the substantival, the infinitive or infinitive phrase is actually used in place of a substantive. In the verbal, the infinitive or infinitive phrase usually makes a further assertion in addition to the main verb. Most often it functions as an adverbial phrase to modify or clarify the assertion of the main verb. It is called the verbal infinitive because its verbal aspects are primary.

1. *Infinitive of Purpose.* The infinitive indicates the aim or purpose of the action or state expressed by the main verb. It is the equivalent of a clause. Purpose is expressed by the infinitive alone, the infinitive with τοῦ, the infinitive with εἰς τό, the infinitive with πρὸς τό, the infinitive with ὥστε, and the infinitive with ὡς. Two examples of each one are given below.

μὴ νομίσητε ὅτι ἦλθον καταλῦσαι τὸν νόμον. (Matt. 5:17)
Do not think that I came *for the purpose of destroying* the law.

ἀνήγαγον αὐτὸν εἰς Ἰεροσόλυμα παραστῆσαι τῷ κυρίῳ. (Luke 2:22)
They brought him to Jerusalem *in order to present* (him) to the Lord.

ὁ παλαιὸς ἡμῶν ἄνθρωπος συνεσταυρώθη, ἵνα καταργηθῇ τὸ σῶμα τῆς ἁμαρτίας, τοῦ μηκέτι δουλεύειν ἡμᾶς τῇ ἁμαρτίᾳ. (Rom. 6:6)
Our old man was crucified with (him), so that the body of sin might be destroyed, *so that* we *might* no longer *serve* sin.

ἡγοῦμαι πάντα ζημίαν εἶναι . . . τοῦ γνῶναι αὐτόν. (Phil. 3:8, 10)
I consider all things to be loss . . . *in order to know* him.

ἔπεμψα εἰς τὸ γνῶναι τὴν πίστιν ὑμῶν. (I Thess. 3:5)
I sent *in order to know* your faith.

ἐπιποθῶ ἰδεῖν ὑμᾶς, ἵνα τι μεταδῶ χάρισμα ὑμῖν πνευματικὸν εἰς τὸ στηριχθῆναι ὑμᾶς. (Rom. 1:11)
I long to see you so that I may impart to you some spiritual gift *so that* you *may be strengthened.*

προσέχετε τὴν δικαιοσύνην ὑμῶν μὴ ποιεῖν ἔμπροσθεν τῶν ἀνθρώπων πρὸς τὸ θεαθῆναι αὐτοῖς. (Matt. 6:1)
Beware of practicing your righteousness before men *for the purpose of being seen* by them.

συλλέξατε πρῶτον τὰ ζιζάνια καὶ δήσατε αὐτὰ εἰς δέσμας πρὸς τὸ κατακαῦσαι αὐτά. (Matt. 13:30)
Collect first the weeds and bind them into bundles *in order to burn* them.

ἤγαγον αὐτὸν ἕως ὀφρύος τοῦ ὄρους ἐφ᾽ οὗ ἡ πόλις ᾠκοδόμητο αὐτῶν, ὥστε κατακρημνίσαι αὐτόν. (Luke 4:29)
They led him to the brow of the hill upon which their city was built *in order to throw* him *down from the cliff.*

ἔδωκεν αὐτοῖς ἐξουσίαν πνευμάτων ἀκαθάρτων ὥστε ἐκβάλλειν αὐτά. (Matt. 10:1)
He gave them authority over unclean spirits *so that* (they) *might cast* them *out.*

εἰσῆλθον εἰς κώμην Σαμαριτῶν, ὡς ἑτοιμάσαι αὐτῷ. (Luke 9:52)
They entered into a village of the Samaritans *in order to prepare* for him.

οὐδενὸς λόγου ποιοῦμαι τὴν ψυχὴν τιμίαν ἐμαυτῷ ὡς τελειῶσαι τὸν δρόμον μου. (Acts 20:24)

I do not consider my life to be of any value (or) precious to myself *so that* (I) *may complete* my course.

2. *Infinitive of Result.* The infinitive indicates what results from the action of the main verb. Sometimes the distinction between purpose and result is quite clear. In other instances it is not so clear. When the result is conceived by the speaker or writer as intended it is difficult to distinguish from purpose. The construction employs the infinitive alone, the infinitive with τοῦ, the infinitive with εἰς τό, and the infinitive with ὥστε. Two examples of each will be given.

διὰ τί ἐπλήρωσεν ὁ Σατανᾶς τὴν καρδίαν σου ψεύσασθαί σε τὸ πνεῦμα τὸ ἅγιον καὶ νοσφίσασθαι ἀπὸ τῆς τιμῆς τοῦ χωρίου; (Acts 5:3)
Why has Satan filled your heart (and) *as a result* you *have lied* to the Holy Spirit and *have kept back something* from the price of the land?

ἐνίκησεν ὁ λέων ὁ ἐκ τῆς φυλῆς ᾽Ιούδα . . . ἀνοῖξαι τὸ βιβλίον. (Rev. 5:5)
The Lion of the Tribe of Judah has conquered (and) *as a result has opened* the book.

ἐὰν ἀποθάνῃ ὁ ἀνήρ, ἐλευθέρα ἐστὶν ἀπὸ τοῦ νόμου, τοῦ μὴ εἶναι αὐτὴν μοιχαλίδα γενομένην ἀνδρὶ ἑτέρῳ. (Rom. 7:3)
If her husband should die, she is free from the law (and) *as a result* she *is* not an adulteress if she marries another man.

οὐδεὶς ἐπιθήσεταί σοι τοῦ κακῶσαί σε. (Acts 18:10)
No man shall attack you (and) *as a result harm* you.

μὴ βασιλευέτω ἡ ἁμαρτία ἐν τῷ θνητῷ ὑμῶν σώματι εἰς τὸ ὑπακούειν ταῖς ἐπιθυμίαις αὐτοῦ. (Rom. 6:12)
Let not sin reign in your mortal bodies (and this) *result in* your *obeying* its lusts.

διαθήκην προκεκυρωμένην ὑπὸ τοῦ θεοῦ ὁ μετὰ τετρακόσια καὶ τριάκοντα ἔτη γεγονὼς νόμος οὐκ ἀκυροῖ, εἰς τὸ καταργῆσαι τὴν ἐπαγγελίαν. (Gal. 3:17)
The law, which came into being four hundred and thirty years later, does not annul the covenant which was previously established by God (and) *as a result destroy* the promise.

ἐν οἷς ἐπισυναχθεισῶν τῶν μυριάδων τοῦ ὄχλου, ὥστε καταπατεῖν ἀλλήλους ... (Luke 12:1)
In the meantime, when the thousands of the multitude had come together (and) *as a result trod* upon each other ...

ἡ πίστις ὑμῶν ἡ πρὸς τὸν θεὸν ἐξελήλυθεν, ὥστε μὴ χρείαν ἔχειν ἡμᾶς λαλεῖν τι. (I Thess. 1:8)
Your faith in God has gone out, (and) *as a result* we *have* no need to say anything.

3. *Infinitive of Time.* This use of the infinitive indicates the relative time at which the action of the main verb took place.

(1) Antecedent Time. The word "before" will be used in the translation. This construction employs the infinitive with πρὸ τοῦ, πρὶν, or πρὶν ἤ. Two examples of each will be given.

πρὸ τοῦ σε Φίλιππον φωνῆσαι ὄντα ὑπὸ τὴν συκῆν εἶδόν σε. (John 1:48)
Before Philip *called* you I saw you while you were under the fig tree.

πρὸ τοῦ ἐλθεῖν τινας ἀπὸ Ἰακώβου μετὰ τῶν ἐθνῶν συνήσθιεν. (Gal. 2:12)
Before certain ones *came* from James he used to eat with the Gentiles.

Κύριε, κατάβηθι πρὶν ἀποθανεῖν τὸ παιδίον μου. (John 4:49)
Lord, come down *before* my daughter *dies.*

πρὶν ἀλέκτορα φωνῆσαι τρὶς ἀπαρνήσῃ με. (Matt. 26:34)
Before the cock *crows* you will deny me three times.

πρὶν ἤ δὶς ἀλέκτορα φωνῆσαι τρίς με ἀπαρνήσῃ. (Mark 14:30)
Before the cock *crows* twice you will deny me three times.

μνηστευθείσης τῆς μητρὸς αὐτοῦ Μαρίας τῷ Ἰωσήφ, πρὶν ἤ συνελθεῖν αὐτοὺς εὑρέθη ἐν γαστρὶ ἔχουσα. (Matt. 1:18)
While Mary his mother was engaged to Joseph, *before* they *came together,* it was discovered that she was pregnant.

(2) Contemporaneous Time. The word "while" will usually be used in the translation. The infinitive with ἐν τῷ is employed.

ἐθαύμαζον <u>ἐν τῷ χρονίζειν</u> ἐν τῷ ναῷ αὐτόν. (Luke 1:21)
They were marveling *while* he *tarried* in the temple.

ἐγένετο <u>ἐν τῷ εὐλογεῖν</u> αὐτὸν αὐτοὺς διέστη ἀπ᾽ αὐτῶν.
(Luke 24:51)
It came to pass *while* he was *blessing* them he departed from them.

<u>ἐν τῷ καθεύδειν</u> τοὺς ἀνθρώπους ἦλθεν αὐτοῦ ὁ ἐχθρός.
(Matt. 13:25)
While men *slept* his enemy came.

<u>ἐν τῷ ὁμιλεῖν</u> αὐτοὺς καὶ <u>συζητεῖν</u> καὶ αὐτὸς Ἰησοῦς ἐγγίσας
συνεπορεύετο αὐτοῖς. (Luke 24:15
While they *talked* and *discussed* Jesus himself drew near and
went along with them.

<u>ἐν τῷ ὑποτάξαι</u> αὐτῷ τὰ πάντα οὐδὲν ἀφῆκεν αὐτῷ
ἀνυπότακτον. (Heb. 2:8)
When he *subjected* all things to him he left nothing not subjected to him.

(3) Subsequent Time. The word "after" is ordinarily used in
the translation. This construction employs the words μετὰ τό
with the infinitive.

φοβήθητε τὸν <u>μετὰ τὸ ἀποκτεῖναι</u> ἔχοντα ἐξουσίαν ἐμβαλεῖν
εἰς τὴν γέενναν. (Luke 12:5)
Fear the one who *after killing* has power to cast into hell.

παρέστησεν ἑαυτὸν ζῶντα <u>μετὰ τὸ παθεῖν</u> αὐτόν. (Acts 1:3)
He revealed himself alive *after* he *had suffered.*

<u>μετὰ τὸ ἐγερθῆναί</u> με προάξω ὑμᾶς εἰς τὴν Γαλιλαίαν.
(Matt. 26:32)
After I *have been raised* I will go before you into Galilee.

ὡσαύτως καὶ τὸ ποτήριον <u>μετὰ τὸ δειπνῆσαι</u>, λέγων . . . (I
Cor. 11:25)
Likewise also the cup *after eating* saying . . .

<u>μετὰ τὸ εἰρηκέναι</u> . . . (Heb. 10:15)
After having said . . .

(4) Future Time. The infinitive is used with ἕως τοῦ. The
word "until" is used in the translation.

εὐηγγελίζετο . . . ἕως τοῦ ἐλθεῖν αὐτὸν εἰς Καισάρειαν. (Acts 8:40)
He preached . . . *until* he *came* to Caesarea.

4. *Infinitive of Cause.* The infinitive may be used to answer the question "why?". The word "because" is usually used in the translation. The idea of cause is often expressed by διὰ τό with the infinitive and rarely by τῷ with the infinitive and ἕνεκεν τοῦ with the infinitive (one time each in the New Testament).

διὰ τὸ μὴ ἔχειν ῥίζαν ἐξηράνθη. (Matt. 13:6)
It withered *because* it *had* no root.

οὐκ ἔχετε διὰ τὸ μὴ αἰτεῖσθαι ὑμᾶς. (James 4:2)
You do not have *because* you *do* not *ask.*

Ἰησοῦς οὐκ ἐπίστευεν αὐτὸν αὐτοῖς διὰ τὸ αὐτὸν γινώσκειν πάντας. (John 2:24)
Jesus did not commit himself to them *because* he *knew* all men.

οὐκ ἔσχηκα ἄνεσιν τῷ πνεύματί μου τῷ μὴ εὑρεῖν με Τίτον. (II Cor. 2:13)
I had no rest in my spirit *because* I *did* not *find* Titus.

ἔγραψα ὑμῖν . . .ἕνεκεν τοῦ φανερωθῆναι τὴν σπουδὴν ὑμῶν. (II Cor. 7:12)
I wrote to you *because* your eagerness *was manifested.*

Note: *Some think that* ἐν τῷ λέγειν *in Heb. 8:13 is causal, but this is very doubtful. There is no reason why it cannot have the usual temporal significance.*

5. *Infinitive of Command.* On rare occasions the infinitive may be used in lieu of an imperative. Some would include this use in the infinitive absolute (below). The first two of the examples which follow are clear instances of this use. The others are more doubtful.

εἰς ὃ ἐφθάσαμεν, τῷ αὐτῷ στοιχεῖν. (Phil. 3:16)
Unto that which we have attained, *let us live* by it.

χαίρειν μετὰ χαιρόντων, κλαίειν μετὰ κλαιόντων. (Rom. 12:15)
Rejoice with those who rejoice; *weep* with those who weep.

πρεσβύτας νηφαλίους εἶναι. (Titus 2:2)
Let the aged men *be* sober.

μήτε ἀνὰ δύο χιτῶνας ἔχειν. (Luke 9:3)
Do not *have* two tunics.

ταῦτα ὑπομίμνῃσκε . . . μὴ λογομαχεῖν. (II Tim. 2:14)
Remind (them) about these things . . . that (they) *must* not
argue about words.

6. *Infinitive Absolute.* The infinitive stands alone and has no
relationship to a sentence. The clearest examples of this use are
in the greetings of letters.

οἱ ἀπόστολοι καὶ οἱ πρεσβύτεροι ἀδελφοὶ τοῖς . . . ἀδελφοῖς
τοῖς ἐξ ἐθνῶν χαίρειν. (Acts 15:23)
The brothers who are apostles and elders to the brothers who
are among the Gentiles. *Greeting!*

Κλαύδιος Λυσίας τῷ κρατίστῳ ἡγεμόνι Φήλικι χαίρειν.
(Acts 23:26)
Claudius Lysias to the most excellent governor Felix. *Greeting!*

Ἰάκωβος . . . ταῖς δώδεκα φυλαῖς ταῖς ἐν τῇ διασπορᾷ χαίρειν.
(James 1:1)
James to the twelve tribes in the dispersion. *Greeting!*

ὡς ἔπος εἰπεῖν . . . (Heb. 7:9)
So as to speak (this) word . . .

The Substantival Infinitive

In the following uses of the infinitive its noun aspect is primary. When an infinitive is used substantivally it and the words
connected with it constitute a substantival phrase which theoretically may be used in any of the ways in which an individual
noun or adjective is used, except as a vocative. In actual practice it is possible to contain most of the uses of the substantival
infinitive in the three categories which are treated below.

1. *The Infinitive as the Subject of a Verb.*

πρέπον ἐστὶν ἡμῖν πληρῶσαι πᾶσαν δικαιοσύνην. (Matt. 3:15)
To fulfill all righteousness is fitting to us.

τὸ ζῆν Χριστὸς καὶ τὸ ἀποθανεῖν κέρδος. (Phil. 1:21)
To live (is) Christ and *to die* (is) gain.

τὸ θέλειν παράκειταί μοι, τὸ δὲ κατεργάζεσθαι τὸ καλὸν οὔ.
(Rom. 7:18)
To will is present in me, but *to do the good thing* (is) not.

τὸν λόγον ἐκράτησαν πρὸς ἑαυτοὺς συζητοῦντες τί ἐστιν τὸ ἐκ
νεκρῶν ἀναστῆναι. (Mark 9:10)
They kept the word to themselves questioning what is *the resurrection from the dead.*

ἀνένδεκτόν ἐστιν τοῦ τὰ σκάνδαλα μὴ ἐλθεῖν. (Luke 17:1)
For offenses not to come is impossible.

Note: *The infinitive here is in the genitive as is indicated by the
article* τοῦ. *Yet it functions as though it were a subject nominative. There is also at least one place in the New Testament where
an infinitive with the article* τό *appears to function as a predicative nominative of an understood verb.* (Phil 1:22) *"If I am to live
in the flesh."*

2. *The Infinitive as the Direct Object of a Verb.* In the first
three examples the infinitive functions as an accusative of
direct object, in the fourth as a genitive of direct object, and in
the fifth as an ablative of direct object. There is apparently no
example in the New Testament of the infinitive being used as a
dative of direct object. The infinitive in indirect discourse
should be included in this category. The entire indirect statement functions as the direct object of the main verb. The sixth
and seventh examples illustrate this use. Also to be included in
this category is the so-called complementary infinitive which
occurs with certain verbs which cannot take a direct object as
such but which require an infinitive to complete their meaning.
See examples eight and nine.

οὐ παραιτοῦμαι τὸ ἀποθανεῖν. (Acts 25:11)
I do not refuse *to die.*

νυνὶ καὶ τὸ ποιῆσαι ἐπιτελέσατε. (II Cor. 8:11)
Now also complete *the doing* (of it).

θεός ἐστιν ὁ ἐνεργῶν ἐν ὑμῖν καὶ τὸ θέλειν καὶ τὸ ἐνεργεῖν.
(Phil. 2:13)

God is the one who works in you both *to will* and *to work.*

ἔλαχε τοῦ θυμιᾶσαι. (Luke 1:9)
He obtained by lot *the privilege of making the sacrifice.*

μὴ κωλύετε αὐτὰ ἐλθεῖν πρός με. (Matt. 19:14)
Do not prevent *them from coming to me.*

. . . οἵτινες λέγουσιν ἀνάστασιν μὴ εἶναι. (Mark 12:18)
. . . who say *that there is no resurrection.*

ὁ ὄχλος ὁ ἑστὼς καὶ ἀκούσας ἔλεγεν βροντὴν γεγονέναι.
(John 12:29)
The crowd which stood and heard said *that it had thundered.*

σῴζειν εἰς τὸ παντελὲς δύναται. (Heb. 7:25)
He is able *to save* to the uttermost.

. . . δεόμενοι ἵνα κατισχύσητε ἐκφυγεῖν ταῦτα. (Luke 21:36)
. . . praying that you might have strength *to escape* these things.

3. *The Infinitive as a Modifier.*

(1) Of Substantives. The infinitive may modify nouns or
adjectives. When it modifies a noun it functions as an adjective
or a substantive in the genitive case (examples one and two), or
it may modify the noun by being in apposition with it (examples
three and four). When the infinitive modifies an adjective it
functions much like an adverbial genitive of reference (examples five and six).

ἐγὼ χρείαν ἔχω ὑπὸ σοῦ βαπτισθῆναι. (Matt. 3:14)
I have a need *to be baptized* by you.

ἦλθεν ἡ ὀργή σου καὶ ὁ καιρὸς τῶν νεκρῶν κριθῆναι καὶ δοῦναι
τὸν μισθὸν τοῖς δούλοις σου. (Rev. 11:18)
Your wrath has come, and the time *for the dead to be judged* and
for giving the reward to your servants (has come).

τοῦτο κρίνατε μᾶλλον, τὸ μὴ τιθέναι πρόσκομμα τῷ ἀδελφῷ ἢ
σκάνδαλον. (Rom. 14:13)
Rather decide (to do) this, *namely not to put a stumbling block*
or *a hindrance* in (the way of) your brother.

θρησκεία καθαρὰ καὶ ἀμίαντος . . . αὕτη ἐστίν, ἐπισκέπτεσθαι
ὀρφανοὺς καὶ χήρας ἐν τῇ θλίψει αὐτῶν, ἄσπιλον ἑαυτὸν τηρεῖν
ἀπὸ τοῦ κόσμου. (James 1:27)
Pure and undefiled religion is this, *namely to visit orphans and
widows* in their affliction (and) *to keep oneself unstained* from
the world.

ἐλευθέρα ἐστὶν ᾧ θέλει γαμηθῆναι. (I Cor. 7:39)
She is free *to marry* whom she wishes.

οὐκ εἰμὶ ἱκανὸς κύψας λῦσαι τὸν ἱμάντα τῶν ὑποδημάτων
αὐτοῦ. (Mark 1:7)
I am not worthy *to loose the strap* of his sandals after I have
stooped down.

(2) Of Verbs. When an infinitive explains, limits, or modifies a verb it is said to be epexegetical. (Some grammarians also
apply this term to the infinitive which modifies a substantive.)
This category includes what some grammarians refer to as the
infinitive of indirect object. There is some question, however,
about the necessity and legitimacy of this category. To a greater
or lesser degree most adverbial infinitives are epexegetical, i.e.,
they modify a verb. It is possible to explain all of the following
examples in some other way, namely as adverbial infinitives of
purpose or result.

παρέδωκεν αὐτοὺς ὁ θεὸς εἰς ἀδόκιμον νοῦν, ποιεῖν τὰ μὴ
καθήκοντα. (Rom. 1:28)
God gave them up to a reprobate mind *to do those things which
are not proper.*

ἐπικατάρατος πᾶς ὃς οὐκ ἐμμένει πᾶσιν τοῖς γεγραμμένοις
ἐν τῷ βιβλίῳ τοῦ νόμου τοῦ ποιῆσαι αὐτά. (Gal. 3:10)
Accursed is everyone who does not continue in all the things
which have been written in the book of the law *to do them.*

παρέδωκεν αὐτοὺς ὁ θεὸς ἐν ταῖς ἐπιθυμίαις τῶν καρδιῶν αὐτῶν
εἰς ἀκαθαρσίαν τοῦ ἀτιμάζεσθαι τὰ σώματα αὐτῶν. (Rom. 1:24)
God gave them up *to dishonor their bodies* in the lusts of their
hearts for uncleanness.

. . . ἵνα ὁ θεὸς ἀνοίξῃ ἡμῖν θύραν τοῦ λόγου, λαλῆσαι τὸ
μυστήριον τοῦ Χριστοῦ. (Col. 4:3)

... so that God might open for us a door for the word *to speak the mystery* of Christ.

ἡ ἀδελφή μου μόνην με κατέλιπεν <u>διακονεῖν</u>. (Luke 10:40)
My sister has forsaken me *to serve* alone.

PARTICIPLE

The participle is a verbal adjective. As such it has some of the characteristics of a verb and some of the characteristics of an adjective. Like a verb the participle has tense and voice (but not mood or person); it may be modified by an adverb, and it may have a direct object (but not a subject). Like an adjective it may be declined according to case, gender, and number. Most important is the fact that the participle can be used in the very same ways in which an adjective can be used (see above pages 70-72).

The Attributive Participle

The attributive participle directly modifies or limits or describes a noun or pronoun by attaching a verbal idea to it. The attributive participle agrees with the noun it modifies in case, gender, and number just as an adjective does. The attributive participle may be used with or without an article. If there is an article, and there usually is, the participle is of course in the attributive position following the article.

ἡ εἰρήνη τοῦ θεοῦ <u>ἡ ὑπερέχουσα</u> πάντα νοῦν φρουρήσει τὰς καρδίας ὑμῶν. (Phil. 4:7)
The peace of God *which surpasses* all understanding will protect your hearts.

... Κορνήλιος, ἑκατοντάρχης ἐκ σπείρης <u>τῆς καλουμένης</u> Ἰταλικῆς ... (Acts 10:1)
... Cornelius, a centurion of the cohort *which is called* the Italian (cohort) ...

οὗτός ἐστιν ὁ ἄρτος ὁ ἐκ τοῦ οὐρανοῦ <u>καταβαίνων</u>. (John 6:50)
This is the bread *which comes down* from heaven.

σὺ λάλει ἃ πρέπει τῇ ὑγιαινούσῃ διδασκαλίᾳ. (Titus 2:1)
Speak what is proper for *sound* doctrine.

... ἔδωκεν ἄν σοι ὕδωρ ζῶν. (John 4:10)
... He would have given to you *living* water.

The Substantival Participle

The participle, like an adjective, may be used in the place of
a noun or other substantive. The participle itself then functions as a noun. Its case, gender, and number are determined
by its use in the sentence. It may be used in most of the ways in
which a noun is used, e.g. as a subject nominative, as a dative
of indirect object, as an accusative of direct object, etc. It may
be used with or without an article. It always stands in the attributive position.

ὁ φιλῶν πατέρα ἢ μητέρα ὑπὲρ ἐμὲ οὐκ ἔστιν μου ἄξιος.
(Matt. 10:37)
The one who loves father or mother more than me is not worthy
of me.

προσετίθεντο πιστεύοντες τῷ κυρίῳ. (Acts 5:14)
Believers were added to the Lord.

σκοπεῖτε τοὺς οὕτω περιπατοῦντας καθὼς ἔχετε τύπον ἡμᾶς.
(Phil. 3:17)
Take note of *the ones who live* just as you have us for an example.

μακάριος ὁ ἀναγινώσκων καὶ οἱ ἀκούοντες τοὺς λόγους τῆς
προφητείας καὶ τηροῦντες τὰ ἐν αὐτῇ γεγραμμένα. (Rev. 1:3)
Blessed is *the one who reads* and *those who hear* the words of
this prophecy and *those who keep the things which stand written* in it.

... ἵνα ἀπόκρισιν δῶμεν τοῖς πέμψασιν ἡμᾶς. (John 1:22)
... so that we may give an answer *to those who sent* us.

The Predicative Participle

The participle, just like an adjective, may stand in the predicate following a linking verb and do two things: make an additional assertion about the subject of the linking verb and
complete the meaning of the linking verb itself. The participle
agrees with the subject in case, gender, and number. The case

will always be nominative. Participles in this category may function simply as predicate adjectives (the first three examples), or they may be part of a periphrastic conjugation (the fourth and fifth examples).

This use of the participle must not be confused with that of a substantival participle which just happens to be a predicate nominative (e.g. in Luke 7:19—σὺ εἶ ὁ ἐρχόμενος; Are you the one who is coming?). The substantival participle which is a predicate nominative usually follows an article, is the equivalent of a noun, and is merely in apposition with the subject. The predicative participle is never used in connection with an article, is the equivalent of an adjective, and makes an additional assertion about the subject.

ἤμην ἀγνοούμενος τῷ προσώπῳ ταῖς ἐκκλησίαις τῆς Ἰουδαίας. (Gal. 1:22)
I was *unknown* by face to the churches of Judea.

πρέπον ἐστὶν ἡμῖν πληρῶσαι πᾶσαν δικαιοσύνην. (Matt. 3:15)
It is *fitting* for us to fulfill all righteousness.

ἐγενόμην νεκρὸς καὶ ἰδοὺ ζῶν εἰμι εἰς τοὺς αἰῶνας τῶν αἰώνων. (Rev. 1:18)
I was dead and behold I am *living* for ever and ever.

Note: *The adjective* νεκρός *and the participle* ζῶν *function in exactly the same way: they complete the meaning of the copula (the linking verb) and make an additional assertion about the subject.*

ἦν ἐκβάλλων δαιμόνιον. (Luke 11:14)
He *was casting out* a demon.

πεπεισμένος ἐστιν Ἰωάννην προφήτην εἶναι. (Luke 20:6)
It (the multitude) *stands persuaded* that John was a prophet.

The Adverbial Participle

The participle, just like an adjective, sometimes modifies a verbal idea rather than a noun and is therefore used like an adverb. This use of the participle is often referred to as the circumstantial participle because it describes the circumstances under which the action of the main verb takes place. The adverbial or circumstantial participle always stands in the predicative position. It can be distinguished from the predicative participle by the fact that it is not required to complete the thought of the main verb. It and the words related to it are the equivalent of a dependent clause which could be removed without serious damage to the sentence. The predicative participle is absolutely necessary in the structure of the sentence.

The adverbial use of the adjective is comparatively rare and quite simple. The adverbial use of the participle is frequent and complicated. The various ideas which may be expressed by the adverbial participle are not inherent in the participle itself but arise from its relationship to the main verb and even to the larger context. The adverbial participle may be subdivided as follows in accordance with the thought expressed.

1. *The Temporal Participle.* This is perhaps the most frequent use of the adverbial participle. Most circumstantial participles have at least some element of the temporal idea, and it is for this reason that attention is usually focused upon the temporal idea when the beginning student is first exposed to participles. When the temporal idea predominates the participle is said to be a temporal participle. It indicates the time at which the action of the main verb takes place. The participle itself, just like the subjunctive, optative, imperative, and infinitive, is timeless. Its time is relative to that of the main verb. Generally speaking, however, the present participle will be translated by using "while" or "as," the aorist participle by "when," "since," or "after."

πῶς οὖν ἐλογίσθη; ἐν περιτομῇ ὄντι ἢ ἐν ἀκροβυστίᾳ; (Rom. 4:10)
How therefore was it reckoned? *While he was* in a state of being circumcised or a state of not being circumcised?

ἀποταξάμενος αὐτοῖς ἐξῆλθον εἰς Μακεδονίαν. (II Cor. 2:13)
When I departed from them I went away into Macedonia.

ἐλθὼν ἐκεῖνος ἐλέγξει τὸν κόσμον περὶ ἁμαρτίας. (John 16:8)
When that one shall come he will convict the world about sin.

ἐλθόντες λέγουσιν αὐτῷ . . . (Mark 12:14)
When they came they said to him . . .

σὺ νηστεύων ἄλειψαί σου τὴν κεφαλήν. (Matt. 6:17)
As for you, *when you fast* anoint your head.

2. *The Telic Participle.* This use of the participle indicates the purpose of the action of the main verb. Such expressions as "so that," "for the purpose of," and "in order to" may be used in the translation. Purpose is expressed by both the future and the present participles.

. . . ὃς ἐληλύθει προσκυνήσων εἰς Ἰερουσαλήμ. (Acts 8:27)
. . . who had come to Jerusalem *for the purpose of worshipping.*

δι᾽ ἐτῶν πλειόνων ἐλεημοσύνας ποιήσων εἰς τὸ ἔθνος μου παρεγενόμην. (Acts 24:17)
After many years I returned *in order to make* gifts to my nation.

εἰς Δαμασκὸν ἐπορευόμην ἄξων καὶ τοὺς ἐκεῖσε ὄντας δεδεμένους εἰς Ἰερουσαλήμ. (Acts 22:5)
I came to Damascus *so that I could lead* the ones who were there in bonds to Jerusalem.

ἀπέστειλεν αὐτὸν εὐλογοῦντα ὑμᾶς. (Acts 3:26)
He sent him *to bless* you.

ἦλθον εἰς Καφαρναοὺμ ζητοῦντες τὸν Ἰησοῦν. (John 6:24)
They came to Capernaum *in order to seek* Jesus.

3. *The Causal Participle.* The ground or reason or cause of the action of the main verb is indicated by this use of the participle. The words "because," "since," or "for" appear in the translation. The use of ὡς with a causal participle injects the idea of supposition.

ἡμέρας ὄντες νήφωμεν. (I Thess. 5:8)
Let us be sober *because we are* of the day.

πάλιν ὁ Πιλᾶτος προσεφώνησεν αὐτοῖς, θέλων ἀπολῦσαι τὸν Ἰησοῦν. (Luke 23:20)
Pilate addressed them again, *because he wanted* to release Jesus.

ἡ εὐσέβεια πρὸς πάντα ὠφέλιμός ἐστιν, ἐπαγγελίαν <u>ἔχουσα</u>
ζωῆς. (I Tim. 4:8)
Piety is profitable for all things *because it holds* a promise of
life.

ἐχάρησαν οἱ μαθηταὶ <u>ἰδόντες</u> τὸν κύριον. (John 20:20)
The disciples rejoiced *because they had seen* the Lord.

γνώμην δίδωμι <u>ὡς ἠλεημένος</u> ὑπὸ κυρίου πιστὸς εἶναι. (I
Cor. 7:25)
I give my opinion *because I have received mercy* by the Lord to
be faithful.

4. *The Conditional Participle.* This kind of participle functions as the protasis of a conditional sentence. It is translated by
the word "if." The participle indicates a condition which must
be fulfilled before the action of the main verb can take place.

πῶς ἡμεῖς ἐκφευξόμεθα τηλικαύτης <u>ἀμελήσαντες</u> σωτηρίας;
(Heb. 2:3)
How shall we escape *if we neglect* such a great salvation?

μόνον ἀξίως τοῦ εὐαγγελίου τοῦ Χριστοῦ πολιτεύεσθε, ἵνα
<u>εἴτε ἐλθὼν</u> καὶ <u>ἰδὼν</u> ὑμᾶς <u>εἴτε ἀπὼν</u> ἀκούω τὰ περὶ ὑμῶν, ὅτι
στήκετε ἐν ἑνὶ πνεύματι. (Phil. 1:27)
Only conduct yourselves in a manner worthy of the Gospel of
Christ so that *whether I come* and *see* you or *whether I am away* I
may hear the things concerning you that you are standing fast in
one spirit.

θερίσομεν μὴ <u>ἐκλυόμενοι</u>. (Gal. 6:9)
We shall reap *if we do* not *give out.*

τί ὠφελεῖται ἄνθρωπος <u>κερδήσας</u> τὸν κόσμον ὅλον ἑαυτὸν δὲ
<u>ἀπολέσας</u>. (Luke 9:25)
What does a man benefit *if he gains* the whole world and
loses himself?

οὐδὲν ἀπόβλητον μετὰ εὐχαριστίας <u>λαμβανόμενον</u>. (I Tim. 4:4)
Nothing (is to be) rejected *if it is received* with thanksgiving.

5. *The Concessive Participle.* This use of the participle indicates the unfavorable circumstances despite which the action of
the main verb takes place. The participle and the words con-

nected with it constitute the protasis of a concessive sentence. Some such word as "although" will be used in the translation. The participle may be used with or without a concessive particle such as καίπερ, καὶ γε, and καίτοι.

ὀφείλοντες εἶναι διδάσκαλοι διὰ τὸν χρόνον, πάλιν χρείαν ἔχετε τοῦ διδάσκειν ὑμᾶς τινά. (Heb. 5:12)
Although you ought to be teachers by this time, you have a need for someone to teach you.

. . . ὃς ἐν μορφῇ θεοῦ ὑπάρχων οὐχ ἁρπαγμὸν ἡγήσατο τὸ εἶναι ἴσα θεῷ. (Phi. 2:6)
. . . who *although he was* in the form of God did not consider being equal with God something to be grasped.

τυφλὸς ὢν ἄρτι βλέπω. (John 9:25)
Although I was blind now I see.

καίπερ ὢν υἱὸς ἔμαθεν ἀφ᾽ ὧν ἔπαθεν τὴν ὑπακοήν. (Heb. 5:8)
Although he was a son he learned obedience from the things which he suffered.

. . . ζητεῖν τὸν θεὸν εἰ ἄρα γε ψηλαφήσειαν αὐτὸν καὶ εὕροιεν, καὶ γε οὐ μακρὰν ἀπὸ ἑνὸς ἑκάστου ἡμῶν ὑπάρχοντα. (Acts 17:27)
. . . so that they may seek God if perchance they might feel after him and find him, *although he is* not far from each one of us.

6. *The Instrumental Participle.* The participle indicates the means (or agent) by which (or by whom) the action of the main verb is carried out. The word "by" will ordinarily be found in the translation.

τίς ἐξ ὑμῶν μεριμνῶν δύναται προσθεῖναι ἐπὶ τὴν ἡλικίαν αὐτοῦ πῆχυν ἕνα; (Matt. 6:27)
Which one of you *by means of being anxious* can add one cubit to his height?

ἐκεῖ διεσκόρπισεν τὴν οὐσίαν αὐτοῦ ζῶν ἀσώτως. (Luke 15:13)
There he wasted his property *by living* recklessly.

ἐν ᾧ πέπονθεν αὐτὸς <u>πειρασθείς</u>, δύναται τοῖς πειραζομένοις βοηθῆσαι. (Heb. 2:18)
Because he himself has suffered *by being tempted,* he is able to help those who are being tempted.

... ἥτις ἐργασίαν πολλὴν παρεῖχεν τοῖς κυρίοις αὐτῆς <u>μαντευομένη</u>. (Acts 16:16)
... who was bringing much gain to her masters *by means of telling fortunes.*

ἑαυτὸν ἐκένωσεν μορφὴν δούλου <u>λαβών</u>, ἐν ὁμοιώματι ἀνθρώπων <u>γενόμενος</u>. (Phil. 2:7)
He emptied himself *by means of taking* the form of a servant, *by appearing* in the likeness of mèn.

7. *The Modal Participle.* The modal participle indicates the manner in which the action of the main verb takes place. It like the instrumental participle is sometimes translated with the word "by," and the difference between the two is not great. For example, the participles in Phil. 2:7 (above) may indicate manner rather than means. The modal participle may employ the particle ὡς.

ἀκούσας ὁ νεανίσκος τὸν λόγον ἀπῆλθεν <u>λυπούμενος</u>. (Matt. 19:22)
When the young man heard this word he went away *sorrowing.*

ἐλάλει <u>εὐλογῶν</u> τὸν θεόν. (Luke 1:64)
He began to speak, *blessing* God.

ἕτεροι <u>διαχλευάζοντες</u> ἔλεγον ... (Acts 2:13)
Others *mocking* were saying ...

πυκτεύω ὡς οὐκ ἀέρα <u>δέρων</u>. (I Cor. 9:26)
I fight not as if *beating* the air.

ἦν διδάσκων αὐτοὺς ὡς ἐξουσίαν <u>ἔχων</u>. (Mark 1:22)
He was teaching them as *one who had* authority.

8. *The Complementary Participle.* Some verbs express a thought which is incomplete in itself and which requires either an infinitive or a participle to complete it. Therefore the complementary participle completes the idea expressed by the main verb. Interestingly enough the participle may agree in

case, gender, and number with either the subject or the direct object of the main verb. The participle in indirect discourse (last three examples) belongs in this category.

ἐγένετο ὅτε ἐτέλεσεν ὁ Ἰησοῦς <u>διατάσσων</u> τοῖς δώδεκα μαθηταῖς αὐτοῦ, μετέβη ἐκεῖθεν. (Matt. 11:1)
It came to pass when Jesus had finished *teaching* his twelve disciples, he departed from that place.

ἀφανίζουσιν τὰ πρόσωπα αὐτῶν ὅπως φανῶσιν τοῖς ἀνθρώποις <u>νηστεύοντες</u>. (Matt. 6:16)
They disfigure their faces so that they may appear to men *to be fasting.*

μειζοτέραν τούτων οὐκ ἔχω χαράν, ἵνα ἀκούω τὰ ἐμὰ τέκνα ἐν τῇ ἀληθείᾳ <u>περιπατοῦντα</u>. (III Jo. 4)
I have no greater joy than this, that I may hear *that* my children *are walking* in the truth.

πᾶν πνεῦμα ὃ ὁμολογεῖ Ἰησοῦν Χριστὸν ἐν σαρκὶ <u>ἐληλυθότα</u> ἐκ τοῦ θεοῦ ἐστιν. (I Jo. 4:2)
Every spirit which confesses *that* Jesus Christ *has come* in flesh is from God.

ἀκούσας Ἰακὼβ <u>ὄντα</u> σιτία εἰς Αἴγυπτον ἐξαπέστειλεν τοὺς πατέρας ἡμῶν. (Acts 7:12)
When Jacob heard *that there was* grain in Egypt he sent our fathers.

9. *The Circumstantial Participle.* A participle may be used to indicate an action which accompanies the action of the main verb. The action indicated by the participle constitutes a rather loose addition to that of the main verb. The participle indicates something else that happened, an additional fact or thought, an incidental fact. There is no certain parallel in English, and it is difficult to translate literally. The best procedure is to translate the participle as though it were a finite verb and to connect it to the main verb by supplying the word "and." The genitive absolute (fifth example) is in fact a circumstantial participle although it also may express other ideas such as time.

ἐδίδασκεν ἐν ταῖς συναγωγαῖς αὐτῶν, <u>δοξαζόμενος</u> ὑπὸ πάντων. (Luke 4:15)

He was teaching in their synagogues *and was being praised* by all.

ὁ Παῦλος ... ἐξέπλει εἰς τὴν Συρίαν ... <u>κειράμενος</u> ἐν Κεγχρεαῖς τὴν κεφαλήν. (Acts 18:18)
Paul sailed to Syria *after having cut off* his hair at Cenchreae.

ἐκήρυσσεν <u>λέγων</u> ... (Mark 1:7)
He preached *and said* ...

ἀπεκρίθη αὐτοῖς ὁ Ἰωάννης <u>λέγων</u> ... (John 1:26)
John answered them *and said* ...

ταῦτα αὐτοῦ <u>λαλοῦντος</u> πολλοὶ ἐπίστευσαν εἰς αὐτόν. (John 8:30)
While he *was saying* these things many believed on him.

10. *The Imperatival Participle.* This use is not found in classical Greek and is rare in the Koine. The participle is used independently like a finite verb in the imperative mood.

τὸ θυγάτριόν μου ἐσχάτως ἔχει, ἵνα <u>ἐλθὼν</u> <u>ἐπιθῇς</u> τὰς χεῖρας αὐτῇ. (Mark 5:23)
My little daughter is near death so that *you must come* (and) *put* your hands upon her.

<u>ἀποστυγοῦντες</u> τὸ πονηρόν, <u>κολλώμενοι</u> τῷ ἀγαθῷ. (Rom. 12:9)
Hate evil; *hold fast* to the good.

τὸ αὐτὸ εἰς ἀλλήλους <u>φρονοῦντες</u>, μὴ τὰ ὑψηλὰ <u>φρονοῦντες</u> ἀλλὰ τοῖς ταπεινοῖς <u>συναπαγόμενοι</u>. (Rom. 12:16)
Think the same thing about one another; *do* not *think about* the high things, but *associate* with the humble.

οἱ οἰκέται <u>ὑποτασσόμενοι</u> ἐν παντὶ φόβῳ τοῖς δεσπόταις. (I Pet. 2:18)
Servants, *submit yourselves* in all fear to your masters.

Note: *There may also be examples of a participle being used independently as an indicative. The matter is disputed by grammarians. Much depends upon whether one supplies an anacoluthon or treats the participle as it stands in the sentence. Certainly no participle should be explained as an independent participle if there is any other way to explain it.*

PART III
ASPECTS OF GREEK
SENTENCES

Thus far the concern of this book has been the syntax of words or small clusters of words as they relate to other parts of the sentence. In this part the purpose is to deal with the larger aspect of Greek sentences. This includes kinds of sentences and clauses, phrases, and substantives as they are used to expand the subject and predicate within sentences. Some particles are dealt with as they relate to certain kinds of clauses or phrases. No attempt is made to deal with all particles. They can be studied as individual words by consulting a lexicon.

KINDS OF SENTENCES

A sentence in English is a group of words consisting of a subject and predicate which conveys a thought. In Greek a sentence can consist of a single word because the finite verb by personal endings can indicate its subject. ἐφοβήθησαν. (John 6:19) *They were afraid. (Note that this verb is more easily translated into English by using a copula.)*

Both in Greek and English elements of the sentence may be omitted from the text. When this is done the context must supply the understood portions of the sentence. δώδεκα. (Mark 8:19) *Twelve.* This one word is a sentence only in relation to Jesus' question, *How many baskets of scraps did you take up?* Both the subject and predicate are understood. *(We took up) twelve (baskets full).*

The purpose of this section is to survey basic sentence types that are recognizable to students. Often these basic sentence types will be developed by additional modifiers and explanatory elements. These types provide the basic framework into which these modifiers are introduced. Word order in Greek is not as important as in English. More will be said about word order in the discussion of specific types.

Simple Statements

The simplest form of a sentence consists of a subject and verb. In Greek this can be a verb alone (see above). The subject may also be expressed by a noun or a noun substitute. These simple statements most often have modifiers of the simple subject or verb or both.

ἐδάκρυσεν ὁ ᾿Ιησοῦς. (John 11:35)
Jesus wept.

ὁ λόγος τοῦ θεοῦ ηὔξανεν καὶ ἐπληθύνετο. (Acts 12:24)
The Word of God increased and multiplied.

ἐξεκλείσθη. (Rom. 3:27)
It is excluded.

ἔρχεται ἡ μήτηρ αὐτοῦ. (Mark 3:31)
His mother came.

Diagramming is a simple method of illustrating the kind of sentence being dealt with. The diagram of the simple statement is as follows.

ὁ ᾿Ιησοῦς	ἐδάκρυσεν		Jesus	wept

ἡ μήτηρ	ἔρχεται		mother	came
αὐτοῦ			His	

Note: *The article is often diagramed as an adjective under the substantive with which it is used. In order to simplify diagraming and because the article is not used in the same way in all instances in Greek and English, it is diagramed here with the substantive with which it is used both in Greek and in English.*

Sentences with Connective Verbs

This kind of sentence has a verb which connects the subject to other words which identify or describe the subject. These verbs are described often as *equative* or *linking* (see above page 4). Adjectives are often used to describe an aspect of the subject. Sometimes the connective verb is understood rather than expressed.

σὺ εἶ ὁ Χριστός. (Mark 8:29)
You are the Anointed One.

θεὸς ἦν ὁ λόγος. (John 1:1)
The Word was God.

ὑμεῖς ἐστε τὸ ἅλας τῆς γῆς. (Matt. 5:13)
You are the salt of the earth.

ἐγὼ φωνὴ βοῶντος ἐν τῇ ἐρήμῳ. (John 1:23)
I (am) a voice of one crying in the wilderness.

ἡ μαρτυρία σου οὐκ ἔστιν ἀληθής. (John 8:13)
Your testimony is not true.

The diagram of the sentence with a connective verb is:

ὁ λόγος | ἦν\θεός   The Word | was\God

Note: *When the article is used with one of two nominatives connected by a copulative verb, the noun with the article is the subject nominative. If one of the two nouns is a proper name, it is the subject. If a pronoun is joined with a noun, the pronoun is the subject.*

Sentences with Objects of the Verb

Transitive verbs are verbs which require a direct object to complete their meanings. In Greek the object of most verbs is in the accusative case (see above pages 49-52). Some verbs, however, take objects in the genitive (above page 20); and others take objects in the dative (above page 37). The normal order in

English sentences is subject, verb, and object. In Greek the order is often varied.

There are sentences in Greek which have two accusatives (see pages 51-52 above). Two examples of the double accusative will be used here. Example three is of a primary and secondary accusative, while four is a personal and impersonal accusative.

ἐκάλεσεν αὐτούς. (Matt. 4:21)
He called them.

ἐλάμβανον πνεῦμα ἅγιον. (Acts 8:17)
They received the Holy Spirit.

Δαυὶδ κύριον αὐτὸν καλεῖ. (Luke 20:44)
David called him Lord.

εἶχον Ἰωάννην ὑπηρέτην. (Acts 13:5)
They had John (as) an assistant.

Examples one and three may be diagramed as follows.

(He)	ἐκάλεσεν	αὐτούς	He	called	them
Δαυὶδ	καλεῖ	αὐτὸν\κύριον	David	called	him\Lord

Note: Lord *is what some grammarians call an object complement or a secondary object (see above page 51).*

Sentences with Indirect Objects

Many transitive verbs also have indirect objects. The indirect object denotes the person or thing for whom or to whom something is done. The normal order in English is subject, verb, indirect object, and direct object; although the order is frequently subject, verb, direct object, and indirect object as in example one below. This order may be varied for emphasis by putting the indirect object first. *For an ungrateful man, I gave my time!* The order in Greek is often varied as in the examples below. In Greek the dative case is used for the indirect object (see above pages 32-33).

The use of the preposition πρός with the accusative case in Greek sometimes comes close to the dative of indirect object as in Acts 1:7. εἶπεν πρὸς αὐτούς, ... *He said to them,* ... The direct quote is the object of the verb and πρὸς αὐτούς denotes those to whom the words were spoken. However, the most frequent construction in Greek for the indirect object is the dative.

ἐλάλησεν αὐτοῖς πολλά. (Matt. 13:3)
He spoke many things to them.

πάντα ἀποδώσω σοι. (Matt. 18:26)
I will repay you all things.

ταῦτα ἔγραψα ὑμῖν ... (I Jo. 5:13)
I have written you these things ...

ἔδωκας αὐτῷ ἐξουσίαν ... (John 17:2)
You gave him authority ...

σοφίαν λαλοῦμεν ἐν τοῖς τελείοις. (I Cor. 2:6)
We speak wisdom to those who are mature.

These sentences are diagramed as follows.

(I)	ἀποδώσω	πάντα		I	will repay	all things
	\σοι				\you	

Interrogative Sentences

Interrogative sentences employ all of the forms discussed above. Often they will have either an interrogative pronoun (τίς, ποῖος, πόσος, and ποταπός) or an interrogative adverb (ποῦ, ὅπου, πῶς, ὅπως, ἆρα, πότε, ἕως πότε, πόθεν, etc.). When no other indicator is present, whether the sentence is a question or not must be determined by the context. Modern editors of the Greek text signal questions by inserting the question mark (;) at the end of the sentence. Often the answer that the speaker expects to his question is indicated in Greek by the particle used with the question. ἆρα and μή expect negative answers, and οὐ expects the affirmative (see the last two examples below). The following are examples of questions which represent a variety of types.

μεμέρισται ὁ Χριστός; (I Cor. 1:13)
Is Christ divided?

Note: *In Greek this has to be diagramed as a simple sentence, while in English it is diagramed as a copulative sentence.*

σὺ τίς εἶ; (John 8:25)
Who are you?

τί με πειράζετε; (Mark 12:15)
Why are you tempting me?

οὐκ εἰμὶ ἀπόστολος; (I Cor. 9:1)
Am I not an apostle? (Yes.)

μὴ ἀπώσατο ὁ θεὸς τὸν λαὸν αὐτοῦ; (Rom. 11:1)
Did God reject his people? (No.)

Questions without an interrogative word are diagramed as though they were simple affirmations.

ὁ Χριστὸς	μεμέριτσαι		Christ	is divided

Others are diagramed as follows.

σὺ	εἶ \τίς		you	are\Who
(you)	πειράζετε \τί	με	you	are tempting \Why	me

Questions which are deliberative use the subjunctive (see above page 119) or optative mood (see above page 125). They are diagramed also according to which type of sentence they represent.

Commands and Requests

Commands and requests are normally expressed in Greek by the imperative mood; however, there are other means by which they are expressed. They may be expressed by the future indicative (see above pages 97, and 115) or by the subjunctive of exhortation or prohibition (see above pages 118-119). Infinitives and participles can also be used in the expression of commands and requests. Each of these may be diagramed as one of the basic sentence types above by arranging the word order as it would be in a declarative sentence. For example:

ἀγαπῶμεν ἀλλήλους. (I Jo. 4:7)
Let us love one another.

(We)	ἀγαπῶμεν	ἀλλήλους	(We)	love	one another

The commands and requests expressed by sentences with the imperative mood also use all of the types of sentences discussed above as illustrated by the following examples.

ἀκολούθει μοι. (Mark 2:14)
Follow me.

χαίρετε. (Matt. 5:12)
Rejoice.

βοήθησον ἡμῖν. (Mark 9:22)
Please help us.

ἀγαπᾶτε τοὺς ἐχθροὺς ὑμῶν. (Matt. 5:44)
Love your enemies.

ἁγιασθήτω τὸ ὄνομά σου. (Matt. 6:9)
Let your name be hallowed.

These may be diagramed as follows.

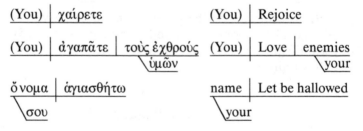

Sentences with Participles and Infinitives

Both participles and infinitives may take the place of nouns, adjectives, or adverbs. They are diagramed as these parts of speech are diagramed, except they are placed on pedestals above the line. Two examples of each are diagramed.

Participles

παράγων εἶδεν Λευίν. (Mark 2:14)
As he passed by, he saw Levi.

ἐπιστραφεὶς ὁ Πέτρος βλέπει τὸν μαθητὴν . . . ἀκολουθοῦντα. (John 21:20)
Having turned, Peter saw the disciple *following.*

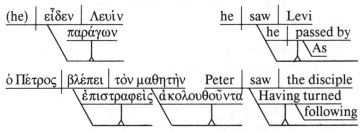

Note: *In adverbial participles, the subject of the main verb is in most instances the subject of the action of the participle. When it is not, the construction is an absolute (see pages 17-18 and 58-59).*

Infinitives

ἐμοὶ τὸ ζῆν Χριστός. (Phil 1:21)
For me *to live* is Christ.

τοῦτο μόνον θέλω μαθεῖν ἀφ' ὑμῶν. (Gal. 3:2)
I wish *to learn* only this from you.

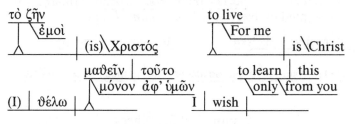

Complex Sentences

Complex sentences have one independent clause and at least one dependent clause. A dependent clause (subordinated) is a group of words with a subject and predicate which serves as a part of speech (noun, adjective, or adverb) in a sentence. The basic structure of a complex sentence may be the same as those described above except for the presence of a dependent clause. The following examples illustrate complex sentences in which the clauses function in different ways.

Note: *See above pages 120-124 for clauses which use the subjunctive mood, pages 126-127 for clauses which use the optative, and page 130 for those which use the imperative.*

Adverbial Clauses

ὅτε εἶδον αὐτόν, ἔπεσα πρὸς τοὺς πόδας αὐτοῦ. (Rev. 1:17)
When I saw him I fell at his feet.

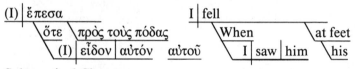

Substantival Clauses

ὅσοι εἰς Χριστὸν ἐβαπτίσθητε, Χριστὸν ἐνεδύσασθε. (Gal. 3:27)
You who were baptized into Christ have put on Christ.

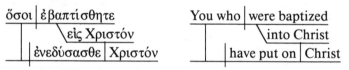

Adjectival Clauses

ἐποίησεν δώδεκα, οὓς καὶ ἀποστόλους ὠνόμασεν. (Mark 3:14)
He appointed twelve, *whom he also named apostles.*

(He) | ἐποίησεν | δώδεκα   He | appointed | twelve

(he) | ὠνόμασεν | οὓς ἀποστόλους   he | named | whom apostles

Compound Sentences

Compound sentences consist of two or more independent clauses joined by a conjunction or conjunctions. The most common conjunctions in the New Testament are καί, δέ, τέ, ἤ, ἀλλά, οὔτε, and οὐδέ. Each part of a compound sentence is diagramed according to the type of sentence it is. They are then linked together with a dotted line on which the conjunction is written.

ἠκολούθει αὐτῷ ὄχλος πολύς, καὶ συνέθλιβον αὐτόν. (Mark 5:24)
A great crowd followed him, and they were crowding him.

ὄχλος	ἠκολούθει	αὐτῷ		A crowd	followed	him
\πολύς				\great		
καὶ				and		
(they)	συνέθλιβον	αὐτόν		they	were crowding	him

THE EXPANSION OF THE SUBJECT

The *subject* of a sentence is usually defined as a noun or noun substitute which denotes that about which the sentence makes an assertion. It answers the question Who? or What? before the verb. The *complete subject* (or expanded subject) is the subject and its modifiers. The purpose in this section is to deal with the various parts of speech which function in the expanded subject of the sentence. Many of these have been dealt with separately in Part I. Often reference will be made to examples found elsewhere, but the examples will not normally be repeated in this section.

By the Use of Adjectives and Adverbs

Many examples may be cited where adjectives are used to modify the subject (see page 71 example two and examples one and two below). Many adjectives are used substantively as subjects (see page 72 example one and example three below). Occasionally adverbs will be used to modify subjects (examples four and five below). The adverb πλησίον is often used as a substantive in the New Testament. As such it may modify the subject as in Rom. 13:10 (ἡ ἀγάπη τῷ πλησίον—*Love for the neighbor).* This is better treated under substantives in the various cases (see below).

ἡ ἐντολὴ ἡ παλαιά ἐστιν ὁ λόγος. (I Jo. 2:7)
The *old* commandment is the word.

ὁ λόγος ὁ σὸς ἀλήθειά ἐστιν. (John 17:17)
Your word is truth.

ὁ δίκαιος ἐκ πίστεως ζήσεται. (Rom. 1:17)
The righteous by faith shall live.

ἡ ἄνω Ἰερουσαλὴμ ἐλευθέρα ἐστίν. (Gal. 4:26)
The Jerusalem *which is above* is free.

ἡ ὄντως χήρα . . . ἤλπικεν ἐπὶ θεόν. (I Tim. 5:5)
The *one who is really* a widow . . . has placed (her) hope in God.

By the Use of Nouns and Pronouns

The subject of a Greek sentence is always a noun or noun substitute. Nouns and pronouns are used to expand the subject. They are used in all cases and may function to modify words or complete the thought of other modifiers.

In the Nominative Case

The noun or pronoun may function in the nominative case in apposition with the simple subject (see page 7).

Ἰούδας Ἰσκαριὼθ ὁ εἷς τῶν δώδεκα ἀπῆλθεν. (Mark 14:10)
Judas Iscariot, *one* of the twelve, went forth.

ἐγὼ Ἰωάννης, ὁ ἀδελφὸς ὑμῶν, . . . ἐγενόμην ἐν τῇ νήσῳ τῇ καλουμένῃ Πάτμῳ (Rev. 1:9)
I John, *your brother,* was on the Island which is called Patmos.

In the Genitive Case

The genitive case is especially useful for modifying words in the subject since it is the case of description (see page 8). The genitive may be used in the expanded subject both with and without a preposition. Often an adjective can be substituted for the word in the genitive case. ἀποκαλυφθῇ ὁ ἄνθρωπος τῆς ἀνομίας. (II Thess. 2:3) *The man of lawlessness* is revealed, or *The lawless man* is revealed. Sometimes the genitive is used with an article which functions as the subject (see page 79 for an example). The following examples illustrate the variety of uses of the genitive in the expanded subject.

ὁ λόγος ὁ τοῦ σταυροῦ τοῖς ἀπολλυμένοις μωρία ἐστίν. (I Cor. 1:18)
The word *of the cross* is foolishness to those who are perishing.

ἡ ἐκκλησία καθ' ὅλης τῆς Ἰουδαίας ... εἶχεν εἰρήνην. (Acts 9:31)
The church *throughout all Judea* had peace.

Note: *Though the substantive with the proposition tells where, it is modifying the subject and not the verb.*

ἡ μαρτυρία σου οὐκ ἔστιν ἀληθής. (John 8:13)
Your witness is not true.

τὸ μαρτύριον τοῦ Χριστοῦ ἐβεβαιώθη ἐν ὑμῖν. (I Cor. 1:6)
The testimony *about Christ* was confirmed among you.

ἡ ἀγάπη τοῦ θεοῦ ἐκκέχυται ... (Rom. 5:5)
The love *of God* has been poured out ...

In the Ablative Case

The idea of separation or source makes the ablative suited to describe the subject. The basic function is still to describe, but the element of separation is indicated strongly.

τινὲς τῶν Φαρισαίων εἶπαν ... (Luke 6:2)
Some *of the Pharisees* said ...

πᾶσα προφητεία γραφῆς ἰδίας ἐπιλύσεως οὐ γίνεται. (II Pet. 1:20)
No prophecy *from Scripture* is (a matter) of private interpretation.

ὥστε οἱ ἐκ πίστεως εὐλογοῦνται σὺν τῷ πιστῷ Ἀβραάμ. (Gal. 3:9)
So, those who (are justified) *by faith* are being blessed with faithful Abraham.

οὐδεὶς ἐξ αὐτῶν ἀπώλετο. (John 17:12)
Not one *of them* has perished.

χωρὶς νόμου ἁμαρτία νεκρά. (Rom. 7:8)
Sin *apart from law* (is) dead.

In the Dative Case

On rare occasions a substantive in the dative is used to modify a word in the expanded subject. Two examples are given on page 35 above under the dative of possession.

ἐξεκομίζετο τεθνηκὼς μονογενὴς υἱὸς τῇ μητρὶ αὐτοῦ. (Luke 7:12)
A dead man, an only son *of* his *mother,* was being carried out.

ἐμοὶ τὸ ζῆν Χριστός. (Phil. 1:21)
Living *for me* (is) Christ.

Note: ἐμοί *may modify the whole sentence.*

In the Locative Case

The locative case is sometimes used to modify substantives in the expanded subject.

οἱ ἐν τῇ Ἰουδαίᾳ φευγέτωσαν . . . (Matt. 24:16)
The ones *in Judea* must flee . . .

πάτερ ἡμῶν ὁ ἐν τοῖς οὐρανοῖς . . . (Matt. 6:9)
Our Father *in heaven* . . .

τὶς ἐν τῷ συνεδρίῳ Φαρισαῖος . . . (Acts 5:34)
A certain Pharisee *in the Sanhedrin* . . .

ἐγὼ Ἰωάννης, ὁ ἀδελφὸς ὑμῶν καὶ συγκοινωνὸς ἐν τῇ θλίψει καὶ βασιλείᾳ καὶ ὑπομονῇ ἐν Ἰησοῦ, ἐγενόμην ἐν τῇ νήσῳ τῇ καλουμένῃ Πάτμῳ. (Rev. 1:9)
I John, your brother and participant *in the tribulation* and *kingdom* and *endurance* in Jesus, was on the Island which is called Patmos.

In the Instrumental Case

The use of the instrumental is rare in the expanded subject. One example of the instrumental of association with σύν in the subject is given on page 48. An instrumental of agency which modifies an adjective in the subject is given on page 49. The example below has an instrumental of association modifying a participle in apposition to the subject.

... ἀνήρ τις ... Κορνήλιος ... φοβούμενος τὸν θεὸν σὺν παντὶ τῷ οἴκῳ ... εἶδεν ... (Acts 10:1-3)
A certain man, Cornelius who *with all his house* feared God, saw ...

In the Accusative Case

The accusative is used rarely in the expanded subject to modify nouns. In the two examples below it indicates extension in the first and relationship in the second. The accusative is sometimes used as the object of a substantival or adjectival participle in the subject (example one under the attributive participle and one under the substantival participle pages 143-144).

εὑρέθη μοι ἡ ἐντολὴ ἡ εἰς ζωὴν αὕτη εἰς θάνατον. (Rom. 7:10)
The very commandment *which (should be) unto life* was found for me (to be) unto death.

τινὲς τῶν καθ᾽ ὑμᾶς ποιητῶν εἰρήκασιν ... (Acts 17:28)
Certain of *your own* poets have said ...

By the Use of Phrases

A phrase is a group of words which does not have subject and predicate but functions as a part of speech within a sentence. In English prepositional phrases are usually treated in this category. In this book substantives with prepositions are not treated separately from other substantives (see part I); therefore, they are treated under the sections on the use of nouns and pronouns in the subject (pages 164-167) and in the predicate (pages 172-174). Many English grammars also include verb phrases. The equivalent to this in Greek is the participle used predicatively (see pages 144-145).

In this section infinitives and participles with words used with them are treated as to their function in the expanded subject. They have been described as to their possible functions on pages 133-143 and 144-152 respectively.

Participial Phrases

Participial phrases which are used to expand the subject are adjectival or substantival. Example one under attributive participles on page 143 illustrates the participle which modifies the subject. Examples one and two under substantival participles on page 144 illustrate the participle as the subject. Other examples of each kind of participle in the subject are given below (example one has adjectival participles and two and three have substantival).

ἀνήρ... Κορνήλιος, ... εὐσεβὴς καὶ φοβούμενος τὸν θεὸν... ποιῶν ἐλεημοσύνας ... καὶ δεόμενος τοῦ θεοῦ ... εἶδεν ἐν ὁράματι... ἄγγελον τοῦ θεοῦ. (Acts 10:1-3)
Cornelius, a religious man and *one who feared* God, *gave* alms, and *prayed* to God, saw in a vision an angel of God.

ὁ ἄνωθεν ἐρχόμενος ἐπάνω πάντων ἐστίν. (John 3:31)
The one who comes from above is above all. (Literally: *The* from above *coming one...*)

ὁ κλέπτων μηκέτι κλεπτέτω. (Eph. 4:28)
The one who steals must steal no more.

Infinitival Phrases

The infinitive is used often as a substantive and functions as the subject (see pages 139-140 above for examples). Two examples are given here where an infinitive modifies the subject.

ἐπλήσθη ὁ χρόνος τοῦ τεκεῖν αὐτήν. (Luke 1:57)
The time *for her to give birth* arrived.

ἐξῆλθεν δόγμα παρὰ Καίσαρος Αὐγούστου ἀπογράφεσθαι πᾶσαν τὴν οἰκουμένην. (Luke 2:1)
A decree *to enroll all the world* went out from Caesar Augustus.

By the Use of Clauses

A clause is a group of words which conveys a thought by means of a predicate and a subject and which functions as a part of a sentence. The main sentence is often referred to as an independent clause (see page 118 above). Clauses that are used within the sentence are subordinated clauses (see above page 120). In this section and the section on clauses used in the predicate (below pages 175-184), the subordinated clauses are dealt with.

Subordinated clauses are used because of the need to make a further assertion about some part of the sentence. By their very nature clauses are modifiers and function most frequently as adjectives or adverbs. They may, like adjectives, take the place of nouns.

Relative Clauses

The clause most frequently used in the subject is the relative. It may function as a substantive or as an adjective.

The relative clause is most often introduced and related to the sentence by the relative pronoun ὅ ς. The relative pronoun is sometimes combined with the indefinite pronoun τις (ὅστις, ἥτις, or ὅ τι) with little or no change in meaning. Other pronouns which introduce relative clauses are οἷος and ὅσος. When a pronoun introduces a relative clause, it serves as a part of speech within the clause, i.e., as subject, object, or modifier. ὃς οὐκ ἔστιν καθ' ἡμῶν, ὑπὲρ ἡμῶν ἐστιν (Mark 9:40). *Whoever is not against us* is for us. The relative pronoun ὅς functions as subject of the relative clause, and the relative clause functions as the subject of the sentence.

The relative clause may have a verb in the indicative or subjunctive mood. When the subjunctive mood is used in the relative clause, the clause may have a dual function of stating or implying a condition and taking the place of the subject (see example one at the top of page 122).

The variety of uses of the relative clause in the subject is indicated in the following examples.

ὃς ἂν πίῃ ἐκ τοῦ ὕδατος, ... οὐ μὴ διψήσει εἰς τὸν αἰῶνα, ἀλλὰ τὸ ὕδωρ ὃ δώσω αὐτῷ γενήσεται ἐν αὐτῷ πηγὴ ὕδατος. (John 4:14)
Whoever drinks of the water, will never thirst; but the water *which I shall give him* will become in him a well of water.

Note: *The first clause functions as the subject of the sentence, while the second clause modifies the subject* ὕδωρ. *The first clause also expresses a condition. The antecedent to* ὅς *is indefinite and must be understood.*

ἄξιός ἐστιν <u>ᾧ παρέξῃ τοῦτο</u>. (Luke 7:4)
He *for whom you should do this* is worthy.

Note: *The relative pronoun is in the dative case because of its function in the clause. The antecedent of* ᾧ *is the subject of* ἐστιν. *Thus, the relative clause modifies the subject (compare this with the substantive in the dative on page 166 above and the next example). The relative clause also implies a result of being worthy (see pages 121-122).*

ἐσαλεύθη ὁ τόπος <u>ἐν ᾧ ἦσαν συνηγμένοι</u>. (Acts 4:31)
The place *in which they were gathered* was shaken

ἐξέστησαν οἱ ἐκ περιτομῆς πιστοὶ <u>ὅσοι συνῆλθαν τῷ Πέτρῳ</u>. (Acts 10:45)
The believers from among the Jews *who came with Peter* were amazed.

ἔσται θλῖψις μεγάλη <u>οἵα οὐ γέγονεν ἀπ᾽ ἀρχῆς κόσμου ἕως τοῦ νῦν</u>. (Matt. 24:21)
There will be a great tribulation *such as has not happened from the beginning of the world until now*. (Literally: A great tribulation *which has never been . . .* will be.)

<u>ὃ ἔχει</u> ἀρθήσεται ἀπ᾽ αὐτοῦ. (Matt. 13:12)
That which he has will be taken from him.

Clauses Introduced by Adverbial Particles

Some adverbial particles introduce clauses which modify nouns. Particles such as ὅτε and ὅταν often introduce clauses which modify nouns that denote time. Particles like ὅπου, ποῦ, οὗ, and ὅθεν sometimes introduce clauses which modify nouns that denote place. The occurrence of such clauses is rare in the subject. Note that the adverbial particles which introduce the clauses function to modify the verbs within the clauses.

ἐλεύσονται ἡμέραι <u>ὅτε ἐπιθυμήσετε μίαν τῶν ἡμερῶν τοῦ υἱοῦ τοῦ ἀνθρώπου ἰδεῖν</u>. (Luke 17:22)

Days will come *when you will desire to see one of the days of the Son of Man.*

Note: *The clause introduced by* ὅτε *modifies* ἡμέραι *which is a period of time.*

ἔρχεται ὥρα ὅτε . . . προσκυνήσετε τῷ πατρί. (John 4:21)
The hour is coming *when . . . you will worship the Father.*

ἐλεύσονται ἡμέραι <u>ὅταν ἀπαρθῇ ἀπ' αὐτῶν ὁ νυμφίος.</u> (Mark 2:20)
Days will come *when the bridegroom is taken from them.*

ἐν Ἱεροσολύμοις ἐστὶν ὁ τόπος <u>ὅπου προσκυνεῖν δεῖ</u>. (John 4:20)
The place *where it is necessary to worship* is in Jerusalem.

ἐγγὺς ἦν ὁ τόπος τῆς πόλεως <u>ὅπου ἐσταυρώθη ὁ Ἰησοῦς.</u> (John 19:20)
The place in the city *where Jesus was crucified* was near.

Clauses Introduced by Subordinating Conjunctions

The subordinating conjunctions which are used in the New Testament as part of the subject are ὅτι and ἵνα. They are used in the subject infrequently. The conjunction ὅτι must be distinguished from the relative pronoun, neuter, singular, ὅ followed by τι (Luke 10:35). One way of distinguishing them is to note that the relative functions as a part of speech within the clause it introduces, while the conjunction merely introduces the clause. Most editors of modern Greek texts print the neuter singular relative and the indefinite pronoun separately (ὅ τι).

ἐν τῷ νόμῳ τῷ ὑμετέρῳ γέγραπται <u>ὅτι δύο ἀνθρώπων ἡ μαρτυρία ἀληθής ἐστιν.</u> (John 8:17)
It is written in your own law *that the testimony of two men is true.* (Literally: *That the testimony of two men is true* is written in your own law.)

πῶς πληρωθῶσιν αἱ γραφαὶ <u>ὅτι οὕτως δεῖ γενέσθαι;</u> (Matt. 26:54)
How can the Scriptures *(which say) that it must be so* be fulfilled?

πῶς γέραπται ἐπὶ τὸν υἱὸν τοῦ ἀνθρώπου <u>ἵνα πολλὰ πάθῃ καὶ ἐξουδενηθῇ;</u> (Mark 9:12)
How is it written about the Son of Man *that he must suffer many things and be despised?*

Note: *In English "it" is often introduced for the subject of passive verbs in questions. For the diagram of such questions see page 159.*

ἐμοὶ εἰς ἐλάχιστόν ἐστιν ἵνα ὑφ᾽ ὑμῶν ἀνακριθῶ. (I Cor. 4:3)
It is a very small thing for me *that I should be judged by you.*
(Literally: *That I should be judged by you* is a very small thing for me.)

THE EXPANSION OF THE PREDICATE

The predicate of a sentence makes an assertion about the subject or completes the subject. The predicate consists of a verb and its direct object(s), its indirect object(s), and their modifiers. Sentences which use a copulative verb may have complements (nouns, adjectives, adverbs, phrases or clauses). Transitive verbs with a direct object may also have an object complement (page 157 above). The words which complete or modify the verb may also have modifiers consisting of nouns (in all cases), adjectives, and adverbs.

By the Use of Nouns and Pronouns

Substantives in all cases are used in the predicate. When in the oblique cases they often function much like adverbs in that they answer such questions as "how?", "when?", "where?", "why?", "how much?", "how many?", etc.

In the Nominative Case

Nominatives are used in the predicate as verb complements or in apposition (see above page 7). Five examples of predicate nominatives are given on page 4.

In the Genitive Case

A noun in the genitive case may function to modify nouns, pronouns, other modifiers, or the verb itself (many such examples are given on pages 8-9). Genitives, like adjectives and adverbs, may also function to complete a copulative verb (see the last example on page 9). The genitive often functions as the object of some verbs (see page 20).

In the Ablative Case

Because the ablative is used to show separation or source (see page 20), it is frequently used to modify the verb or some part of the predicate. The ablative is often used in the predicate to answer the questions "whence?", "where?", "by whom?", "by what means?", and "for what reason?". The ablative also functions to express comparison because of its emphasis upon separation or distinction. Adequate examples of all of these uses in the predicate are given on pages 21-31.

In the Dative Case

The primary function of the dative is as the indirect object of the verb. It also functions as direct object of certain verbs. Adequate examples are given on pages 31-37.

In the Locative Case

The primary function of the locative is to indicate location. The location may be in space, time, or sphere. Examples are given on pages 37-42.

In the Instrumental Case

Words in the instrumental case express means, cause, manner, measure, association, and agency. Adequate examples of all of these functions are illustrated on pages 42-49.

In the Accusative Case

The accusative functions with the most variety of any case used in the predicate. Its predominant use is as object of the verb. As such it limits the action of transitive verbs to the substantive in the accusative case. Examples are listed on pages 49-52. See the diagram for objects on pages 156-157. Other functions for substantives in the accusative case are as adverbs telling "how much?", "how many?", "how far?", "why?", and "for what cause or purpose?". The accusative is used also in specialized ways such as oaths, concession, comparison, and relationships showing advantage or disadvantage. Adequate examples of these functions are found on pages 52-63. Most of the words (with or without prepositions) will be diagramed as adverbs (see page 162). Some will be diagramed as adjectives modifying substantives used in the predicate (see page 160).

By the Use of Adjectives and Adverbs

Many examples can be cited where adjectives are used to modify substantives in the predicate (page 71 examples three and four). They also function to complete the copulative verb (examples one and three under "predicatively" page 71). Adjectives may function also as direct objects (example one page 72), indirect objects (example one below), or with prepositions adverbially (example two below). Some adjectives also function as adverbs without a preposition (see examples on page 72). Adverbs function in the predicate to modify the verbal idea or the verb itself. They may show manner (example four below), place (example five below), or time (example six below).

ὅσα ἔχεις πώλησον καὶ δὸς τοῖς πτωχοῖς. (Mark 10:21)
Whatever you have sell (it) and give (it) *to the poor.*

ἐρωτῶ . . . ἵνα τηρήσῃς αὐτοὺς ἐκ τοῦ πονηροῦ. (John 17:15)
I ask . . . that you may keep them *from the evil one.*

εἰς τὰ ἴδια ἦλθεν. (John 1:11)
He came *unto his own (home).*

δωρεὰν ἐλάβετε, δωρεὰν δότε. (Matt. 10:8)
Freely you have received, *freely* give.

. . . θερίζων ὅπου οὐκ ἔσπειρας καὶ συνάγων ὅθεν οὐ διεσκόρπισας. (Matt. 25:24)
. . . Reaping *where* you have not sown and gathering *where* you have not scattered.

Μαρία ἡ Μαγδαληνὴ ἔρχεται πρωῒ . . . εἰς τὸ μνημεῖον. (John 20:1)
Mary Magdalene came *early* . . . to the tomb.

By Use of Phrases

Phrases as they are dealt with in this section are infinitive or participial phrases (see above page 167).

Participial Phrases

All uses of the participle listed on pages 143-152 appear in the predicate. In the predicate the participle appears as a substantive, an adjective, or an adverb. The great variety in the use of the adverbial participles is seen in the examples on pages 145-152.

Infinitival Phrases

The infinitive is used in the predicate in all of its functions listed on pages 132-143. Adequate examples are given for all of its uses in the predicate. References to the adverbial accusative of reference on pages 55-57 will illustrate how the accusative case is used to indicate the subject of the action expressed by the infinitive. When no such accusative is used with the infinitive, the subject of the main clause is also the subject of the action expressed by the infinitive. Compare the two examples below. The infinitive also may take an object in the accusative case.

γινώσκειν ὑμᾶς βούλομαι . . . (Phil. 1:12)
I want *you to know* . . . (ὑμᾶς indicates who will know.)

τοῦτο μόνον θέλω μαθεῖν ἀφ' ὑμῶν, . . . (Gal. 3:2)
This only do I want *to learn* from you, . . . (τοῦτο is the object of the infinitive. "I" is the subject of the action of the infinitive.)

By the Use of Clauses

The clauses which are in the subject are also used in the predicate (pages 168-172 above) as well as clauses introduced by other particles.

Relative Clauses

Relative clauses are used in the predicate to take the place of substantives or to modify substantives. The relative clause may also indicate purpose, result, or condition even when it is grammatically in the form of an adjective or substantival clause (see above page 169). In addition to the relatives listed on page 169, τίς sometimes functions as a relative pronoun. Not all clauses introduced by τίς are indirect questions. Some function in the same way as ὅς (example three below).

The variety of functions of the relative clause in the predicate is illustrated by these examples.

κράτει ὃ ἔχεις. (Rev. 3:11)
Hold fast *that which you have.*

μνημονεύετε τοῦ λόγου οὗ ἐγὼ εἶπον ὑμῖν. (John 15:20)
Remember the word *which I spoke to you.*

Note: *The relative pronoun* οὗ *is in the genitive case by attraction to* λόγου *rather than in the accusative case as we would expect since it is the direct object of* εἶπον.

οὐκ ἔχουσιν τί φάγωσιν. (Matt. 15:32)
They do not have *anything to eat.*

Note: *It is easier to translate the clause into English as an infinitive.* Literally, it is translated, *They do not have* anything which they may eat. *Compare this with the next example.*

εἶπέν μοι πάντα ἃ ἐποίησα. (John 4:39)
He told me everything *which I had done.*

ἡ ἐντολὴ ἡ παλαιά ἐστιν ὁ λόγος ὃν ἠκούσατε. (I Jo. 2:7)
The old commandment is the word *which you heard.*

ἐν ᾧ ἔρχομαι ἐγὼ ἄλλος πρὸ ἐμοῦ καταβαίνει. (John 5:7)
While I am coming, another goes down before me. (Literally: *In the time in which I am coming . . .*)

Note: *The relative clause, like a substantive, is used with a preposition. The same is true of* ἄχρι ἧς *in Matt. 24:38. This transforms these relative clauses into adverbial clauses. See also Acts 1:11:* ἐλεύσεται ὃν τρόπον ἐθεάσασθε αὐτὸν πορευόμενον. He will come *in the manner which you saw him go. The use of the noun* τρόπον *causes the relative to function as an adverb.*

Clauses Introduced by Adverbial Particles

Some adverbial particles are listed on page 170. Several others function in the predicate such as ἄρχι(ς), ἐπάν, ἐπειδή, ἕως, ὡς (as an adverb), ἡνίκα, and πρὶν ἤ (rare). Clauses introduced by these function like adverbs. They tell where and when. Occasionally they modify substantives which indicate time or place. These clauses are often discussed under the headings of temporal and local clauses. The following examples illustrate the variety of functions.

ἄλλο ἔπεσεν ἐπὶ τὸ πετρῶδες <u>ὅπου οὐκ εἶχεν γῆν πολλήν</u>. (Mark 4:5)
Other (seed) fell upon rocky ground *where it had not much earth.*

<u>ὅπου ἐὰν εἰσέλθῃ</u> εἴπατε τῷ οἰκοδεσπότῃ . . . (Mark 14:14)
Wherever he enters say to the householder . . .

Note: *The adverbial particle followed by the subjunctive with ἐάν makes the clause contingent. The clause then becomes a conditional clause, but it also indicates place. Contrast it with the examples above and below.*

εἰς τὸν οἶκόν μου ἐπιστρέψω <u>ὅθεν ἐξῆλθον</u>. (Matt. 12:44)
I will return to my house *whence I came out.*

οὐκ ἔγνωσαν <u>ἕως ἦλθεν ὁ κατακλυσμός</u> . . . (Matt. 24:39)
They did not know *until the flood came* . . .

ἴσθι ἐκεῖ <u>ἕως ἂν εἴπω σοι</u>. (Matt. 2:13)
Stay there *until I tell you.*

Note: *As with example two above the particle ἄν and the subjunctive make the clause contingent. The time indicated by ἕως becomes indefinite. Compare this example with the one above in which the aorist indicative is used and the one below in which the present indicative is used.*

εὐθὺς ἠνάγκασεν τοὺς μαθητὰς αὐτοῦ . . . προάγειν, . . . <u>ἕως αὐτὸς ἀπολύει τὸν ὄχλον</u>. (Mark 6:45)
Immediately he compelled his disciples . . . to go forth . . . *while he dispersed the crowd.*

ἦν αὐτῷ κεχρηματισμένον . . . μὴ ἰδεῖν θάνατον <u>πρὶν ἢ ἂν ἴδῃ τὸν Χριστὸν κυρίου</u>. (Luke 2:26)

It had been revealed to him that he would not see death *until (before) he had seen the Anointed of the Lord.*

ὡς ἦλθον πρὸς αὐτὸν οἱ Σαμαρῖται, ἠρώτων αὐτὸν μεῖναι παρ' αὐτοῖς. (John 4:40)
When the Samaritans came to him, they asked him to remain with them.

Note: *This example has the aorist tense in the clause (see John 2:9; Luke 5:4; etc.). The present is sometimes used with* ὡς *and is translated "while" or "as" (see Acts 1:10). When either* ἄν *or* ἐάν *is used with* ὡς *the time becomes contingent in the future (see Rom. 15:24 or Phil. 2:23).*

Comparative Clauses

Particles which introduce comparative clauses are ὡς, ὡσεί, ὥσπερ, καθώς, and καθάπερ. These clauses modify the verb of the main clause by showing manner or circumstance. They may also be used to explain or to function as predicate complements for copulative sentences.

Often comparative clauses will be elliptical. The omitted elements in the clause, as in English, must be understood (see examples three and four). The particles which introduce these clauses may be correlated with οὕτως (example five). The verb in the comparative may be in the subjunctive mood. This seems to differ little from the use of the indicative mood (example six).

ὀψόμεθα αὐτὸν καθώς ἐστιν. (I Jn. 3:2)
We shall see him *as he is.*

ἔκραξεν φωνῇ μεγάλῃ ὥσπερ λέων μυκᾶται. (Rev. 10:3)
He cried out with a loud voice *as a lion roars.*

ὅτε ἤμην νήπιος, ἐλάλουν ὡς νήπιος. (I Cor. 13:11)
When I was a child I spoke *as a child (speaks).*

... ἵνα ὡς τάχιστα ἔλθωσιν πρὸς αὐτόν. (Acts 17:15)
... that they should come to him *as quickly (as they could come).*

ὡς ἀμνὸς ἐναντίον τοῦ κείραντος αὐτὸν ἄφωνος, οὕτως οὐκ ἀνοίγει τὸ στόμα αὐτοῦ. (Acts 8:32)

As a lamb before his shearers is dumb, so he did not open his mouth.

οὕτως ἐστὶν ἡ βασιλεία τοῦ θεοῦ <u>ὡς ἄνθρωπος βάλῃ τὸν σπόρον ἐπὶ τῆς γῆς.</u> (Mark 4:26)
Thus the Kingdom of God is *as if a man should cast seed upon the ground.*

Clauses Introduced by Subordinating Conjunctions

The subordinating conjunctions which are used to introduce clauses in the predicate are ἵνα, ὅτι, and ὅπως. In the predicate these clauses indicate cause, purpose, and result. Even in the subject (pages 168-172), these clauses functioned as substantives or adjectives and indicated oughtness and necessity.

When the negative is used with these conjunctions, μή is used with ἵνα and ὅπως, and οὐ with ὅτι (except at John 3:18).

Clauses Introduced by ὅτι. One use of ὅτι is to introduce both direct and indirect discourse (examples one and two). Such clauses are often called objects of verbs of saying or perception. With direct speech ὅτι functions much like quotation marks in English and is not translated. When ὅτι introduces indirect discourse (examples two and three), it is translated "that." ὅτι is used also with some nouns or pronouns to further explain or to give the content of the words (example four). This conjunction is used often to introduce causal clauses (example five). As such it functions like the adverbial particles (above page 177). ὅτι sometimes appears in the compounds διότι and καθότι with little or no difference in function (example six).

λέγουσιν αὐτῷ ὅτι <u>Πάντες ζητοῦσίν σε.</u> (Mark 1:37)
They said to him, *"All people are seeking you."*

μαρτύρομαι πάλιν παντὶ ἀνθρώπῳ περιτεμνομένῳ <u>ὅτι ὀφειλέτης ἐστὶν ὅλον τὸν νόμον ποιῆσαι.</u> (Gal. 5:3)
I bear witness again to every man who is being circumcised *that he is obligated to do the whole law.*

ἤρξατο διδάσκειν αὐτοὺς <u>ὅτι δεῖ τὸν υἱὸν τοῦ ἀνθρώπου πολλὰ παθεῖν.</u> (Mark 8:31)
He began to teach them *that the Son of Man must suffer many things.*

ἔστιν αὕτη ἡ ἀγγελία..., ὅτι ὁ θεὸς φῶς ἐστιν... (I Jn. 1:5)
This is the message..., *that God is light*...

οὐκ ἤφιεν λαλεῖν τὰ δαιμόνια, ὅτι ᾔδεισαν αὐτόν. (Mark 1:34)
He did not permit the demons to speak, *because they knew him.*

...ἦν... ἀδημονῶν διότι ἠκούσατε ὅτι ἠσθένησεν. (Phil. 2:26)
He was troubled *because you heard that he was sick.*

Clauses Introduced by ἵνα. The subordinating conjunction most often used in the New Testament to introduce purpose clauses is ἵνα (see examples on pages 120-121 above and example one below). Purpose clauses are often referred to as final clauses. Result clauses also use ἵνα (see above page 121). Both purpose and result clauses employ the subjunctive mood and a subordinating conjunction (see page 120). This conjunction is also used to introduce substantival clauses which function as objects of verbs which express a wish, desire, warning, exhortation, permission, or command (see pages 123-124 and examples two and three below). Example two is indirect discourse, but example three shows the ἵνα clause only as object of the verb. The ἵνα clause may also explain or modify certain nouns or adjectives which express need, desire, command, time, or exhortation (examples four and five). This includes ἵνα clauses which function as predicate nominatives (see page 123). This clause is also used with demonstrative pronouns (example six).

ἐπιποθῶ ἰδεῖν ὑμᾶς, ἵνα τι μεταδῶ χάρισμα ὑμῖν πνευματικὸν εἰς τὸ στηριχθῆναι ὑμᾶς. (Rom. 1:11)
I long to see you, *in order that I may share some spiritual gift with you* in order that you may be strengthened.

Note: *The infinitive phrase* εἰς τὸ στηριχθῆναι *functions to show purpose as does the* ἵνα *clause. These constructions are often parallel in Greek (see page 133 above).*

συνεβουλεύσαντο ἵνα τὸν Ἰησοῦν δόλῳ κρατήσωσιν καὶ ἀποκτείνωσιν. (Matt. 26:4)
They were taking counsel *that (how) they might take Jesus by deceit and put him to death.*

οὐκ ἤφιεν ἵνα τις διενέγκῃ σκεῦος διὰ τοῦ ἱεροῦ. (Mark 11:16)

He did not allow *anyone to carry anything throught the temple.*
(Literally: . . . *that anyone might carry . . .*)

ἔδωκα αὐτῇ χρόνον ἵνα μετανοήσῃ. (Rev. 2:21)
I gave her time *that she should repent.*

οὐκ εἰμὶ ἐγὼ ἄξιος ἵνα λύσω αὐτοῦ τὸν ἱμάντα τοῦ ὑποδήματος.
(John 1:27)
I am not worthy *that I should loose the strap of his sandal.*

τοῦτο προσεύχομαι, ἵνα ἡ ἀγάπη ὑμῶν . . . περισσεύῃ . . .
(Phil. 1:9)
I pray for this, *that your love . . . may abound . . .*

Clauses Introduced by ὅπως. The ὅπως clause is used often to
indicate purpose (see above pages 120-121 and examples one
and two below). The ὅπως clause also functions to complete
verbs of asking, request, or intention (examples three and four
below). These are, in reality, indirect discourse.

ὁ κύριος ἀπέσταλκέν με, . . . ὅπως ἀναβλέψῃς καὶ πλησθῇς
πνεύματος ἁγίου. (Acts 9:17)
The Lord sent me, . . . *in order that you may receive sight and be
filled with the Holy Spirit.*

Note: *A few examples of* ὅπως *with* ἄν *may be found in the New
Testament. The addition of* ἄν *seems only to make the clause
more general* (see Luke 2:35).

. . . τοῦ δόντος ἑαυτὸν . . . ὅπως ἐξέληται ἡμᾶς . . . (Gal. 1:4)
. . . the one who gave himself . . . *so that he might rescue us . . .*

δεήθητε τοῦ κυρίου τοῦ θερισμοῦ ὅπως ἐκβάλῃ ἐργάτας εἰς τὸν
θερισμὸν αὐτοῦ. (Matt. 9:38)
Pray the Lord of the harvest *that he send workers unto his harvest.*

οἱ Φαρισαῖοι εὐθὺς μετὰ τῶν Ἡρῳδιανῶν συμβούλιον ἐδίδουν
κατ’ αὐτοῦ ὅπως αὐτὸν ἀπολέσωσιν. (Mark 3:6)
The Pharisees with the Herodians immediately took counsel
against him, *how they might destroy him.*

Conditional Clauses

Conditional clauses function as part of the predicate in that
they give a condition under which the action of the verb can

take place or a reason or cause for the action of the verb taking place or not taking place.

The various kinds of conditional sentences have been referred to under the syntax of the moods (first class, page 117; second class, page 117; third class, page 121; and fourth class, pages 126-127). The purpose in those references was to illustrate uses of the moods. In this section the purpose is to define the conditional clauses and to illustrate their function as part of the sentence. Additional examples are given for the second and third classes. Five examples are given for the first class.

First Class Condition. In the first class condition the speaker assumes that the condition stated in the protasis *(the if clause)* is a reality. Because of this assumption, the speaker uses εἰ plus the indicative mood in the protasis. The apodosis *(the main clause)* may use the indicative, subjunctive, or the imperative mood. It may be a direct statement, a question, an exhortation, a command, or a request. The verb in the apodosis may be in any tense.

εἰ κεκοίμηται σωθήσεται. (John 11:12)
If he has fallen asleep, he will be cured.

εἰ τὴν ἴσην δωρεὰν ἔδωκεν αὐτοῖς ὁ θεὸς . . . , ἐγὼ τίς ἤμην
δυνατὸς κωλῦσαι τὸν θεόν; (Acts 11:17)
If God gave the same gift to them . . . , who was I to be able to forbid God?

εἰ ζῶμεν πνεύματι, πνεύματι καὶ στοιχῶμεν. (Gal. 5:25)
If we live by the Spirit, let us also walk by the Spirit.

εἰ υἱὸς εἶ τοῦ θεοῦ, εἰπὲ τῷ λίθῳ τούτῳ ἵνα γένηται ἄρτος.
Luke 4:3)
If you are the Son of God, command this stone to become bread.

εἴ τις ἔχει ὦτα ἀκούειν ἀκουέτω. (Mark 4:23)
If anyone has ears to hear, let him hear.

Second Class Condition. In the second class condition the speaker assumes that the condition in the protasis is untrue. The apodosis states what would have been true in the event that the protasis had been true. This is a graphic way of depicting the failure or untruth of the other person's position or argument.

In the protasis of the second class condition εἰ is used with a past tense in the indicative mood. The apodosis usually has ἄν and a past tense of the indicative mood (see discussion and examples on page 117).

εἰ ἤμεθα ἐν ταῖς ἡμέραις τῶν πατέρων ἡμῶν, οὐκ ἄν ἤμεθα αὐτῶν κοινωνοὶ ἐν τῷ αἵματι τῶν προφητῶν. (Matt. 23:30)
If we had been in the days of our fathers, we would not have been partners with them in the blood of the prophets.

εἰ ἐπιστεύετε Μωϋσεῖ, ἐπιστεύετε ἄν ἐμοί. (John 5:46)
If you had believed Moses, you would believe me.

εἰ ἠγαπᾶτέ με ἐχάρητε ἄν. (John 14:28)
If you loved me, you would have rejoiced.

Third Class Condition. The speaker in the third class condition considers that the condition stated in the protasis has the possibility (or even probability) of becoming a reality. Therefore, he uses ἐάν or ἄν and the subjunctive mood in the protasis. The present, future, and aorist indicatives are all used in the apodosis. The present imperative also occurs frequently in the apodosis, but the aorist subjunctive occurs only rarely.

The statement in the apodosis becomes a reality only when the conditions stated in the protasis are met. The great variety of uses in the apodosis is because of the differences of what the speaker expects to happen. Examples on page 121 above have in the apodosis the future indicative (indicating that the speaker considered that the result would follow the fulfillment of the condition) and the perfect (indicating that the result would be a reality at the time of fulfillment). Compare the examples below.

ἐάν τις τὸν ἐμὸν λόγον τηρήσῃ, θάνατον οὐ μὴ θεωρήσῃ εἰς τὸν αἰῶνα. (John 8:51)
If anyone keeps my word, he will never see death forever.

Note: *The speaker obviously wanted to stress the reality of the apodosis should the protasis be fulfilled.*

ἐὰν ἐν τῷ φωτὶ περιπατῶμεν ... , κοινωνίαν ἔχομεν μετ᾽ ἀλλήλων. (I Jn. 1:7)
If we walk in the light..., we have fellowship with one another.

Note: *The speaker conceives that there probably are people actually walking in the light; thus, they are having fellowship.*

ἐὰν ἔλθῃ πρὸς ὑμᾶς δέξασθε αὐτόν. (Col. 4:10)
If he comes to you, receive him.

Note: *This apodosis states what the speaker surely wanted should the protasis ever become a reality.*

Fourth Class Condition. The fourth class condition does not occur in the New Testament in a complete form (see above, page 126).

By the Use of Indirect Discourse

Indirect discourse has been referred to in other places in this book. In this section, the various kinds of indirect discourse are brought together and illustrated as a part of the predicate.

Indirect discourse takes the form in Greek of three basic forms of direct discourse: assertions, questions, and commands. It appears that the verb used in indirect speech is normally reported in the same tense and mood as was used by the original speaker. The person of the verb in indirect discourse, however, is determined by the relationship of the one reporting the discourse to the original speaker. If the original speaker is reporting the discourse, he uses the first person. If another person is reporting the discourse to the original speaker, he uses the second person. If another is reporting the discourse to a third person, he uses the third person.

The following examples are organized around the means used to express indirect discourse. Normally two examples are given. Where one means is used to introduce more than one kind of discourse, additional examples are given.

Employing a ὅτι Clause

The ὅτι clause is used to report indirect assertions (see page 179).

ἐγὼ πεπίστευκα ὅτι σὺ εἶ ὁ Χριστός. (John 11:27)
I believe *that you are the Christ.*

ἡμεῖς ἠλπίζομεν ὅτι αὐτός ἐστιν ὁ μέλλων λυτροῦσθαι τὸν
Ἰσραήλ. (Luke 24:21)
We were hoping *that he was the one who was going to free Israel.*

Note: *The use of the second person in the first example is
because the speaker is speaking to the original speaker, and the
use of the third person in the third example is because the original statement is being reported to a third party. Note the use of
the present tense in both. The direct statement in both requires
the present. The present in the second example is translated into
English by the past.*

Employing a ἵνα or ὅπως Clause

In addition to ὅτι, both ἵνα and ὅπως function as conjunctions to introduce indirect discourse; however, they introduce
indirect commands or requests (see pages 179-181).

παρήγγειλεν αὐτοῖς ἵνα μηδὲν αἴρωσιν εἰς ὁδόν . . . (Mark 6:8)
He commanded them *to take nothing for the journey* . . .

Note: *The ἵνα clause is translated more clearly into English by
the infinitive. In many of their functions infinitives and ἵνα
clauses were interchangeable in Greek.*

προσηύξαντο περὶ αὐτῶν ὅπως λάβωσιν πνεῦμα ἅγιον.
(Acts 8:15)
They prayed for them *that they might receive the Holy Spirit.*

Employing a Clause Introduced by τί

The τί clause is used in indirect questions. Not every use of τί
as a relative is an indirect question (see pages 175-176 above),
but there are some instances when it is so used with verbs of perception. Luke 12:5 is sometimes cited as a direct command put
in the form of an indirect question (example three). The original command would be, "Fear him." It is also possible to see
this as only an indirect question. The direct question could
have been "Whom should I fear?"

ἦλθον ἰδεῖν τί ἐστιν τὸ γεγονός. (Mark 5:14)

They came to see *what had happened.*

Note: *The direct question was, "What has happened?"*

οὐ ᾔδει τί ἀποκριθῇ. (Mark 9:6)
He did not know *what he should answer.*

ὑποδείξω ὑμῖν τίνα φοβηθῆτε. (Luke 12:5)
I will show you *whom you should fear.*

Employing an Infinitive

Infinitives are often used to express indirect discourse. In this use the infinitive functions as the direct object of verbs of saying and perception (see above pages 140-141). The two examples cited under the infinitive as direct object are both examples of indirect assertions. The infinitive is commonly used for indirect commands.

τῷ Παύλῳ ἔλεγον διὰ τοῦ πνεύματος <u>μὴ ἐπιβαίνειν εἰς</u>
<u>Ἱεροσόλυμα</u>. (Acts 21:4)
They were telling Paul through the Spirit *not to go to Jerusalem.*

παραγγέλλομεν ὑμῖν . . . <u>στέλλεσθαι ὑμᾶς ἀπὸ παντὸς ἀδελφοῦ</u>
<u>ἀτάκτως περιπατοῦντος</u>. (II Thess. 3:6)
We command you *to keep away from every brother living in idleness.*

Employing a Participle

The participle often functions substantivally as the direct object of transitive verbs (see page 144). When it is the object of verbs of saying or perception, it is used to report indirect discourse.

ἀκούομεν <u>τινας περιπατοῦντας ἐν ὑμῖν ἀτάκτως</u>. (II Thess. 3:11)
We are hearing *that certain ones are walking among you disorderly.*

ἀκούσας Ἰακὼβ <u>ὄντα σιτία εἰς Αἴγυπτον</u> . . . (Acts 7:12)
When Jacob heard *that there was grain in Egypt* . . .

SUBJECT INDEX

Ablative, see Case.
Absolute, nominative, 5f.;
    genitive, 17f.; accusative,
    58f.
Accidence, xiii.
Accusative, see Case.
Active, see Voice.
Adjective, 70ff.; in subject,
    163.
Adverbs, adverbial preposi-
    tions, 70ff.; in the subject,
    163f.; in the predicate,
    174ff.; in clauses, 170f.,
    177f.
Agency, ablative, 24ff.
Aktionsart, 82f.
Aorist, see Tense.
Apposition, 7; genitive of, 16f.
Article, 73ff.; diagramed, 155;
    with copulative verb, 156.
Augment, 90, 99, 108.

Case, 2-3; the cases, 3-64;
    nominative, 3ff.; genitive,
    8ff,; genitive absolute, 17;
    ablative, 21ff.; dative,
    31ff.; root idea, 20f.; loca-
    tive, 37ff.; instrumental,
    42ff.; accusative, 49ff.;
    absolute, 58f.; vocative,
    64.
Clauses, 168ff.-175ff.; with
    subjunctive, 118ff.; with
    optative, 126f.
Commands, in imperative
    mood, 127ff.; in future
    indicative, 97, 115f.; in

subjunctive mood, 118f.;
    diagramed, 159f.
Comparison, ablative, 27f.;
    accusative, 61, 122;
    clauses, 178f.
Complex sentences, 161f.
Compound sentences, 162f.
Conditional clauses, 181ff.,
    indicative mood in, 117;
    subjunctive, 121; optative,
    126f.; imperative, 130.
Conjunctions, subordinating,
    171f., 179f.; coordinating,
    162f.
Copulative verbs, 156.

Dative, see Case.
Diagrams, 155ff.
Direct Object, accusative,
    49ff.; dative, 37; genitive,
    20; diagramed, 156f.

Finite verbs, 131.
Future, see Tense.

Gender, 1.

Imperfect, see Tense.
Imperative, see Mood.
Indicative, see Mood.
Indirect discourse, with infini-
    tive, 140f.; ὅπως clause,
    179f.; in the predicate,
    184ff.
Indirect objects, 32f.; dia-
    gramed, 157f.; with πρός,
    157f.

Infinitive, defined, 132f.; uses, 133ff.; diagramed, 161.

Instrumental, see Case.

Linking verbs, see Copulative verbs.

Locative, see Case.

Means, ablative, 26f.; instrumental of, 42f.

Measure, adverbial genitive, 11f.; accusative, 52ff.; instrumental, 45ff.

Middle, see Voice.

Mood, 114ff.; indicative, 114ff.; subjunctive, 118ff.; optative, 124ff.; imperative, 127ff.

Morphology, xiii.

Noun, 70; see Substantive.

Number, in substantives, 1; in verbs, 131.

Oaths, accusatives, 57f.

Optative, see Mood.

Participle, 143ff.; diagramed, 161.

Passive, see Voice.

Perfect, see Tense.

Person, 130f.

Phrases, in the subject, 150f.; in the predicate, 175.

Pluperfect, see Tense.

Predicate, 172ff.; see Verb.

Prepositions, 2f.; proper prepositions, 60ff.; adverbial prepositions, 67ff.

Prohibition, with subjunctive, 118f.; imperative, 127f.

Pronoun, 80, see Substantive.

Questions, indicatives, 115; subjunctive, 119; optative, 125f.; diagramed, 158f.

Sentences, 154ff.

Subject, 163ff.

Subjunctive, see Mood.

Substantive, 1-64, defined, 1.

Syntax, xiii.

Tense, 82ff.; meaning, 82f.; tenses: present, 83ff.; imperfect, 90ff.; future, 95ff.; aorist, 98ff.; perfect, 104ff.; pluperfect, 108f.

Time, adverbial genitive, 10f.; locatives of time, 39f.; instrumental of measure, 45f.; adverbial accusative, 52ff.

Verb, 82-152; defined, 82, 172; kinds, 131ff.

Vocative, see Case.

Voice, 109ff.; active, 110f.; middle, 111f.; passive, 113.

SCRIPTURE INDEX

Matthew	page	Matthew	page
1:12	12	5:17	119, 133
18	136	19	122
21	97	20	25, 119
22	26	21	97, 116
		24	22
2:1	18	29	21
2	115	32	23
4	77, 86	37	28
5	77	38	30
7	74	43	97
10	50	44	160
13	177	48	97
22	20, 30		
		6:1	49, 134
3:1	88	2	90
6	26	5	121
8	14	6	127
11	22, 27	7	44
11	60, 96	9	160, 166
14	93, 141	11-12	128
15	139, 145	13	72, 128
17	24, 102	16	151
		17	147
4:3	123	19	127
4	116	25	36
11	95	27	149
15	23	31	119
19	22	34	119
21	9, 50, 157		
		7:4	118
5:1	73	17	87
3	41, 71		
11	72	8:3	99
12	22, 160	24	27, 91
13	156	25	84
14	13	32	128
15	54		

Matthew	page	Matthew	page
9:18	103	15:32	62, 176
21	121	38	71
38	181		
		16:13	115
10:1	134		
8	174	17:9	18
14	22	12	35
24	61	14	18
29	11, 22		
32	37	18:14	123
35	29	15	22, 104
37	61, 144	17	76
		21	97
11:1	151	26	32, 158
5	72	33	94
7	27		
11	25	19:5	63, 98
16	98	12	62
21	117	14	141
26	64, 79	22	150
12:7	108	20:3	38
24	49	6	52
31	16	13	11
36	6	19	40
44	177		
		21:19	53
13:3	32, 158	42	26
6	138	43	96
12	170		
24	77	23:5	59
25	137	30	183
29	48, 77	31	34
30	134	32	128
34	23		
46	106	24:16	166
		20	10, 39
14:2	77	21	170
8	38	28	122
21	23	30	19, 96
24	13	33	38, 123
25	40, 53	38	176
		39	177
15:23	22		
25	37	25:5	17, 92
29	54	6	106

Matthew	page	Mark	page
25:24	174	2:20	171
27	116	27	62
34	25		
46	71	3:6	181
		14	162
26:2	59	31	155
4	113, 180	34	7, 38
9	94		
18	88	4:4	54
28	78	5	177
32	137	7	115
34	136	8	46
38	12	23	182
39	52	26	122, 179
51	9	36	88
54	171	41	50
55	62		
63	20, 91	5:4	42
71	80	11	39
		13	24
27:8	11	14	185
11	115	23	152
24	22, 115	24	163
31	51	32	95
45	11	34	55
63	89		
		6:8	185
28:1	11, 22	11	23
15	11	19	34
		23	12
Mark		34	51
1:7	142, 152	35	78
13	19	40	54
14	75	45	177
19	72	48	54
21	88, 95		
22	44, 150	7:4	111
24	115	15	24
30	88	28	23
34	180	31	53
37	179		
		8:2	7
2:5	89	19	154
10	13	29	156
14	160, 161	31	179
18	35		

Mark	page	Luke	page
9:6	186	1:8	13
10	140	9	141
12	171	13	116
22	128, 160	15	13
28	17	20	11, 28
30	13	21	40, 137
31	89	45	26
40	169	57	168
		62	125
10:1	109	64	150
13	32		
18	71	2:1	168
21	174	4-5	112
48	46	15	13, 118
52	105	21	5
		22	133
11:16	180	26	177
22	16	35	181
24	104	37	53
		41	40
12:2	31	49	91
14	119, 147		
15	159	3:2	11
18	141	10	119
33	27	15	126
41	13		
		4:3	182
13:3	13	13	11
20	117	14	13
30	123	15	151
		16	35
14:6	34	18	29
10	164	22	8, 44
14	177	29	134
30	39, 136	41	108
72	56		
		5:3	31, 50
15:6	93	4	178
16	13	5	11
23	94	19	12
		27	54
16:6	103		
		6:1	42
Luke		2	165
1:1	100	11	125
6	13	13	31

Luke	page	Luke	page
6:37	120	12:5	137, 185
37-38	129	5	186
42	118	7	27
		8	37
7:4	122, 170	10	62
6	91	11	76
12	166	15	111
19	145	41	57
35	101	52	35
38	43		
39	117	13:2	61
		7	84
8:2	109	8	54
4	27	9	116
13	54		
26	13	14:7	113
27	46		
41	4	15:2	47
		13	149
9:3	139	17	43
9	90	25	20
14	55	27	90
25	148	29	37, 85
32	48		
38	35	16:16	14
46	126	19	55
47	39	24	31
52	134		
57	122	17:1	140
		21	13
10:1	53	22	170
4	53	27	91
7	75		
11	34	18:7	10, 53
19	13	9	41
30	38	11	31
35	171	12	10, 85
40	57, 143	13	73
		31	36
11:14	145	42	15
23	29		
37	48	19:4	12
41	55	7	48
		11	13
12:1	136	26	11
3	28	44	28

Luke	page	John	page
19:46	52	1:22	144
		23	156
20:6	145	26	152
26	13	27	181
44	157	28	23
		29	88
21:4	35	30	14, 29
19	15	32	106
26	38	39	39
36	141	45	79, 24
		48	136
22:6	22		
15	45	2:9	178
23	125	10	71
35	22	19	129
49	98	20	46
54	110	24	60, 138
23:4	76	3:2	24
15	48	7	119
20	147	16	74
26	22	17	25, 77
		18	107, 179
24:1	39	28	89
10	9	29	60
15	137	31	74, 168
21	46, 185	36	37
41	28		
46	104	4:4	12
51	137	5	14
		6	28
John		8	109
1:1	54, 78, 156	10	144
2	4	11	71
5	4	14	169
6	5, 35	20	116, 171
7	59, 120	21	171
10	38	27	40
11	174	31	93
12	9	34	123
14	4, 14, 100	39	176
15	22, 29, 106	40	178
16	74	43	74
17	75	45	50, 110
18	105	49	136
19	110, 115	52	100

John	page	John	page
5:6	85	11:54	13
7	84, 176		
11	71	12:29	107, 141
37	105	32	22
46	183		
		13:6	86
6:2	34, 13	13	5
11	74		
17	109	14:3	88
19	52, 154	26	96
24	147	28	88, 183
35	120		
44	40	15:6	101
50	143	8	103
66	19	12	123
68	64	19	117
71	9	20	176
		27	85
7:13	16		
24	51	16:8	146
45	76	19	72
48	31	28	24
52	87, 130		
		17:1	64
8:13	156, 165	2	158
16	123	6	105
17	171	11	128
25	159	12	31, 165
30	152	14	24
33	106	15	22, 174
51	183	17	164
9:25	149		
		18:16	108
10:7	9		
11	71	19:1	110
18	21	2	38
28	120	3	79, 93
29	105	15	119
40	72	20	171
		24	118
11:12	182		
26	115	20:1	174
27	185	12	39
35	155	20	148
49	10	28	79

John	*page*	Acts	*page*
21:6	28	8:15	185
10	103	17	157
15	9	18	61
20	161	20	124
		21	13
		27	147
Acts		31	125
1:3	137	32	178
4	23	40	138
5	110		
7	158	9:15	8
10	178	17	181
11	176	21	109
22	16	31	13, 165
24	79	38	39
2:13	150	10:1	143
19	95	1-3	167, 168
26	41	30	11
38	60	45	170
3:2	93	11:5	13
8	95	17	182
10	59	19	13, 35
16	22	23	44
25	63, 80	28	11
26	32, 147		
		12:2	43
4:9	18	6	22
31	170	23	28
		24	155
5:3	135		
4	100	13:5	51, 157
14	144	6	13
21	54	19	111
24	125		
28	105	14:4	48, 77
31	38	23	109
34	49, 166		
35	33	15:12	100
		19	75
7:12	151, 186	23	139
14	46	28	23
26	93	29	21
43	22		
60	100	16:3	111

Acts	page	Acts	page
16:13	22	25:11	106, 112
16	150	11	140
18	53, 89	22	116
37	45		
		26:1	89, 95
17:6	90	3	58, 60
7	29	11	93
11	126	22	22
15	178	28	86
27	149	29	23, 125
28	60, 167	32	117
29	116		
31	36, 49	27:8	39
		14	24
18:10	135	22	23
13	62	34	18
18	152	43	21, 100
25	55		
		Romans	
19:1	75	1:1	6, 7
13	57, 73	6	25
26	12	7	6, 25
32	29	9	41
		11	134, 180
20:15	13	17	164
24	134	18	15
33	20	24	142
		25	61
21:4	186	28	142
21	41		
31	84	2:1	64
		5	8
22:1	64	11	41
4	12	12	41
5	147	15	22
16	113		
21	53	3:1-2	72
22	12	4	125
		5-6	97
23:26	139	23	101
30	102	27	155
24:17	147	4:4	57
19	116	10	146
26	47	11	17

Romans	page	Romans	page
5:5	105, 165	14:9	100
7	98	13	141
14	99	23	107
15	72		
18	59	15:2	56
		4	23
6:2	96	5	125
6	8, 134	7	112
12	127, 135	19	14
14	97	22	92
		24	178
7:2	121	26	31
3	98, 135		
8	165	16:17	63
10	167	19	36, 56
18	4, 140	25	16, 46
25	37		
		I Corinthians	
8:3	30	1:6	16, 165
8	37	13	159
12	36	18	165
18	61		
35	15	2:6	32, 158
36	85	13	25, 26
9:3	94	3:6	91, 110
		19	7
10:12	21	21	9
11:1	159	4:3	172
2	36, 47	8	47, 117
7	4	18	103
9	34		
11	121	5:9	32, 113
20	44		
30	43	6:9	127
33	7	12	36
		16	98
12:9	152	18	22
15	138	20	11
16	41, 152		
		7:1	14
13:7	75	7	77
10	163	17	32
		25	148
14:4	36	28	104

I Corinthians	*page*	II Corinthians	*page*
7:36	128	4:3	35
39	107, 142	7	23
8:7	44	5:1	17
13	110	5	17
		10	57
9:1	159	13	33
19	34	15	33
25	56		
26	150	6:11	104
26-27	86	14	47
		18	63
10:4	93		
30	44	7:12	30, 138
		15	15
11:6	112		
21	85, 90	8:7	124
25	137	11	140
26	85	17-18	102
		18	77
13:4	74	23	15
8	112		
11	178	9:7	87
		14	34
14:8	111		
10	126	10:16	23
20	40		
27	53	11:1	117
31	54		
		12:9	85
15:3	56	11	116
29	98		
37	127	13:7	71
16:1	62	Galatians	
10	74	1:1	25
11	119	4	181
16	111	6	84, 90
		11	89
II Corinthians		13	91
1:1	9	18	99
		22	145
2:1	34	23	72
2	25	24	44
13	107, 138		
13	146		

Galatians	page	Ephesians	page
2:1	11	4:26	130
12	136	28	168
3:2	161, 175	5:25	78
9	165	31	28, 98
10	142	32	124
13	19	33	124
17	135		
19	29		
27	162	6:12	63
		16	47
4:17	50	18	18
20	94, 116	18-19	19
26	164		
		Philippians	
5:3	179	1:5	71
4	86, 103	6	4, 96
12	112, 117	7	59
16	120	9	181
17	121	9-10	60
18	48	12	175
24	9, 79, 101	18	45, 97
25	182	21	140, 161
		21	166
6:1	123	22	112, 140
5	98	27	148
9	148		
12	44, 86	2:6	149
		7	41, 150
Ephesians		13	140
1:4	13	15	13
17-18	58	16	55
		23	57, 178
2:1, 5	58	24	104
4	99	25	102
8	27	26	180
14	4	27	42
20	17		
		3:1	64
3:3	100	8-10	134
20	28	16	138
		17	144
4:1	114		
10	23	4:7	143
11	77	18	24
15	56		

Colossians	*page*	II Timothy	*page*
4:3	18, 142	1:3	18
7-8	102		
10	184	2:9	12
		14	139
I Thessalonians			
1:5	45	4:1	58
6	19	14-15	130
8	136	15	112
2:7	122	Titus	
		2:1	144
3:5	134	2	139
7	36, 115	13	76
4:16	45	Philemon	
17	48	13	94
		19	102
5:5	8		
8	147	Hebrews	
10	48	1:4	46
14	63		
16-18	127	2:3	148
19-20	128	8	137
23	124	14	20
27	58	17	56
		18	150
II Thessalonians			
2:3	164	3:9-10	52
15	55, 114	12	8
3:4	96		
6	186	5:8	149
11	186	12	51, 56, 149
		13	14
I Timothy		14	21
3:1	20		
2	75	6:16	20
13	78		
16	49	7:9	139
		25	141
4:4	148		
8	148	8:13	138
5:5	164	9:3	54
		5	23
6:5	21	26	40

Hebrews	page	I Peter	page
10:15	137	3:6	51
18	30	14	126
		17	126
11:13	99	18	41
17	94		
		4:8	29
12:1	118	14	79
12:4	12		
		5:2	50
13:7	21, 130	8-9	130
24	77	12	130
James		II Peter	
1:1	139	1:20	24, 165
5-6	128		
6	104	2:6	17
11	101	19	48
13	14, 25	22	7, 111
13-15	87		
19	129	I John	
21	127	1:1	106
22	4	5	180
27	142	7	183
2:5	50	2:2	14
10	107	3	43
18	27	5	107
25	45	7	92, 164, 176
		8	84
3:8	14	15	79
4:2	138	3:2	178
7-8	129	8	87
		12	29
5:10	52	20	27
12	29, 58		
		4:2	151
I Peter		7	118, 160
1:1	12	8	4, 78
2	124		
18-19	43	5:1	26
		13	158
2:18	152	16	50
3:1	22	III John	
3	130	4	151

Jude	*page*	Revelation	*page*
7	55	6:6	11
11	12	8	43
14	47		
24	13	8:7	31
Revelation		9:2	27
1:1	6	6	96
3	144	11	5
4	5, 78		
8	78	10:3	178
9	164, 166		
17	162	11:2	22
18	145	5	121
		17	78
2:16	34	18	141
21	181		
		12:6	25
3:11	176	7	132
12	6		
20	104	14:20	22
4:3-4	13	16:9	55
6	13	10	28
10	13		
		21:2	33
5:5	101, 135	25	10
7	106		
11	13